TALLEYRAN

NAPOLEON and
TALLEYRAND

NAPOLEON and TALLEYRAND

The Last Two Weeks

BARBARA NORMAN

STEIN AND DAY/*Publishers*/New York

First published in 1976
Copyright © 1976 by Barbara Norman
All rights reserved
Designed by Ed Kaplin
Printed in the United States of America
Stein and Day/*Publishers*/Scarborough House,
Briarcliff Manor, N.Y. 10510

Library of Congress Cataloging in Publication Data
Makanowitzky, Barbara Norman.
    Napoleon and Talleyrand: the last two weeks.

    1. Napoléon I, Emperor of the French, 1769-1821.
2. Talleyrand-Périgord, Charles Maurice de, Prince de
Bénévent, 1754-1838. I. Title.
DC202.5.M3   944.05   75-11823
ISBN 0-8128-1830-X

"Triumph and disgrace
are never far apart"
—NAPOLEON

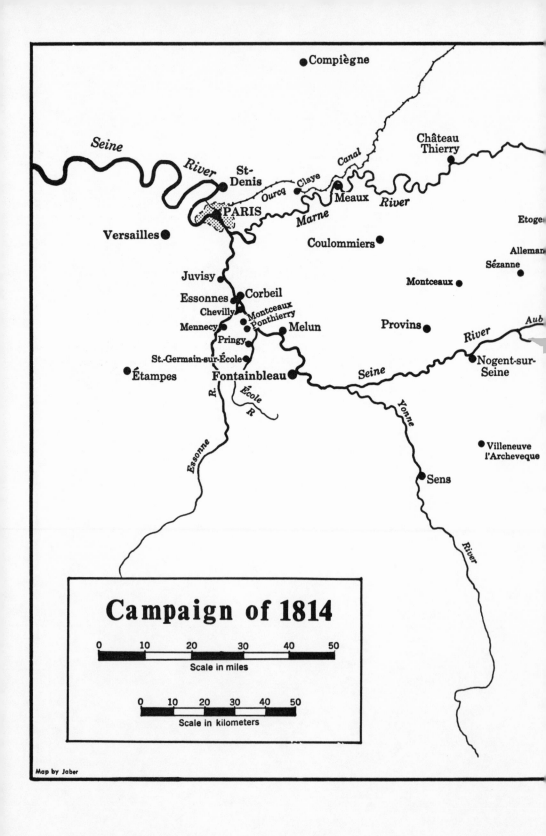

Compiègne

Seine River

Château
Thierry

St-
Denis

Claye

Ourcq

Canal

Meaux

Marne River

Etoges

PARIS

Versailles

Coulommiers

Allemant

Sézanne

Juvisy

Montceaux

Essonnes

Corbeil

Chevilly

Montceaux

Ponthierry

Mennecy

Melun

Provins

Aube

River

Pringy

St.-Germain-sur-École

Nogent-sur-
Seine

Étampes

Fontainbleau

Essonne R.

École R.

Seine

Yonne

Villeneuve
l'Archeveque

Essonne

Sens

River

Campaign of 1814

```
0      10      20      30      40      50
Scale in miles
```

```
0    10    20    30    40    50
Scale in kilometers
```

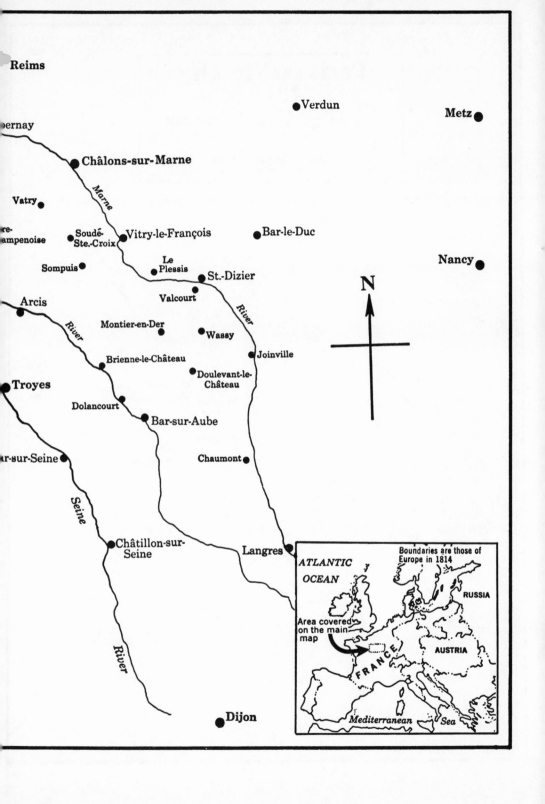

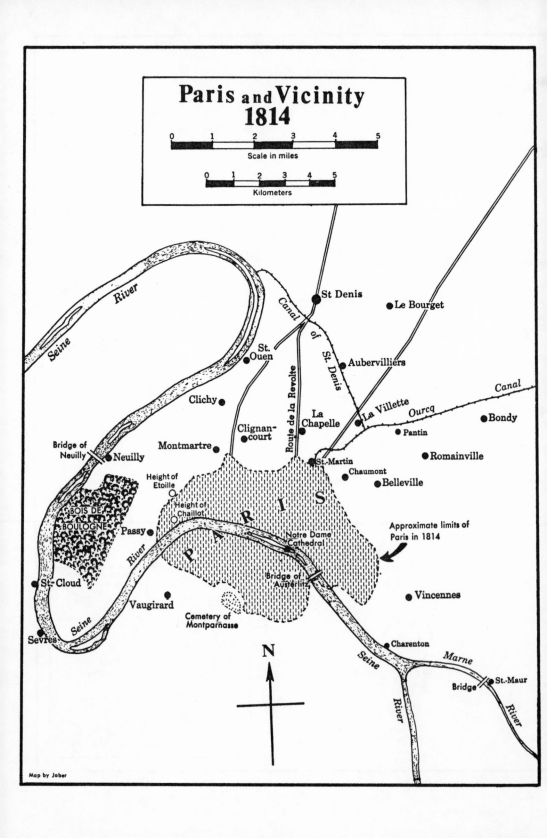

Paris and Vicinity 1814

0 1 2 3 4 5
Scale in miles

0 1 2 3 4 5
Kilometers

Seine River

St Denis

Le Bourget

Canal of St. Denis

St. Ouen

Aubervilliers

Route de la Revolte

Clichy

La Villette

Ourcq Canal

Bondy

Clignan-court

La Chapelle

Pantin

Romainville

Bridge of Neuilly

Montmartre

St.-Martin

Neuilly

Chaumont

Height of Etoile

Belleville

Height of Chaillot

P A R I S

Notre Dame Cathedral

Approximate limits of Paris in 1814

BOIS DE BOULOGNE

Passy

River

Bridge of Austerlitz

St.-Cloud

Vincennes

Vaugirard

Cemetery of Montparnasse

Sèvres

Seine

Charenton

Marne

N

Seine River

Bridge

St.-Maur

River

Map by Jaber

CONTENTS

PREFACE

HUNDREDS OF ACCOUNTS were written by people close to Napoleon and Talleyrand during the eventful days of spring 1814. Marshals, *grandes dames,* valets, statesmen, and mayors left memoirs and diaries. Archives are filled with unpublished records, from police dossiers to Marshal Berthier's register of orders, from diplomatic notes and the operational journals of corps commanders to blood-stained notes carried by couriers.

The wealth of material makes it possible to give details of scenes and conversations documented by those who were there. With few exceptions, quotes and descriptions of scenes are from eyewitnesses, usually from the memoirs of one of the participants. To avoid footnotes, so disturbing to the eye and to the flow of narrative, chapter notes at the end of the book indicate sources.

I wish to thank all those who helped me locate material or allowed me to visit the interiors in which events took place. In France, I am particularly indebted to Bernard Mahieu, *conservateur en chef* of the Archives Nationales, for his aid in finding documents in his own and other repositories; and to the French historian and writer Jean-Baptiste Duroselle, of the Institut de France, for kindly agreeing to read the manuscript. Any errors remain, of course, my own.

INTRODUCTION

HISTORY HAS GIVEN Napoleon's name to his age and glorified his role until his contemporaries often seem to be reduced to bit players beside him. It was not always so. When Napoleon's star was failing in the spring of 1814, the dominant figure in France and all Western Europe was Talleyrand, the brilliant, cynical lame statesman who manipulated heads of state like puppets and juggled the French Emperor's fate in his slender aristocratic hands.

Two men more opposed in character would be hard to find. Napoleon, the single-minded, hot-blooded Corsican, drove himself to the forefront as general at twenty-four, emperor at thirty-four. Talleyrand, the *bon vivant*, gambler, snob, and wit, was a king-maker, not a king, always at work behind the scenes. The two men, once collaborators, alternately admiring and hating one another for sixteen years, engaged in a duel whose outcome shaped the future of France and all Europe.

Talleyrand was once Napoleon's most intimate friend. It was he who helped put Napoleon on the throne, who called Napoleon the most remarkable genius to appear in hundreds of years, who wrote Napoleon in the early days of their collaboration, "My devotion will end with my life."

Yet on March 30, 1814, while still a high official of the empire he had helped to found, Talleyrand turned his back on the Emperor of the French to open the gates of Paris to the enemy Emperor, Alexander of Russia. For seven days, Napoleon had been grasping at victory, preparing for a last battle in which he would win back his place as master of Europe. In the next seven days he lost his empire, his wife, and his son. Louis XVIII gained the throne with the aid of men who had beheaded his brother, Louis XVI. Paris welcomed the enemy army it had dreaded

13

the week before, and Talleyrand emerged from disfavor to become the most influential man in Europe.

For the loss of his empire, Napoleon blamed Talleyrand and Talleyrand blamed Napoleon. "If I had just hanged two men, Talleyrand and Fouché, I would still be on the throne today," Napoleon said from exile on Elba. "*Ah, ce pauvre Napoléon,*" said Talleyrand, "instead of hanging me, he should have listened to me.... Napoleon's greatest traitor was himself."

Was Talleyrand a traitor or, as he claimed, the savior of France? The answer to the question, still debated by historians, lies in the two weeks that begin on March 23 on the plains of Champagne in eastern France.

Part One

NAPOLEON'S GAMBLE

"Victory is within my grasp."
—NAPOLEON at St.-Dizier,
March 23, 1814

I

THE GAMBLE

March 23

IT WAS 3 A.M. on a clear, cold night, March 23, 1814. The small square pink chateau sat on a broad meadow hemmed by forest. Soldiers huddled by bonfires in the clearing. Dozens of candles burned in the upper story of the chateau, where a short, somewhat stout man paced the floor.

Despite the fire, the room was chilly. The man wore a madras kerchief wrapped around his head, a white quilted bathrobe, and white stockings. As he paused a moment by the fire, hands clasped behind his back, an observer would have noticed that his stomach was a bit prominent and his neck a little short, but he was otherwise well proportioned. His traits were regular. His profile, so familiar to all Europe from the coins of the French empire, resembled the classic profile on the coins of another, earlier conqueror to whom he felt akin, Julius Caesar.

Napoleon had dreamed of conquering more territory than Caesar and Alexander the Great combined, but in 1814 he was fighting for survival against a coalition of almost all Europe. Frenchmen, who had come to take Napoleon's victories for granted, were shaken by his recent reverses. In 1812, they had been talking of Napoleon's grandiose plans to march from Moscow to Persia and India as soon as the Tsar signed the peace treaty by the light of his burning capital. Suddenly they learned their emperor had returned to Paris almost alone on a sled, leaving the remnants of his magnificent army of 500,000 to struggle back across a frozen waste. Defeat in Russia was followed by the loss of Germany in

17

1813. One by one Napoleon's allies and the states he had conquered turned on him.

At the beginning of 1814, it had been France's turn to be invaded. The coalition armies attacked from the north, southwest, southeast, and east. It was from the east, however, that they were making their main thrust, along that direct line from the Rhine to Paris that invaders have taken over and over again. Just before Christmas of 1813, two armies totaling 300,000 men crossed the Rhine with three sovereigns riding at their head. Russia's young Tsar, Alexander I, was bent on revenge for Napoleon's invasion of 1812. Stiff and angry King Frederick William of Prussia had a score of humiliations to settle. Last and somewhat reluctant, more often at the rear than the front, came Napoleon's father-in-law, Emperor Francis I of Austria, whose quarrels with France had not ended with Napoleon's marriage to his daughter, Marie-Louise.

Napoleon set out from Paris on January 25 to confront these formidable forces with an army that seldom exceeded 70,000 fighting men. He hardly ever had as many as 30,000 for any single combat. Never had he fought harder. For two months, he averaged twenty or more miles daily with his army, changed headquarters nightly, and inspired his weary men to battle larger, fresher forces almost continuously. Often on horseback from dawn to dark, he spent from midnight to 3 or 4 A.M. each night reading dispatches and issuing the next day's orders.

To a lesser man, the odds might have seemed impossible. To Napoleon, they were a challenge. He had faith in himself and his star, contempt for other men. Though everyone around him was disheartened, as he paced the floor before dawn on March 23, 1814, he felt victory was within his grasp.

The room Napoleon was pacing was a humble one for an emperor. That evening his Imperial Guard had quickly cleared out the chateau's furniture by simply tossing it out the window. Now the room contained the essentials that nightly turned a tent, a corner of a hut, or a room in a palace into Napoleon's campaign study, the center from which he regulated the details of his empire and his army.

Men on Napoleon's staff spoke with awe of his ability to deal from memory with one complex subject after another, as if pulling mental files from neat compartments. Nothing escaped him, from an error of centimes to the loss of a cannon. But Napoleon did not rely on his prodigious memory alone. He furnished and refreshed it constantly with the notebooks, maps, and reports whose daily upkeep was the main duty of his staff.

"The trade of emperor has its tools like any other," he said.

First among these tools on campaign was his traveling library, unloaded from the mules nightly in its partitioned mahogany boxes and stacked, as it was now, on benches around his makeshift study. The twenty volumes of army muster rolls that told him the situation of his armies at all times occupied first place in the library.

"I enjoy reading them the way a young girl enjoys a novel," Napoleon said.

From the rolls, he knew each unit's strength and location. He knew what food supplies, munitions, vehicles, and horses it had, and where the nearest reserves were. If he visited a fort, he knew better than the commander how many cannonballs were in its stores and of what caliber. He could issue orders calling up reinforcements instantly, anywhere, because his notebooks gave him the location of the nearest units with information on their training and battle records. There were detailed records on each officer and subordinate, for the greatest general in the world liked to be able to single out a sergeant at a troop review, tweak his ear affectionately, and recall his part in a famous battle of a dozen years earlier. Touches like this made men still willing to live and die for Napoleon, even men who had lost their blind faith in him.

In addition to the benches holding the traveling library, Napoleon's study contained two tables. A detailed area map, lit by twenty candles, was spread out on one. Rivers and mountains had been clearly outlined by the imperial cartographer, who had just finished moving colored pins to record the latest information on the positions of the opposing armies. A scale ruler and a compass open to measure a day's march on the map lay ready for Napoleon's use.

The second table was piled high with reports. On top were Napoleon's chief of staff's summary of the latest positions of French army units, and his auditor's daily report on enemy positions. Current business of the twenty-four-hour day—reports on enemy movements from scouts, couriers, mayors of nearby towns, local inhabitants, and captured enemy soldiers—was stacked in one corner. The latest army dispatches and the status reports each corps sent headquarters at the end of the day were on the side of the table nearest the map. When these reports had come in sometime after midnight on the twenty-third, Napoleon had been awakened as usual to study them and issue the orders that would set his army on the march before dawn and give him several hours' head start over his sleeping enemy.

"A general-in-chief should never sleep," he said.

Napoleon slept little; his staff slept barely at all. Throughout the night, the tramp of boots on the stairway and the thud of hoofbeats on the drive marked the coming and going of couriers. In the *salon de service* adjoining the study, the cartographer, the aides-de-camp on duty, the equerry, orderlies, and pages napped, fully dressed, on cushions, mattresses, and chairs. They were on call at all hours to work or be sent on a mission, ready to leap to the door at Napoleon's cry, "To horse!" that signaled the departure of the entire army. There was no pattern to the days and nights, no set hour for anything, no forewarning of what would come next. Napoleon's plans changed continually according to events and incoming information. He liked sudden decisions and abrupt departures.

"Keeps men guessing and on their toes," he said.

Napoleon could sleep anywhere, anytime. He could wake up, instantly lucid, dictate an order, and go back to sleep at once. In the middle of a crucial battle, if he decided no substantial change would take place for an hour, he could sleep soundly on the ground. He thrived on activity, returning from campaigns stouter and healthier than before.

"I was made for work," he used to say. "I've never known the limit of my capacity."

For other men, the Emperor's schedule was exhausting. It was particularly hard on the two men Napoleon called on most, now sitting at one of the tables in full uniform, awaiting orders.

Napoleon took a pinch of snuff from a gold box, dribbling most of it on the lapels of his bathrobe. Turning the empty box upside down, he held it out. Baron Fain, secretary and archivist to Napoleon for fifteen of his thirty-six years, scurried to the bedroom behind, brought an identical snuffbox from the row in readiness next to Napoleon's iron camp bed, and sat down again at the table.

Napoleon resumed pacing, his hands joined behind his back again, making his stomach look even rounder. He takes too many hot baths, his secretary thought; that must be what makes him fat because he barely eats and he's so active he wears out everyone around him.

"Write, Berthier!" Napoleon said.

His Most Serene Highness Louis-Alexander Berthier, Marshal of

France, Vice-Constable, Master of the Hounds, Prince of Wagram, Duke of Valengin, Sovereign Prince of Neuchâtel, took up his pen. Short, thick-set, pale-complexioned, and given to wearing clothes as loose-fitting as those Napoleon wore, Berthier was sometimes mistaken for him at a distance. As Napoleon's chief of staff for eighteen years, he had been at his master's side day and night, leading troops and supervising the army in war, leading the hunt and supervising the palace in peace. All his titles were rewards from Napoleon, who had also given him a large yearly income, a mansion in Paris, an estate outside the city, and a pretty young Bavarian princess as his wife.

"But what's the good of it all if you can't enjoy it? It's the tortures of Tantalus," Berthier once said with tears in his eyes.

Now sixty-one, after forty-nine years in the army, he had no time to spend his money, had never set foot in his principality, never relaxed on his estate, barely slept in his Paris town house, and seldom saw his wife and children.

"I want to get to know my children, to make them love me," Berthier wrote on turning sixty. "The greatest joy in life, especially when one grows old, is to be loved."

Marshal Berthier, who usually listened with his finger in his nose, removed it hurriedly to take down Napoleon's staccato dictation, spit out impatiently as if he despised the slowness of human speech. Berthier's feather pen raced over sheets of foolscap. No man could catch the full torrent of words, and interrupting was unthinkable. After eighteen years, Berthier had learned to grasp the essence, fill in blanks later with the emperor's favorite phrases, and correct the proper names Napoleon garbled. When Napoleon read the clear copy Berthier transcribed from his scrawled notes, the Emperor would recognize it as his own and correct. In addition to the recurrence of Napoleon's favorite expressions, which he could see coming like a rondo and simply mark with a sign, Berthier was helped by the Emperor's habit of repeating phrases associated with his current plans. On March 23, they were "Sound the tocsin" and "We are arriving on the enemy's rear." Striding faster in rhythm with his words, Napoleon dictated the orders Berthier was to issue.

Send a gendarme in disguise to Metz, another to Nancy, and one to Bar with letters for the mayors. Tell them we are arriving on the rear of the enemy, that the moment has come to rise in mass, sound the tocsin,

blockade all commanders of fortresses and enemy commissaries, fall
upon convoys, and seize the enemy's stores and reserves. . . . Write the
commander of Metz to get his garrison together and come meet us. . . .

"We'll soon send the enemy scuttling," Napoleon boasted.

The moment had come for which Napoleon had been waiting
throughout the campaign. For almost three months, his 70,000 men had
held off 300,000 invaders. Too weak to confront either of the two
invading armies in a pitched battle, he had resorted to the tactics that had
won him fame fighting in Italy for the French Republic two decades
earlier: divide and conquer.

"The essence of strategy with a weaker army," Napoleon wrote in
1797, "is always to have more force at the decisive point than the
enemy." Outmanuevering, outguessing, outmarching the enemy,
Napoleon attacked him piecemeal, often when the enemy least suspected
he was near. Terrierlike he worried the Allied armies, slashed a flank,
harried a straggling line, routed a weak center. Napoleon's soldiers were
exhausted, but his tactics were successful.

He could not win the war that way, however. He could only keep
the Allies from winning it, and only for a time. Napoleon would run out
of soldiers long before the Allies did.

His plan for victory was based on another of his favorite tactics, an
attack on the enemy rear. In a rear attack, he also faced only a part of his
enemy's forces with all of his own, but he had the added advantage that
the enemy's defense was weakened by being in reverse. Furthermore, a
rear attack cut off the enemy's supply lines and communications, his link
with his reserves, and his path of retreat. Napoleon's goal throughout the
campaign had been to make a sufficiently strong and persistent attack on
the Allies' rear to trap their armies in France or send them racing for the
Rhine. Napoleon knew a superior army could be defeated by being cut
off in a hostile, distant country; it had happened to him in Russia. It
could happen to Tsar Alexander and his allies now, in France.

What had so far prevented Napoleon from pursuing his plan until
the Allies retreated across the Rhine was a lack of men. He was facing
not one but two Allied armies marching separately: the Grand Allied
Army under the command of Prince Schwarzenberg and the smaller,
tougher Army of Silesia under old Marshal Blücher. Napoleon was
unable to attack both armies from the rear simultaneously, and he did

not have enough men to protect Paris adequately from one while attacking the other. Each time Napoleon attacked the rear of one of the Allied armies, its commander instantly retreated eastward to protect his communications, supplies, and reserves, while the second Allied army advanced on Paris. When Napoleon turned back to rescue the capital, his move would give the retreating army time to recover and launch a new offensive. Napoleon would cut that short in turn by moving to the rear, and the pattern would be repeated again.

Four times in the winter of 1814, one or the other of the Allied armies had gotten close enough to the capital to shake Paris with the roar of cannon, and four times Napoleon had forced the Allies to retreat by marching on their rear.

Circumstances had changed for Napoleon on March 23. Just six days prior to that, Prince Schwarzenberg's army had been within three days' march of Paris, driving before it the slight forces Napoleon had been able to spare to protect the capital. Once again, Napoleon had moved east to threaten the advancing army's rear. Schwarzenberg had fled toward Germany at once in what amounted to panic.

Napoleon's success in sending 100,000 men into a rout by a maneuver with a marching army of 30,000 can only be explained by the almost superstitious terror he inspired in his enemies. Rumors of his approach sent huge armies flying helter-skelter. He had only to appear before his own troops to goad the most discouraged to incredible feats. Napoleon estimated his presence on the battlefield as worth 100,000 men, though his rival, Wellington, felt 40,000 to be a more accurate figure.

On the eighteenth of March, Schwarzenberg's alarm was greater than ever before for several reasons. First, the peasants in the eastern part of France, exasperated by Allied requisitions and destruction, were attacking the invaders more and more boldly. Rumor had it that the Swiss were about to turn on the Allies too and cut off the possibility of a retreat through Basel. Lastly, the Army of Silesia had been immobilized for days at Laon, eighty-four miles from Paris, by the illness of its commander, Blücher. Though his own forces were three or four times larger than Napoleon's, Schwarzenberg was terrified at the thought of fighting the French without Blücher's army by his side.

"I admit I tremble," he wrote his wife. "What if I were beaten! What a triumph for Napoleon!"

One of the Russian aides-de-camp wrote, "We no longer know what we want," while a general admitted, "The confusion and dismay at headquarters are impossible to imagine."

Allied officers and soldiers felt surrounded. How would they ever escape from this hostile country if Napoleon got all the way to their rear, to St.-Dizier, and blocked their retreat with his united forces? The British Military Commissioner to the Allied Armies wrote Britain's foreign secretary that every Allied officer was longing for peace, and that Schwarzenberg himself at times wished he were back in safety on the Rhine.

"The fact is, our operations are very singular," Commissioner Lord Burghersh concluded. "We are afraid of fighting."

The Allies' greatest fears were about to be realized. On the twenty-third, Napoleon was preparing to move to St.-Dizier from the chateau of Plessis. He counted on being able to carry his plan through to victory this time. He had already received reports of Schwarzenberg's rapid retreat. He knew Schwarzenberg's timidity as a general well, for the prince had been under his command in Russia in 1812 when Austria was still an ally of France. Napoleon was certain of being able to continue drawing Schwarzenberg's Grand Allied Army after him, and for the first time he felt he could head east without worrying about an attack on Paris. It would take a bold man to lead the Army of Silesia against Paris while Schwarzenberg was in full retreat. Blücher was the only man capable of doing it, and Blücher was ill. Under the circumstances, Napoleon wrote, it was "absurd" to think Blücher would attempt an offensive alone against Paris: "Blücher would have to be mad to try anything serious." Besides, if Napoleon's appearance on the Aube had sent Schwarzenberg into a panic-stricken rout, imagine how he would react when he learned Napoleon had crossed the Marne and reached St.-Dizier! He would be calling on Blücher to join him, and the two commanders would be grateful to be allowed to reach the Rhine. Nevertheless, Napoleon was cautious. "Twenty-four hours can bring about many changes in a military situation," he said. "I am going to St.-Dizier to wait."

Cautious he might be, but his voice was buoyant as he dictated orders to Berthier at Plessis. The cavalry was to ride in all directions to make French forces appear greater and wider spread than they were. Orders were sent in duplicate, in triplicate. Horsemen were to gallop from town to town in the east to arouse resistance forces. Everyone—peasants, partisan bands, army detachments—would join in pursuing and harassing the enemy, capturing his couriers, occupying bridges, blocking defiles. As Napoleon developed his ideas, his animation increased. His sentences exploded, one after another. He twisted his right arm and pulled at his cuff as he always did when absorbed.

He was a far different man from the one Berthier had seen just two days earlier, after his defeat at Arcis-sur-Aube.

The battle of Arcis had been a total mistake. Both Napoleon and the Allies were just passing through, Napoleon on his way east to cut off Schwarzenberg's army, Schwarzenberg on his way east to prevent Napoleon from doing so. Neither had wanted to confront the other, and both had at first refused to believe the other was there. Schwarzenberg was convinced the French troops he saw across the Aube were merely detached units, and Napoleon was certain Schwarzenberg could not have retreated rapidly enough to have reached Arcis with his army. Both were wrong, but for Napoleon, the consequences were much graver.

When Napoleon discovered his error, 120,000 Allied soldiers were descending upon his army of 30,000, trapped in a hollow with no suitable retreat. Behind them lay only lowlands, a river, and a swamp, all in full view of the enemy charging down the hills opposite.

The French fought courageously. Napoleon, always in the center of the fray, acted as if he had given up hope of winning and wanted only to die on the field. Sword in hand, he led charges and pointed cannon. He was sometimes surrounded by the enemy. He escaped a saber thrust by a miracle, and once he forced his horse over the lighted fuse of a shell about to explode. The horse was killed, but Napoleon was unhurt.

At noon on the second day of battle, after thirty hours of combat, the Allies were ranged on the hills in a defensive position, ready to receive the last desperate charge they were certain the French would make. Schwarzenberg, always cautious, was determined to take full advantage of his position by waiting for Napoleon to make the first move.

On the French side, Napoleon, far from preparing to attack, was sitting with bowed head and dreamy expression on a chair by the narrow bridge over the Aube. For two hours he sat there, raising his head from time to time to praise and encourage his men as they picked their way through the narrow streets of the half-burned town, clambered over the corpses of men and horses, and filed past him in a thin, vulnerable line, heading away from the enemy. Beyond the town, the French still had to cross a raised road a thousand paces long over a swamp. Yet, in one of the more curious pauses of military history, Schwarzenberg and his 120,000 men stood by, awaiting a charge. Napoleon had gambled his army on the assumption Schwarzenberg would refuse to believe the French capable of attempting a daylight retreat in the face of such odds. When the Allies attacked, it was too late. Almost all the French had escaped.

In all, Napoleon had lost 3000 or 4000 men. He could ill afford their loss, but he had saved his army. The battle of Arcis renewed Napoleon's contempt for his enemy. Schwarzenberg had not only let the French slip away, he had allowed them to proceed north.

And now Napoleon was about to lead them to victory from Plessis.

Throughout the early-morning hours on March 23, Napoleon's aides-de-camp left the chateau with orders calling in his scattered troops for an all-out gamble to defeat the invaders. The forces Napoleon had left on the Aube to hold back the Allies would march north to join him. Marshals Marmont and Mortier, whom he had left near Paris to delay any advance on the capital, would join him from the west with their 17,000 men. The 60,000 to 70,000 men garrisioned in French fortresses in Metz, Verdun, and elsewhere along the Rhine, the Meuse, and the Moselle, would break through enemy blockades to join him from the east. His light cavalry units were already fanning northeast to open communications with the garrisons.

Napoleon was close to those strongholds in the chateau of Plessis. He would be closer still that night at St.-Dizier, ten miles farther east, as he awaited the gathering of his troops. Before the week was out, reinforced by his garrisons and supported by the populace of Burgundy, Franche-Comté, and of Alsace and Lorraine on both sides of the Vosges Mountains, he would hurl his united army against the enemy rear. The Allies would be pinned inside France without supplies, reserves, or communications. Demoralized, their escape cut off, they would wait helplessly while Napoleon moved back to the Rhine, gathered fresh supplies and reinforcements, and dictated a triumphant peace from Germany.

"I am closer to Munich than the Allies are to Paris," Napoleon said. "They thought the lion was dead and all they had to do was piss on him. I'll surprise them with my victories yet!"

While Napoleon confidently put his plan for victory into operation from Plessis, a lone carriage lurched across the gutted roads of Champagne bearing a man anxious to bring him bad news. This was the man Napoleon had talked to most over the last few years, about everything and everyone—his wife, the heads of Europe, the past, the future, war and peace, his plans and regrets. Napoleon talked, but he listened less and less. If he won't listen to me now, the man in the carriage thought, he's ruined, and he'll pull France down in ruins with him. Napoleon's chief equerry and foreign minister, Caulaincourt, Duke of Vicence, urged on the horses.

The beasts sank to their knees in mud, labored over still-frozen ruts, stumbled in holes left by the passing of carts, artillery, horses, and thousands of weary men. It was all but impossible to walk or ride though that mud, much less move armies over it. Yet for over two months, the warring armies had been grunting, bogging down in swamps, dragging, pulling, pushing caissons and supplies and cannon, east to west, west to east. Crossing and recrossing the rivers that dominated this battle-field—the Seine, the Marne, and the Aube—they were buffeted by rain, sleet, hail, and wind.

Sometimes the armies were so close on each others' heels that enemy soldiers lit their bivouac fires from the embers left by Napoleon's men, while the invading Emperor of Russia slept in the bed warmed by Napoleon a night or two before. The network of paths the opposing armies traced covered an egg-shaped area between Paris and the Rhine, widening in the middle across the plains of Champagne and narrowing at either end, Nancy to the east, and Meaux, less than thirty miles from Paris, in the west.

At times, Allied and French lines were so entangled it was impossible to sort them out. Indeed, figuring out where the enemy was and which way he was headed was one of the greatest problems both defender and invader faced. The plains of Champagne are deceptive. You may think you are on flat land or a height from which everything for miles around is visible, yet there can be just enough of a dip over the horizon to hide an entire army. Sometimes Napoleon's army and the enemy's would be a cannon shot apart without knowing it.

Caulaincourt had been scanning the horizon in search of Napoleon's army for the past two days and nights. During the day, he could see twenty or thirty miles across the gently sloping plains that faded into the blue distance. It was a desolate sight. Not a man, not a tree, not a bush. Even in peacetime, you could travel for leagues without seeing a tree or a bush in Champagne. But in peace there were fields golden with grain, green pastures filled with cows, sheep, and goats, and red or gray tracts of plowed land—a bucolic patchwork stretching almost endlessly

under a changeable sky whose scudding clouds and sudden storms
spattered the plain with splotches of dark and light. There was a sweep
to it, a grandeur, and, at the same time, a quiet charm.

Now the empty pastures and unplowed fields presented a monotonous and mournful picture. In a few places, Caulaincourt had seen
women, children, and old men dragging ladders or thorny branches
across the soil, trying to scratch the half-frozen surface enough to give
the grain a place to root. The soil is poor in this part of Champagne,
south of the famous vineyards, but the peasants had always managed to
survive by planting hardy crops like rye, oats, barley, and wheat. Next
year, unless a miracle happened, there would be almost nothing to
harvest.

Poor Champagne, thought Caulaincourt, staring at the ravaged
countryside from his jolting carriage. *Ma fidèle Champagne,* my faithful
Champagne, Napoleon called it. The peasants, outraged by enemy
excesses, were attacking isolated enemy units with pitchforks, picking
up abandoned enemy guns to fire on troops retreating from towns, and
risking their lives to bring news or prisoners to their emperor at his
headquarters. *It can't go on, France cries for peace.* Caulaincourt sighed as
he rolled past stumps of trees on the approach to a town.

Everything that would burn had been burned by 400,000 French
and enemy soldiers seeking fuel in a region that had never had enough
for its inhabitants. The sparse roadside trees and the trees planted in
valleys to hold back floods had all been cut and burned. The farmers'
wooden plows had been burned, along with wooden hoes, pitchforks,
shovels, and carts. The plow horses were gone, stolen by Cossacks,
requisitioned by the invaders or by Napoleon's army—little did it
matter which, they were gone.

The villages were as gloomy as the countryside. In some that
Caulaincourt's carriage passed, all the houses had been leveled to the
height of a man. The straw roofs had been burned, the characteristic
latticed beams of the second stories torn down for fuel. Most houses had
neither doors nor shutters left. The few surviving chickens and pigs had
the run of almost empty courtyards. Stores were closed because there
was nothing to sell. People were idle because there was nothing to do.
They ran out to stare at the man who dared to travel at the risk of being
caught between warring armies or robbed and beaten by the bands of
Cossacks terrorizing the countryside. Caulaincourt's passport and visas
(without which no one could move) were closely examined at the

barrier to each town. The traveler himself was besieged with questions by people eager for news, often ignorant of what was happening five miles away.

Caulaincourt's weary horses labored into the hilltop town of Sézanne about midnight on March 23. The posting inn had neither news of Napoleon nor fresh horses. Impatiently, Caulaincourt resigned himself to giving his team a two-hour rest. Two hours, when every moment counted, when the Allies might already be drawing close to Paris.

"I had the fever of despair and death in my heart," Caulaincourt wrote.

He had to find Napoleon quickly and convince him that if he did not give in now, it would be too late; all chance to negotiate peace would be irrevocably lost.

Napoleon had ignored Caulaincourt's warning that the peace conference at Châtillon-sur-Seine would be broken off if he refused the Allies' demands. Now it had happened. To hear Napoleon talk, you would think the peace talks were in distant Prussia, not 150 miles from Paris. You would think Napoleon commanded huge armies rather than decimated corps of exhausted veterans and raw recruits, and that the maps of battlefields he pored over each night were of Silesia or Lithuania, not France.

When would he face reality? Caulaincourt had come to dread his master's victories more than his losses because victories encouraged Napoleon's blind obstinacy. Every time Napoleon won a battle, he was less willing than ever to hear talk of concessions. As if a victory over one enemy corps counted, when masses of Allies covered France, converging from all sides! Besides, when Napoleon won a battle in one place, his generals were usually losing one somewhere else, because there weren't enough forces to go around.

"Everyone was saying the same thing," said Caulaincourt, "everyone at Napoleon's headquarters as well as in Paris. Everyone was discouraged, not because of daily dangers, but because there was no foreseeable end to them."

Only Napoleon could put an end to the dangers by making peace, and he refused.

A month earlier, Caulaincourt had gotten a message at Châtillon from one of Napoleon's most prominent generals, Belliard, who had fought in every imperial campaign. "Tell Caulaincourt we don't have an army anymore," Belliard had said. "Tell him the only hope we have left lies with him."

"Never was a man in a more painful position than I," Caulaincourt wrote in his journal. "If I agreed to sign what the Allies demanded, I was a traitor, a coward. If signing would have saved France, I would have signed anyway, but it wouldn't. Having forbidden me to commit myself to the Allies without his consent, Napoleon would refuse to ratify what I signed. Within a week, everyone would have been dissatisfied. They would all have thought the Allies had demanded so much only because I had been weak. The charitable would call me too yielding; the others would call me a traitor, and Napoleon's army, crying for peace now, would have cried treason!"

Napoleon saw as clearly as Caulaincourt that the country would soon come to detest the man who signed the peace it clamored for.

"France needs peace," he said, "but the peace the enemy wants to impose would bring more misery than the most devastating war.... What would I be to the French once I signed their humiliation?... Can I leave France smaller than I found it after all our struggles, bloodshed, and victories? Never! Could I, without being a traitor or a coward?... You're afraid of continuing the war," Napoleon told Caulaincourt, "but what I fear is other, more certain dangers you don't see.... I prefer to gamble on war, however desperate the odds!"

If Napoleon was determined to put the fate of his empire on the barrel of his last cannon, Caulaincourt was equally determined to save France, the empire, and the Emperor at the conference table. Now that peace talks had broken down, he was certain the Allies would stop vacillating and fight in earnest. They would head straight for Paris to overthrow Napoleon's government, and Napoleon would be unable to stop them.

Being a diplomat, Caulaincourt tried to find some advantage in the new situation. Perhaps, he told himself, a separate peace plan could be worked out with Austria, apart from her allies. Austria had always been conciliatory; it was her allies who were false, treacherous, and vengeful. How could Austria want to see Napoleon's empire destroyed? Napoleon was the Austrian Emperor's son-in-law, Napoleon's empire was Austria's heritage too. Surely Emperor Francis would not dethrone his own daughter and disinherit his grandson if Napoleon agreed to compromise in time—but there lay the problem. Even if Caulaincourt reached

Napoleon before the Allies got to Paris, there was no certainty that the Emperor would pay any more attention to his arguments than before.

Napoleon had grown increasingly obstinate in recent weeks. Caulaincourt dishonored him, he said. He no longer read Caulaincourt's reports; they bored him. When Caulaincourt urged him to make peace while there was still a chance, Napoleon said peace always came soon enough if it was a dishonorable one. Still, Napoleon's last dispatch, sent from Reims on the seventeenth, had given Caulaincourt a glimmer of hope when he received it just after leaving Châtillon. Caulaincourt had written Austrian Foreign Minister Metternich at once that he had no doubt an understanding could still be reached.

"I hasten to our headquarters in order to see you again the sooner," he concluded.

Two days later, Caulaincourt was still hastening to French headquarters. But where were they? He asked everywhere. No one seemed to know. By moving east to cut off Allied communication lines, the Emperor had cut off his own communications with Paris and the forces he had left to shield the capital. The French general guarding Nogent, sixty miles southeast of Paris, had had no word from or about Napoleon since the Allies had fled east on March 18. Farther on his journey, Caulaincourt heard from two peasants that the Allies had reversed themselves and were marching on Paris again. He pushed on in increasing anguish, champing at delays, sleeping in his jolting carriage.

A postal inspector passed on a rumor that the emperor had headed northwest toward Sézanne, but when Caulaincourt went to the local army headquarters after arriving there on March 23, he found that the colonel in charge knew no more of Napoleon's whereabouts than he did. Indirectly, the colonel had heard that marshals Marmont and Mortier were being attacked northeast of Paris by large forces and had lost contact with Napoleon. Caulaincourt's alarm redoubled. Cossack bands were intercepting all couriers, the colonel told him. Just that evening, twelve miles to the east, near Fère-Champenoise, two couriers had been captured, one of them said to have been carrying a letter to the Emperor from the Empress, along with some government dispatches.

If the courier had gone through Fère-Champenoise, that must be the way to Napoleon's headquarters, Caulaincourt concluded. He set off in that direction with his barely rested horses at 2 A.M. Meeting a grain convoy en route, he joined it for safety, though it was making a slight detour south from the main road toward the little town of Sompuis. A few hours later, he would find himself in a battle for life.

When Caulaincourt joined the grain convoy, Napoleon was still in his study at the chateau of Plessis, checking on the execution of previous orders. He had more and more occasion to complain. Shortages of material were constant, human failures more and more frequent. Since the enemy had crossed the Rhine, his officers no longer obeyed orders instantly and unquestioningly. Napoleon fumed. Where were the horses and wagons? The bread rations? The *eau de vie*? Why hadn't the advance guard reached St.-Dizier?

"Write General St.-Germain," he dictated to Berthier, "that he failed to go to St.-Dizier yesterday as ordered, he must go there early today and reconnoiter to the southwest since that's the direction from which the enemy might approach. Ask General Defrance why he hasn't reported in . . . tell him we should have at least three reports daily. . . . Tell General Sorbier he must send in accounts of the movements of the main artillery twice a day, that we still don't know what time he crossed the ford yesterday or where he is now. . . . Write General Blein the bridge equipment was so badly made we lost an entire day putting it up and then found it almost useless. . . ."

The candles were low and sputtering when Napoleon's thoughts turned at last to Paris.

"Give me a pretty little piece of paper and a good pen," he said. "My good Louise must be able to read me."

My good Louise. All his letters to his wife began either *mon amie* or *ma bonne Louise*. In his illegible scrawl and capricious spelling, Napoleon wrote:

> *Mon amie*, I've been on horseback all these days. The twentieth, I took Arcis-sur-Aube. The enemy attacked me there at 6 P.M. I beat him that same day and killed 4000 of his men. I took two cannon and he took two, which made us even. The twenty-first, the enemy army drew up battle lines to protect convoys heading for Brienne and Bar-sur-Aube. I decided to move toward the Marne against his communications to draw him farther from Paris and get closer to my strongholds. I'll be at St.-Dizier this evening. *Adieu, mon amie*. A kiss for my son.
>
> NAP

He had written his young wife short, reassuring letters like this from Poland, from Russia, from Germany, almost every day that he was away fighting for the past four years. It was, in fact, just four years ago to the day that nineteen-year-old Marie-Louise had crossed the Rhine on her way to marry the man she had been brought up to regard as the scourge of Europe. Trembling outside her father's capital of Vienna in the summer of 1809 while Napoleon occupied it in triumph, the young archduchess was looked upon as a little lamb sacrificed to interests of state.

"I'll do everything my dear papa wishes," Emperor Francis I's dutiful daughter said when the alliance was proposed.

Poor Iphigenia, the Austrian courtiers called her, but by the time she reached the Rhine in March 1810, she was more bored than apprehensive. Travel was slow and arduous in those days, even for a future empress. Marie-Louise looked forward to the end of the trip.

"I'm really anxious to see the Emperor," she said. When she met him at last, she found him "surprisingly gentle for such a formidable man of war," and before a week was out, confessed, "I think I may soon like him very much."

While Marie-Louise was being wooed and won by Napoleon, the ladies of the French court who had escorted her across France gossiped about their new empress with sophisticated malice. She said quite common things, they reported, asked the townspeople wherever they stopped streams of idiotic questions about her aunt, Marie-Antoinette, wanted to hear about the troubles people had had during "that terrible thing, the Revolution," misused French words and phrases she picked up, and exlaimed childishly over the diamonds Napoleon's courtiers wore. When an answer pleased her, she guffawed without parting her teeth. She was more homely than pretty, much too red in the face, her manners were gauche, her clothes impossible. She had a mediocre mind and no wit; her daily *niaiseries* regaled the court. Still, she was a good-natured girl for an Austrian archduchess, the ladies concluded.

Napoleon was delighted with his rosy-fleshed German dumpling. Weeks before she arrived, he was transformed. His generals hardly recognized the conqueror of Europe in this almost effeminate man. His courtiers were amused.

"Our Solomon is learning all the games of childhood while awaiting his Queen of Sheba," one of them wrote.

Then forty-one, Napoleon plunged wholeheartedly into the role of an ardent bridegroom about to marry a woman half his age. He got a new tailor who made him such tight-fitting clothes that Napoleon discarded them soon after his marriage. He tried to look younger, used lotion on his hands, makeup on his face. He lingered in front of mirrors, gave up the snuff that blackened his nostrils, hummed the latest tunes, learned to dance, doused himself with eau de cologne, fixed the curl in the middle of his forehead with pomade, laced his round middle with a waist cincher, and adopted a brisk, youthful walk.

If Napoleon regretted any of Marie-Louise's shortcomings, he was nevertheless happy with her, and he found it easy to make her happy. All she wanted was the sort of life a merchant's daughter in Graz might have enjoyed. She had lessons in drawing, painting, piano, and harp, rode horseback, played cards and billiards, embroidered, and followed to the letter the day Napoleon designed for her. She was up at eight, spent from eight to ten dressing, and received visits of minor importance until eleven-o'clock lunch (eaten in her own apartments if Napoleon did not send for her). After lunch came a ride or a walk in the park "to yawn and stretch awhile under the trees," as she put it. From one to two, she read a few pages of a novel or practiced the piano. Various lessons filled in the afternoon until five-o'clock tea, followed by a few official visits.

Sometimes Napoleon interrupted this routine by dropping in to caress her lapdog, tell her stories in atrocious German, play on her piano, or pose for her to paint his portrait. At six, Marie-Louise joined Napoleon for dinner, but dinner was over in ten or fifteen minutes. Even at a state banquet, Napoleon ate little and fast. Shortly after dinner, he usually returned to his sanctuary to work, leaving the courtiers on duty and the ministers and officials favored with admission to the inner palace circle to amuse the Empress. Marie-Louise's only complaint was that Napoleon's empire kept him much too busy.

"Our Austrian princes do much less work," she said.

"To the Empress," Napoleon said, handing his letter to Baron Fain at Plessis and adding, as he did when in a good mood, "To the lady of my thoughts, the queen of my heart."

Baron Fain sealed it, wrote *"Letter from the Emperor to the Empress"* on it, and called an orderly to send it on its way at once by estafette. Letters sent by estafette passed from one secure hand to another, traveling continuously, outdistancing those sent by courier, since couriers had to stop to eat and sleep. Napoleon's letters to Marie-Louise always went by estafette because he wanted her to be the first to have news of him.

Hers were the letters Napoleon looked for first when a courier arrived, but he had received none for a while. Her letter of the twenty-first and a routine report on her health and activities sent from Paris never reached him, but Napoleon could picture what she was doing without them. When Baron Fain sealed Napoleon's note and Napoleon closed the green silk curtains around his camp bed for two or three hours' sleep, Marie-Louise was asleep in Paris. When she got up, she would follow the same routine Napoleon had established for her when they were first married except that, on occasion, instead of playing whist and billiards in the evenings, Marie-Louise had to preside as regent over a council of ministers. She had been filled with dread when Napoleon appointed her regent of France in March 1813. She wrote her family and confidantes of the burden of governing, the boring councils, the "melancholy role of regent." She envied her sister, still running carefree in the sunlit gardens of Schoenbrunn. The burden did not prove heavy enough to transform the Empress's routine, as the report for Napoleon of March 22 attests:

> The health of the Empress is excellent. Yesterday the weather was so fine she decided to ride her horse. She felt refreshed by the exercise, which she repeated today.
>
> Her Majesty awaited letters from the Emperor all day. She has had none since one of March 20 from Plancy. During the past two days, she has been very gay. She was a little anxious before. When she came back from her ride, she wrote several letters to her family, an occupation that took up the entire afternoon and took the place of drawing. That is an irregularity seldom seen in the Empress's routine, for each hour has its invariable occupation. Yesterday Her Majesty sketched alone; Isabey [her tutor in drawing] has been ill for two days.

Among the letters the Empress wrote home was one Napoleon had asked her to write, in his last letter. It was one of many appeals urging Emperor Francis I to influence his allies to offer peace terms acceptable to Napoleon.

"I would very much like my letters to have a good effect," Marie-Louise wrote her husband on March 21, "but I don't think they will. Papa doesn't pay much attention to me in politics."

Whether she thought Papa François would listen or not, she wrote whenever Napoleon asked her to, conscientiously putting in her own words all he told her to say.

"Don't underestimate the Empress," Napoleon said more than once to Caulaincourt.

Her lack of imagination and sensitivity made her solid, reliable, and firm. Her loyalty was unwavering, her obedience prompt and unquestioning. If Napoleon asked her to review troops, to address the legislative body, to write her father, to receive someone, or to stop receiving someone, she did so at once. Though timid, she was so dutiful that Napoleon believed she would be capable of bold action if he demanded it.

Used to relying on people only for the execution of orders, Napoleon did not ask more of his wife or his regent. Besides, whom could he count on in Paris other than his child wife? Not his brothers King Joseph and King Jérôme, who had lost the kingdoms he gave them. Not the mediocre functionaries he had brought to power, who vacillated over minute decisions, sought Napoleon's approval of every detail, and postponed action as long as possible.

"Posterity will never know how difficult it was to build a monarchy out of the material I had on hand," Napoleon said.

He had not even been able to find reliable advisers for Marie-Louise's guidance in his absence. He cautioned her constantly against the two he appointed. He distrusted the judgment of aging Archchancellor Cambacérès, a man his contemporaries described as worthless in a crisis. He suspected his brother Joseph of trying to seduce Marie-Louise and take empire and empress for himself.

"Joseph is a pygmy who acquired the bad habit of ambition in Spain," Napoleon wrote his wife in mid-March. "Am I destined to be betrayed by him? It wouldn't surprise me."

Napoleon railed at the inaction of his government in almost daily dispatches.

"Has everyone gone mad in Paris? You're all asleep.... I'm no longer obeyed, I'm constantly opposed with buts and ifs and fors...."

He was certain that if his government backed him wholeheartedly, the nation would too.

"The people have energy and a sense of humor," he wrote Joseph. "It is certain leaders who hesitate to fight.... All France would be up in arms by now if it weren't for the cowardice of her ministers."

Napoleon was discovering that incompetence can be as harmful as treachery, and he suspected treachery as well. Sometimes it was hard to tell the difference. "You're either clumsy or disobedient," he wrote Minister of Police Rovigo. He suspected Minister of War Clarke of plotting against him. He knew the commander of the First Paris Division, General Hulin, was pretending he had no arms in order to avoid issuing them to the Parisian National Guard. Talleyrand, Vice Grand Elector and the most intelligent opponent of his war policies, he regarded as his greatest threat.

As long as Napoleon had been victorious, the men he put in office had obeyed him blindly. Now the once obedient raised questions, showed doubts. From hesitating to carry out orders to ignoring them was a short step, and Napoleon was too far from Paris to discipline the culprits. Nevertheless, he did not believe anyone, even Talleyrand, would try to overthrow him.

"How could they? Don't they need me? Aren't they more afraid of a revolution or the return of the Bourbons than of me?"

Napoleon had reason to believe that in his ungoverned, undefended capital with its fickle, mercurial population, he could count only on the loyal obedience of his Austrian wife, Marie-Louise. Therefore it did not matter to him, it neither surprised nor dismayed him, that at twenty-three, Marie-Louise was living exactly as she had lived at nineteen; as regent, exactly as she had as a teen-age empress; in a desperate war, exactly as she had in peacetime. She would be sleeping, he knew, as he rose at six to fight again, but she was loyal. She obeyed. She was *ma bonne Louise.*

As light dawned at 6 A.M., Caulaincourt, staring out the windows of his carriage, at last saw what he had been seeking for two days. Red plumes bobbed from the tall bearskin hats of Napoleon's cannoneers ahead.

Caulaincourt had caught up to an artillery park moving painfully north to join Napoleon at Vitry-le-François. The wheels of the big guns, caissons, and wagons were constantly getting stuck, the white leggings of the artillery men were black with mud, and the column had gotten strung out over almost two miles in the struggle. Caulaincourt joined the tail end, happy to know he was at last nearing Napoleon's headquarters.

As the convoy approached Sompuis, 1700 Russian hussars, dragoons, and lancers galloped down a hill to attack it. Confusion in orders had left the artillery park with an escort of only 250 national guardsmen. The artillery commander formed his few hundred drivers into the traditional defense position, squares of men facing outward with bayonets leveled, officers inside the squares, guns at all four corners. By a miracle, the squares withstood the first savage charge. Over a dozen French subordinate officers and cannoneers on horseback dashed boldly out of the squares to saber the retreating Russians.

It was a brief triumph. When the Russians fired shells on the caissons and blew up several of them, the squares broke apart. The enemy heavy cavalry charged, scattering the French while the Russian light horse rushed to encircle them.

Every Frenchman, including Caulaincourt, would have been killed or captured if a French cavalry detachment on reconnaissance had not heard cannon fire and come to the rescue. The enemy made off with hundreds of prisoners, at least fifteen big guns, and a courier carrying imperial dispatches, but Caulaincourt escaped. Abandoning his slow-moving carriage for the horse of a French cannoneer killed in the fight, he joined his rescuers to continue north toward St.-Dizier. When he caught up to the commander of the artillery and cavalry, Marshal Macdonald, Caulaincourt had a chance to find out what had happened in the last few days' fighting.

Four days earlier, Macdonald and Marshal Oudinot had been within fifty miles of Paris with orders to hold back the advancing Allies. Heavily outnumbered, they were yielding ground steadily when the Allies suddenly began to retreat. Even before new orders arrived from Napoleon, Macdonald realized the only possible explanation for the Allies' retreat was that Napoleon had moved to threaten their rear.

Macdonald followed the enemy east. The Allies, he wrote Napoleon en route, seemed to be heading for Arcis, and so rapidly that he was unable to catch up to their rear guard. Ordered by Napoleon to bring all his troops to Arcis as quickly as possible, Macdonald pressed on, preceded by Oudinot.

Riding ahead of his men along the north bank of the river Aube, Macdonald reached Arcis on the afternoon of the twenty-first. To his astonishment, he saw black masses of enemy covering the hills on the far side of the river, over 100,000 of them, in a motionless semicircle. On his own side of the river, he saw a thin column of French forces retreating north over mercilessly exposed terrain within range of enemy cannon.

Macdonald galloped on. Napoleon was seated by a campfire in the middle of the public square of Arcis.

"What's the reason for withdrawing troops from here?" Macdonald asked.

"The enemy is retreating," Napoleon said. "I am heading for Vitry to cut off their communications. We've got them now, they'll pay for being so rash."

"They're retreating?" Macdonald could not believe his ears. "They're in position just across the river. I saw them massed there myself, and your own retreat is completely exposed. How are you going to stop them if they attack?"

"They won't dare, all they're concerned about is getting back across the Rhine. . . ."

Interrupting Macdonald's protests, Napoleon asked when his troops would arrive.

"Very late tonight."

"Fine. You will support Marshal Oudinot, who will continue to act under your command."

Napoleon told Berthier to take down Macdonald's orders. While he was dictating, Marshal Ney, who had gone to observe the enemy, arrived.

"What are they doing?" Napoleon asked.

"Not moving," said Ney. "Not looking at all as if they mean to attack." Shortly, one of Napoleon's aides galloped up at top speed to announce the enemy was advancing.

"That's impossible," said Napoleon.

Guns boomed. Macdonald, sent by Napoleon to reconnoiter on horseback, found Marshal Oudinot in a critical position with only 7000 men to keep the Allied army from crossing the River Aube in pursuit. Oudinot, whose keenest joy was galloping in front of his troops to urge them on in battle, feared his situation was untenable. He begged Macdonald to hurry back to the emperor for help.

"Otherwise I'm done for," he said.

"Don't expect any help from him," said Macdonald. "All his troops are on the way to Vitry."

Napoleon was, in fact, leaving Arcis at that moment. As one of his aides recalled afterward, the emperor turned back to examine the situation with his spyglass. Uttering a sharp exclamation on seeing

Oudinot's perilous position, he rode on slowly, head down, arms and reins dangling, his gray mare following the other horses without guidance.

When Macdonald got back to Arcis, he found Berthier's orders to hold the enemy back until further notice. There was no time to think, only to fight. Enemy soldiers were already pouring across the bridge over the Aube. Oudinot's troops were falling back. Raking the enemy with artillery fire, under the joint leadership of the two marshals, the French managed to repulse the enemy and hack the bridge to bits. In the meantime, Macdonald's 20,000 men arrived and were posted to cover as best they could the three-mile stretch along the river opposite the Allies.

The marshals waited uneasily, fearing another attack after dark. In his dispatch from headquarters at Sompuis that night, Napoleon ordered them to hold firm for two or three days. The marshals worried, grumbled, and held firm. Oudinot had survived thirty-four wounds and fifty-seven campaigns. Macdonald, bad-tempered and outspoken, was as stubborn as he was brave. In leaving them to do the impossible, Napoleon knew they would do or die.

Dawn revealed the Allies still in position across the river, and there they remained all through the twenty-second. On new orders, Marshals Oudinot and Macdonald slipped away just before midnight, heading north to join Napoleon at Vitry. After stopping to camp for just a few hours, Macdonald continued north, once again in the position of rear guard. Harassed all day by Allied detachments, he was afraid the main body of the Allied army, which he glimpsed from time to time, might reach the Marne River before he did and block his crossing.

"If they do, my contact with the Emperor will be cut off again," Macdonald told Caulaincourt as they rode on to Vitry. "If the Allies attack us now, we're finished."

Though Macdonald was convinced he was being followed north by the whole Allied army, some of his officers believed the units they saw were only isolated detachments, masking the movement of the main body. Caulaincourt, certain the main body was marching on Paris, agreed with them. When he reached Vitry and learned that the presence of a stubborn enemy garrison in that town had led Napoleon to continue east, Caulaincourt hurried ahead of Macdonald. Just before five in the afternoon, Caulaincourt came upon the headquarters of Marshal Ney, who was keeping watch on the enemy garrison in Vitry and a ford over the Marne where Napoleon had crossed twenty-four hours earlier.

Caulaincourt continued with an escort of lancers of the Imperial Guard and a fresh horse Ney found for him—a sorry nag belonging to a subordinate officer, but a horse nevertheless.

At midnight, after traveling almost continuously for sixty-six hours over a circuit of 166 miles, a gloomy and exhausted Caulaincourt reached St.-Dizier. He did not have to ask the way to the palace, as Napoleon's headquarters were always called, even if in a tent. Napoleon had stopped in the same house before, at the very beginning of the campaign. Caulaincourt rode straight to the modest home of the mayor of St.-Dizier, a two-and-a-half story dwelling in a row of similar houses. Dismounting in the courtyard, he rushed upstairs. A murmur of voices rose behind him. His thin, worried face told everyone negotiations for peace had failed.

Caulaincourt found the emperor having a jolly midnight supper with Marshal Berthier. The army would have a good day tomorrow, Napoleon felt.

"The pear is ripe, time to pick it," he said, using one of his favorite expressions.

St.-Dizier was the site of his first victory of the campaign two months ago. It was a fitting place from which to launch the maneuver that would drive the Allies out of France for good.

St.-Dizier offered several strategic advantages. It was close to the eastern strongholds and to the border areas Napoleon counted on to rise *en masse* against the enemy. It lay between the two main lines of operation of the Allied armies, the road through Switzerland that Schwarzenberg had taken to the south and the road from Strasbourg that Blücher had taken to the north. And it was not so far from Paris that Napoleon could not rush back there if his plans went awry and the enemy marched on the capital instead of pursuing him. There was some risk, of course. Never before had Napoleon moved to the enemy rear without leaving sizable forces to protect Paris, but this time he needed all his men with him in order to succeed. At worst, he thought, the capital might have to resist for a day or so until he could come to the rescue.

Napoleon had been weighing his next move since his midday arrival at St.-Dizier. He was in any case obliged to await the arrival of the troops of Oudinot and Macdonald before taking action. He hoped, too, to hear of the arrival at Châlons, to the north, of the corps of Marmont and Mortier that he had called back from the vicinity of Paris.

At four-thirty that afternoon he wrote out his alternatives to clarify his thoughts. Though he reviewed all possibilities once more, he had practically committed himself to the strategy of attacking the Allied rear when he crossed the Marne the day before, and his choice was now one of tactics. He was certain Schwarzenberg was following him, but was not sure whether the Austrian was marching in his footsteps through Sompuis and Vitry or had gone eastward via Brienne and Wassy to intercept him as he marched east toward his strongholds.

While Napoleon waited, army scouts and civilian volunteers scurried northeast, southeast, east, and southwest on reconnaissance missions. Officers disguised as woodsmen or peasants went to border regions to organize resistance. Prisoners were interrogated, mayors of nearby towns questioned. Pins were moved on maps, new details were added. Orders continued to flow.

Napoleon needed only a week to carry through his plan. It would take that long to gather in his forces, finish organizing the peasant uprising and mass levy of national guards, and harass the trapped Allies into surrender. The beginning augured well. Good news of successful advances was coming in from commanders of the eastern garrisons. Inhabitants of the border provinces were responding to the stirring call, "If the enemy comes, let the land that bore you be his tomb." The battle of Arcis had proved that, even with vastly inferior forces, Napoleon's appearance still inspired terror in the enemy. His jubilant reception in St.-Dizier that noon proved he still inspired enthusiasm in his people.

Here, as everywhere Napoleon went, anxiety and defeatism turned to noisy and naïve confidence. People flocked around his horse, reached out to touch it, and crowded around him all the way to the gateway of the mayor's house. Optimism swept the surrounding countryside. The enemy was no longer feared, he was hunted down. Peasants outdid each other in taking prisoners and bringing them to the Emperor, who often questioned both captives and captors personally to add details of hills, hollows, and road conditions to the map he carried in his head.

Despite the efforts of Napoleon's scouts and spies, information about the Allies remained exasperatingly sketchy and contradictory through most of the twenty-third. "The enemy is concentrating at Brienne ... retreating to Langres.... Emperor Alexander slept at Montier-en-Der.... Macdonald is pressed closely in his retreat toward Vitry by the entire Allied Army...." A scout Napoleon sent to Sompuis the afternoon of the twenty-third was unable to get through because of the presence of enemy troops. Were they isolated units or part of the main army?

At last, soldiers brought in two intercepted dispatches, one in Russian and one in German, taken from a courier en route from Allied headquarters to the beseiged enemy commander in Vitry. Napoleon called in his translator. Both dispatches directed the Vitry commander to hold out if attacked and assured him the Allies were following Napoleon step by step.

Soon after, encouraging reports began pouring in from Napoleon's advance guard. Joinville and Chaumont, once key points along Allied lines of communication, were in French hands. While Allied reserves were being evacuated eastward, the enemy army was following Napoleon so closely that the Allied sovereigns made their headquarters the night of the twenty-third at Sompuis, where Caulaincourt and the artillery park had been attacked that morning. Tsar Alexander slept in the house in which Napoleon had slept two nights before.

Napoleon made an abrupt change in tactics. He would leave the Allies heading northeast in pursuit of a phantom. Rather than going directly to his strongholds as the Allies expected, he would make a surprise move south, returning to the Aube at Bar, many miles east of Arcis. This move would allow him to reestablish communications with Paris south of the new Allied position and to complete his blockade of Allied communications with Germany. By the time the Allies discovered his new plan and came back, worn out by a useless march north, Napoleon would be ready for them. In contrast to his position at Arcis, this time he would be protected, not trapped, by the Aube River, and his ranks might have swollen to 135,000. He was certain of overwhelming the enemy.

Napoleon summoned his cartographer, Colonel Athalin. Bending over the map, sometimes stretched out full length on it with the colonel full length by his side, he calculated the army's movements over the next three days with the aid of a compass opened to mark seventeen to twenty miles on the map (or a march of twenty-two to twenty-five miles, taking curves in the road into account). Turning his compass from point to point, Napoleon determined the army's final disposition on the Aube and the defensive and offensive positions of the various units en route. While Colonel Athalin placed pins in the new positions, Napoleon dictated orders giving the hour of departure, route, rate of march, and day's objective for each unit—all with the speed and accuracy that made his marching orders famous.

The army was to head south on the road from St.-Dizier to Bar-sur-Aube at dawn on the twenty-fourth. Macdonald, whose troops had just finished crossing the Marne, was to form a rear guard at St.-Dizier in case the enemy should try to head that way from Vitry. The night of the twenty-fourth, imperial headquarters would be at Doulevant, twenty-one miles south of St.-Dizier, with wings toward Bar and Chaumont. The remainder of the troops would bivouac at various points up to ten miles north of Doulevant. During the twenty-fourth, the light cavalry would fan out still farther to intercept retreating enemy reserves and artillery, capture supplies, and create panic. To deceive the Allies, word was to be spread among prisoners of war that the French army was marching northeast toward Metz and the eastern strongholds.

Napoleon finished sending his orders just half an hour before Caulaincourt's midnight arrival. If Napoleon was surprised to see his foreign minister, he gave no sign of it. Without asking a single question, he went on talking of his plans with Berthier while gulping his usual supper of lentil or bean salad, a bit of meat, some bread, and Chambertin wine.

"I cut the Allies' communications. They have masses of men, but no support. I rally part of my garrisons, I crush some of their corps. The slightest reverse can spread havoc. . . . With the Burgundians in the mood they are in after being sacked by the Russians and Prussians, they'll drive the enemy out of France. The enemy will be massacred. That's the way to negotiate peace."

Turning to Caulaincourt, he added, "My high officials and ministers are running scared. . . . You're all milktoasts. . . . I alone understand the French people. . . . You'll see, the entire population will be up in arms in a week, and we'll have to rescue the enemy from its excesses. Anyone who looks remotely foreign will be massacred. We're going to fight, Caulaincourt. If the nation backs me, the enemy is nearer ruin than I am. If I lose, falling with glory is better than accepting dishonorable terms. But Schwarzenberg is following in my footsteps. You got here just in time, you're about to see some fine action."

"He was so absorbed in his military plans that nothing I could say swayed him," Caulaincourt wrote in his journal that night. "He was so involved in strategy that he overlooked my last letters completely, so certain the Allies were following him that he wouldn't listen when I insisted they were marching on Paris, that there might not be time left to negotiate, that all was about to be lost. How could I convince him when he was so sure he was on the eve of triumph?"

Napoleon had said: "Even if the Allies tried to occupy a city of 700,000, what chance would they have, surrounded by a more or less hostile population? Deprived of their communications, running out of ammunition, cut off from their supplies and reserves?"

Besides, he insisted, they would never dare march on Paris while he was threatening their rear.

Through the night and again the following morning, Caulaincourt continued to badger Napoleon to sue for peace.

"I tried, I fought—anyone would have thought I was arguing with an enemy. Discouraged, I did not give up. Rebuffed, I returned to the charge, renewed, redoubled my arguments. He at last agreed it was necessary to reopen negotiations, but because he refused to decide on the means of doing so, nothing was done."

Napoleon insisted the Allies never intended to negotiate. All they wanted was to use talk of peace to undermine French will, bring the country to its knees, and partition it.

"You're a dupe, Caulaincourt," Napoleon said. "I know Metternich and the Russians. Make one concession today and tomorrow they'll be back demanding more...."

Napoleon, his entourage complained, refused to recognize the limits of the possible. But had he been the sort of man who listened to harbingers of ill omen like Caulaincourt, flying in like an old crow with "the fever of despair and death in his heart," he would never have become master of Europe. As emperor of France, Napoleon had achieved the impossible. Was it *possible* for a penniless Corsican lieutenant to become a general at twenty-four, emperor of France at thirty-four?

Before invading France, the Allies had said it was impossible for Napoleon to put up any resistance. For months, he had not only resisted, he had more than once been on the verge of forcing the Allies to retreat across the Rhine. How often in the past had he not stolen victory with a handful of men over crushingly superior forces? The odds might be against him, but Napoleon not only intended to win, he expected to, and he had an excellent chance.

A great gambler, Napoleon knew his cards and his opponents. His miracles were carefully planned. He foresaw every possible contingency, and never gambled on anything he could find out or calculate. He was always ready to reverse his plans, to make an abrupt switch to one of many alternatives prepared in advance in his study. His secretary, Baron Fain, said that Napoleon spent far more time calculating his moves in case of failure than in case of success. The Allies' ever-changing demands at the conference table had convinced him he could win peace only by fighting. There was nothing Caulaincourt or anyone else could tell him that he had not considered in making his decision.

Though Caulaincourt's predictions of doom had no effect on Napoleon, they reinforced the doubts of his generals at St.-Dizier just as their waning enthusiasm for battle had been revived by Napoleon's jubilance. Caulaincourt was right in saying even Napoleon's generals were crying for peace. They saw the enormous and growing inequality of forces. They saw their ragged corps dwindling, their men increasingly exhausted by forced marches, constant maneuvers, continuous battle. They saw supplies growing scarcer, equipment deteriorating. How long could they drive starving men and dying horses twenty miles a day through the mud?

In the past months, a bold few had tried to convince Napoleon of the futility of continuing the fight, but all had turned tail quickly to escape his fury. Now, they muttered behind his back. Napoleon was exhorting them to pull on their old boots while they were longing for slippers. They were tired of misery, tired of twenty years of warfare, tired of winning victories only to see them compromised on new ventures. They longed for peace to enjoy the fortunes made in war.

"At the age of thirty, one becomes less fit for making war," Napoleon had said. Of the eight marshals remaining under Napoleon's command in the campaign, Berthier was the oldest at sixty-one, Marmont the youngest at forty. Moncey, in Paris, was sixty, Lefebvre, fifty-nine. Ney, Mortier, Oudinot, and Macdonald were in their mid- to late forties. Most of them had enlisted young—at twelve, fifteen, sixteen, seventeen. They had had enough. While Napoleon's energy and genius were rekindled in 1814, his staff had lost its youthful fire.

"Brave men grow old too," said Napoleon's aide-de-camp, Count de Ségur.

After Caulaincourt's arrival, treasonable mutterings in the antechambers of imperial headquarters at St.-Dizier grew loud enough for Napoleon to hear. His marshals and generals were afraid that in turning east they were leaving Paris, their families, houses, and possessions open to the devastation they saw in the countryside around them. And what would the sacrifice bring? Defeat again. What hope was there of victory with these sham battalions without soldiers, marshals without armies?

They criticized Napoleon's strategy: "Why are our soldiers still defending Milan and Barcelona when Paris itself is threatened? We're tossing away every chance to negotiate for a mirage, abandoning Paris to throw ourselves on the Allied rear, risking everything on a single maneuver."

Even if Napoleon's plan succeeded, by a miracle, victory would probably lead only to more risks, more sacrifice, more war. Napoleon boasted of dictating terms from Munich or Vienna. Was there any chance of lasting peace with him? Must they sacrifice everything to one man's stubborn pride? We need peace above all, they said.

Peace at any price was the cry of the country. Peace, the merchants cried, their commerce destroyed. Peace, the peasants cried, their grain stores gone, their ravaged fields unplanted. Peace, the aristocrats protested, their sons, hitherto exempt from draft, conscripted into honor guards. Peace, the wine merchants of Bordeaux clamored, their full barrels unsold in cellars, their ships idled in war-locked harbors. Peace, the Senate and Legislative Assembly cried, blamed by a depleted nation if they voted more resources for defense and blamed again if they refused.

Peace was the cry of Napoleon's ministers, of his brother King Joseph.

"We are on the verge of total collapse," Joseph wrote Napoleon. "Only peace can save us.... The day the people are convinced Your Majesty chose prolonging the war over even a disadvantageous peace, they'll switch sides out of sheer exhaustion.... Paris is unwilling to undertake any real defense and will back the man who allows it to foresee the earliest peace."

The French had fought almost without respite since the revolution of 1789, first against a Europe bent on stamping out the insidious example of revolutionary France, and lastly against a Europe united again to bring imperial France to heel. So long as war meant conquest and glory and was fought outside the country, the French had hailed Napoleon as a hero. Now that he was losing and France was the battlefield, they were tired of war, of demands for sacrifice, of Napoleon himself.

"Peace—do you think I don't want peace too?" Napoleon said. "I'll make peace as soon as it's possible."

How shortsighted men were. How forgetful! Hadn't they learned that ideals alone never moved men and wars aren't won by waiting for volunteers? When revolutionary France was invaded by a European coalition in 1793, the republican government did not rely on popular fervor to drive the enemy out. Men had to be drafted to fight for the Revolution, and even the draft didn't produce more than an inadequate 80,000 to 90,000 men. It took the Terror and the guillotine to raise the 500,000 who drove the invaders out.

Men were such fools. The Senate's efforts to force a compromising peace on him only made true peace more remote by encouraging the enemy to count on France's internal divisions. Couldn't the senators see that? Their peace propaganda did the French cause more harm than any battle lost on the plains of Champagne. Napoleon accused them of bad faith.

"You're seeking publicity and popularity, not the public good," he told them. "The only lasting peace is peace with honor, and with the backing of the nation, I can win it. . . . No one has ever beaten a united France."

Napoleon's call to rise united against the enemy met little response except in areas the Allies had overrun. For Frenchmen living there, as for Napoleon's soldiers, the indifference of Paris and the interior was hard to understand.

"Fire, rape, killing—these are the benefits the self-styled liberators of France bring us," one of Napoleon's subordinate officers wrote home. "If the French only understood their own interests, they would have driven these brigands back across the Rhine in a month."

Napoleon tried to arouse the Parisians' indignation and will to fight. Newspapers warned them to prepare to defend themselves because the city, if taken, would be sacked by Prussians and Cossacks. Colored engravings depicting Cossacks as monsters committing all sorts of outrages went on sale in engraving shops and bookstores. Recitals of Allied excesses were printed in papers and leaflets. Inhabitants of eastern provinces were sent to Paris to give personal accounts of the devastation, pillage, and atrocities they had seen. Parisian diaries of the time often mention these survivors of the war haranguing knots of onlookers in a public square, by a bridge over the Seine, or on the edge of a market.

Napoleon's plan backfired. Parisians were appalled rather than indignant when they heard such tales or saw terrified peasants streaming into the city for refuge with their belongings. More than ever, they wanted Napoleon to make peace so that no such atrocities could occur in their city.

Even Napoleon's government did not seem serious about defending Paris if the war reached it. For two months, instead of preparing the defense of the ciy, Joseph pleaded with Napoleon to make peace, urged his immediate return to Paris, and excused his own inaction by complaining of lack of funds, lack of guns, and lack of precise orders. As late as March 22, Joseph wrote his brother, "General Dejean is impatiently awaiting Your Majesty's approval to start work on the exterior defense of Paris." This, when the enemy had come within thirty miles of Paris more than once. Napoleon had been urging a mass levy in Paris for weeks, but his chief of police was still refusing arms to volunteers on the grounds that "stirring up the populace is the greatest danger of all.... The workers might fight for the government two days in a row and turn on it on the third."

It was a wonder there were any volunteers at all. A patriot would be hard put to maintain his enthusiasm to fight for Paris if he strolled around the city and saw the sorry earthworks hastily erected on the heights of Chaumont and Montmartre outside the city walls, and the flimsy wood pallisades and pair of cannon at some of the city gates. It looked as if the city had been abandoned by the authorities. Had Napoleon abandoned it too? Unless he was able to get to Paris fast, the city could not repel an attack. There had been no official news of him since an article in the government newspaper, Le Moniteur, of the nineteenth announced his plan to arrive at Arcis the following day. Arcis was a long way east. Why invite Allied vengeance by a hopeless gesture of defiance?

Paris waited in a curious apathy. It has always been a city of *flâneurs* and idlers; it was that sort of city in March 1814. People flocked to public places—restless, curious, seeking and passing on the latest rumors. Theaters were full, promenades were full, clothes were elegant. Every afternoon spectators filled chairs lining the main boulevards to watch columns of men leaving to join the army. Whenever the war came close, carriageloads of Parisians drove out to Meaux to see the cannon protecting the approach to the capital, and the Louvre had a rush of visits from people who feared its treasures would soon be carried off by the Allies.

As Napoleon's minister of police, the Duke of Rovigo, put it, Paris, like all unoccupied France, was *"dans le plus grand calme."* People watched, hoarded, gossiped, and waited. The rich and powerful hired masons and carpenters to build special hiding places for their silver and jewels. They packed their families and valuable furniture off to safer sites.

"Cowards!" said Napoleon when he heard that Rovigo had shipped his daughters and furniture to Toulouse. The Parisian populace watched these departures with growing cynicism and followed the empress's carriage closely whenever she drove out the gates of the Tuileries. When she, too, left Paris, they would know the capital was doomed.

No one seemed to give much thought to what occupation or defeat might mean. Paris wanted simply to avoid trouble. Men called up for the National Guard left town, hid, or declared themselves sick. Law and medical students who were to be organized into artillery companies jeered and insulted the commander who came to review them and ended by driving him into ignominious flight. Parisians seemed to regard France's battle for survival as a spectacle at which they planned to remain spectators.

Napoleon was no more alarmed by Parisian indifference than he had been impressed by Parisian enthusiasm years before. Marching to his coronation in 1804, he had remarked to a friend that the cheering crowd would see him to the scaffold with equal enthusiasm the following day.

"It's a fickle public," he said to Caulaincourt at St.-Dizier in the early hours of March 24, 1814. "One brilliant victory and all will be well again."

As for the loud voices in the room next to Napoleon's study, though Baron Fain heard them, Napoleon either did not or pretended not to.

"Men brave in battle sometimes lack two-o'clock-in-the-morning courage," he often said, "and men like Macdonald grumble all the time."

The first signs of success would quell these rebellious voices, and within a week the war would be over.

After three months of fighting, the Allies were no closer to victory. They were moving, daily, farther from Paris. Whether they called it regrouping forces or pursuing Napoleon, the fact is that they had been retreating since March 18. Men, supplies, and heavy artillery were being evacuated pell-mell toward Germany. Allied rear headquarters, moved hastily east from Troyes to Bar-sur-Seine to Bar-sur-Aube, had to be rushed off toward Dijon the night of the twenty-third. Emperor Francis of Austria, fleeing east with the Allied diplomatic crops, narrowly escaped capture by Napoleon's advance cavalry.

News of the Austrian Emperor's flight and the sight of Allied reserves retreating in disorder lowered the invading troops' morale and encouraged the natives' belligerence. The specter of the French army trapped in Russia haunted the Allies more and more vividly. In the words of an English general at Allied headquarters, the Allies were unable to protect their retreat, yet obliged to withdraw.

Schwarzenberg felt his only chance of escape lay in joining Blücher and overtaking Napoleon quickly enough to defeat him in one decisive battle before the entire countryside joined the French army. The prince took comfort in news that Blücher had anticipated orders to join him in the east and was already nearing Châlons. When their advance guards met on the twenty-third, the two Allied armies were united for the first time in the campaign, but they were marching, 200,000 strong, right into Napoleon's trap.

As Schwarzenberg and the King of Prussia rode off from Sompuis on the morning of March 24, Napoleon cried, "To horse," at St.-Dizier, twenty-five miles to the east. Both sides looked forward to a rapid dénouement, but it was Napoleon who held the cards. He was about to fulfill the boast he had made to his legislators on January 1:

"In three months I'll be dead or I'll have driven the enemy back across the Rhine."

II

INTRIGUE

March 24

NAPOLEON'S MOST DANGEROUS enemy was not on the field of battle—he was in Paris. Charles-Maurice de Talleyrand-Périgord stood looking out the long French windows of his salon over the Place de la Concorde, where the heads of Louis XVI, Marie-Antoinette, and two thousand others had rolled off the guillotine's blade two decades before. His immobile face, with its hawk nose and hooded eyes, did not reflect the distaste he felt at the recollection. For him, the Revolution was a meaningless sequence of disorders like all events left to the whims of popular passion—planless, aimless, leaving, in the end, nothing of historical importance. Such regrettable disorder.

Talleyrand's palace, a harmony of pale gray, crystal, and gold leaf, had been turned into a warehouse for saltpeter in 1793, with sweaty workmen dragging sacks up the marble staircase and across the gleaming parquet floors. Now the bloodthirsty rabble were gone from the Place de la Concorde, but Paris still bore the scars of their folly. There were empty, muddy lots in mid-city. Churches and convents stood half burned and abandoned. Notre-Dame and others still bore signs saying "National Property for Sale." Talleyrand had been unable to intervene in the fall of the monarchy, but in 1814, he was determined that the future would not be left to the passions of the populace after the fall of the empire.

He foresaw the end of the empire with regret. What a charming figure Napoleon had been on his triumphal return from Italy, seventeen years ago.

"I liked Napoleon," Talleyrand wrote. "At his début, I was drawn to him by the irresistible attraction a great genius has. . . . Twenty battles won give a pale young man such charm."

When they met in the fall of 1797, Talleyrand was forty-three. Foreign minister under the Directory—last in a series of revolutionary regimes—he was looking for a strong military figure to restore peace and prosperity to France. The role suited Napoleon's ambitions, and the two men set about the overthrow of their government.

Talleyrand took the twenty-eight-year-old hero in hand. He staged Napoleon's public appearances in such a manner as to hide his overweening ambition and ruthlessness. He arranged for Napoleon to be made a member of the mathematical section of the French Academy at a ceremony for which the young general wore the simplest uniform and most modest mien.

"What we should fear," Talleyrand said in his introductory speech, "is not Napoleon's ambition, it is our being unable to tear him away from a studious life in retreat."

Talleyrand arranged parties in Napoleon's honor at which old society and men new to power mixed for the first time. Napoleon was the man to end division, to bring back stability and harmony: that was Talleyrand's message. In 1799, in a coup masterminded by Talleyrand, Napoleon became consul with Talleyrand as his foreign minister.

"If he lasts a year, he'll go far," Talleyrand wrote of his protégé. When Napoleon became counsul for life in 1802, Talleyrand wrote him, "My devotion will end only with my life." He regarded the empire and Napoleon as his creations; he was the first to foresee their demise.

"The end cannot be far off," he wrote his beautiful mistress on March 20, 1814. "If Napoleon were killed, his death would ensure the rights of his son, but so long as he lives, everything is uncertain and no one can foresee what will happen. . . . Burn this letter as soon as you have read it."

Dorothée de Courlande kept Talleyrand's note of March 20, just as she kept the one sent the same day by regular mail in which he complained, for the benefit of the police who would read it, of the nuisance of having his letters delayed twenty-four hours for examination:

"What is there to find? Just that I love you. For the rest, the news I write runs the streets. How annoying to be embarrassed in one's private life when all one wants is to isolate oneself from the affairs of the world."

At sixty, Talleyrand was far from ready to retire, though an appearance of withdrawal from public life was useful to him. He had begun to enjoy the career for which he was so well fitted rather late, having been diverted first by his parents, then by revolution and exile. When Talleyrand was born, only two careers were considered suitable for nobles without fortunes: the army and the church. Talleyrand always thought he would have liked the army, but it was ruled out by a childhood accident that left him severely lame. His injury in a fall from a dresser at the age of four might not have crippled him had it not been neglected. For this, and for other instances of parental indifference, Talleyrand bore resentment all his life. When accused of lack of feeling, he once said: "Everything can be explained by my childhood."

While they denied him affection, the Talleyrand-Périgords watched over their son's advancement in the church for the sake of the family name. By the time the Revolution began, Talleyrand was Bishop of Autun, though as unsuited for the mysticism of the church as he was repelled by its worldliness. He probably felt little regret when he was excommunicated by the Pope for assisting the revolutionary government in its break with Rome, but when that more violent phase of the Revolution known as the Terror forced him to live abroad, he was deprived of the promising political career to which his churchly duties had led him.

In what Talleyrand termed four dull years, his genius and lack of scruples enabled him to make a new fortune in America, largely from land speculation. As one of the first aristocrats pardoned and welcomed back to France under the Directory, he became foreign minister in July 1797, less than eight months after his return. One week later, he wrote his first flattering letter to young General Napoleon in Italy.

What a pity, Talleyrand thought, that his protégé had stopped heeding him and chosen to surround himself with mediocrity. What good is it to be the greatest genius in the world if you're reduced to conversing with an idiot like Secretary of State Maret?

Talleyrand turned from the window to limp across the gleaming floor. It was the hour he devoted daily to consulting his chef, Carême, with whom he discoursed on food and wine with the same subtlety and wit he applied to politics. The greatest chef in the world played no little part in making Talleyrand's house the center of all that was great, important, amusing, and influential, whether the master was in office or out, in favor or disgrace. Napoleon, too impatient to enjoy the pleasures of the table himself, understood their power well enough to have made full use of Talleyrand's genius for receiving.

Talleyrand had served him well. It was at Talleyrand's house that foreign powers were seduced and diplomats induced to make deals and commit indiscretions. In Talleyrand's salons aristocratic émigrés returning to France were integrated into the new-born empire. By nullifying the émigrés as a source of division at home or abroad, Talleyrand had helped Napoleon unite France and make it respectable again in the eyes of Europe's monarchs. And Talleyrand had made the upstart Napoleon respectable by supplying him with aristocratic figureheads to dazzle those monarchs.

"I want some great names," Napoleon said to Talleyrand in making his preparations for the international conference at Erfurt in 1809. "The truth is only they know how to behave at court."

"Sire, you have Monsieur de Montesquiou."

"Fine."

"Prince Sapieha."

"Not bad."

"It seems to me two will be enough," Talleyrand said. "It's a short stay and Your Majesty can have them always at his side."

The *julienne aux pointes d'asperges* and the *ortolans truffés* would complete the nine-course menu nicely. Talleyrand ate only once a day, at six o'clock, but he ate well. The consultation with Carême over, he rang for his carriage. Waiting, he glanced through the *Moniteur*.

France might be fighting for survival on March 24, 1814, but France's official newspaper did not mention it. Although Paris was teeming with rumors of a recent major battle at Arcis, the rupture of peace negotiations, the cutting of communications with Napoleon, and the declaration of Bordeaux for the royalists, there was not a word of such news in the four-page *Moniteur*. Under the heading *Interior* was a report on the review of a provincial urban guard two weeks earlier. Another column and a half listed the appointment of prefects in remote towns. An article on Darwin filled three and a half columns under the heading *Literature*. A review of a newly printed geography filled another four and a half, and stock-market quotations and a list of theater attractions completed the paper.

Talleyrand, the best-informed man in France, had other sources. Foreign newspapers, which even the minister of war was unable to obtain, were smuggled to him by an agent in the police. After reading articles in English papers urging the burning of Paris, he set off in his carriage on his daily round of visits to gather the news of the day.

The city he drove through was not the handsome capital of broad boulevards and long perspectives of today. It was still a dark, walled, medieval town. Most of the streets were narrow, muddy, unpaved, and without sidewalks. Pedestrians walked them in danger for their lives. Professional *décrotteurs* thrived on the filth in the streets, stationing themselves at main intersections to clean mud and manure from boots and clothing for a fee. Because there were few sewers, storms turned some streets into impassable rivers. Neighborhood concierges would throw portable wood bridges over the rushing waters and collect tolls from those wanting to cross.

Napoleon had intended to make Paris the handsomest city in the world, but he had not had time. He turned part of the Louvre into a museum, built four bridges, rebuilt and extended the quays along the Seine, and opened up the Rue de la Paix (then known as Rue Napoléon). He was clearing the slums between the Palais Royal and the Place de la Concorde for the arcaded Rue de Rivoli when war usurped the allotted funds. Piles of rubble, stacks of construction material, and empty scaffolding were visible on Talleyrand's left when he started across the square toward the Seine.

Talleyrand's carriage mingled with caissons and carts bearing wounded. Drums rolled, trumpets sounded, announcing continual parades. The streets were crowded with soldiers. Wagons and guns rumbled over the cobblestones. Paris was the center through which all passed. It was the assembly point for conscripts, troops, supplies, and ammunition; the returning point for wounded from all fronts. Every day increasing numbers of wounded arrived, bloody, hastily bandaged, in rags, some on hobbling horses, some in carts, some on foot, other piled into boats on the Seine. Hospitals overflowed. A typhus epidemic threatened. Every time the Allies drew near the city, shortages of food and supplies were intensified by a rush of refugees from the surrounding countryside.

Talleyrand's first call was at the Ministry of Police on Quai Malaquais. He knew Rovigo had been keeping him under surveillance for years, intercepting and reading his letters on Napoleon's orders. Talleyrand was amused. All Rovigo would find in those letters was what Talleyrand wanted him to read, and all he would see in following him was a cultivated Parisian of means going about his idle rounds. Just a month ago, Rovigo had refused to obey Napoleon's orders to imprison him. How could he arrest Talleyrand? Rovigo had exclaimed in front of

Postmaster General de La Valette. Why, he counted on Talleyrand's daily visits for information on the activities of the exiled Bourbons and their supporters abroad and in the aristocratic quarter of Paris, the Faubourg St.-Germain.

"What is the Emperor thinking of?" Rovigo said. "Don't I have enough royalists to cope with? Does he want to throw the whole Faubourg St.-Germain on my hands? It's Talleyrand who keeps them from doing foolish things. The Emperor will thank me for not executing this order."

Rovigo ignored Napoleon's order but watched Talleyrand more closely. He knew Talleyrand was informed of news passing through the post office by various sources, including the postmaster general himself. He knew Talleyrand's former subordinate at the foreign ministry, Chargé d'Affaires de la Besnardière, was giving away details of diplomatic relations, and he suspected Caulaincourt as well. He knew Talleyrand was in touch with royalists—where else would he get the information Rovigo found so useful? He knew Talleyrand's circle of intimates: the Duke of Dalberg, the Archbishop of Malînes, and Baron Louis were spinning plots. He suspected Talleyrand knew that an agent had been sent from Paris to eastern France in early March to Louis XVIII's brother, the Count d'Artois, but he dismissed the mission as an obscure intrigue of no possible importance.

In Rovigo's words, "I was unable to get anything precise. I knew everyone he received, but his conduct was so artful and he knew how to make it look so natural by seeing men of all opinions and characters one after another that I avoided approaching any of them. The state of affairs was too desperate for them to renounce any favors they thought they had won for the future. Besides, what could they have told me? They would have repeated conversations lacking a single fact or given me their private opinions of Talleyrand's frame of mind, of which I had a good idea already."

Riding around Paris on horseback one day, Rovigo noticed the carriage of the Archbishop of Malînes at the door of Talleyrand's mansion. De Malînes, an ex-diplomat exiled by Napoleon, had returned to Paris like many other exiles when the estate to which he had been banished was overrun by the Allied army. Rovigo decided to burst in on the pair in the hope of catching them plotting against Napoleon.

Instead of having the porte-cochère opened, I dismounted in the street and dashed in on foot. The porter, who knew me, didn't dare stop me. I ran up the stairs, reaching Talleyrand's study without meeting anybody in the antechamber. There he was, *tête à tête* with the archbishop. I entered as abruptly as if I had burst through the window. Conversation stopped dead.... I couldn't help saying, "This time you can't deny it, I've caught you conspiring!" I was right. They laughed, tried to put me off, but when I urged them to go on with their conversation, they couldn't. I left, certain they were plotting, but not sure what.

This ridiculous story is, in Rovigo's own account, the closest he came to obtaining evidence against Talleyrand. It does not say much for him either as minister of police or as zealous supporter of Napoleon. Indeed, the case of Rovigo is one of the more curious in Napoleon's ministry. His memoirs read as though he had been observing a foreign capital in 1814, rather than one under his jurisdiction. He gave up surveillance, he said, because he saw no point in arresting people. It wasn't that he lacked justification for mass arrests—there weren't enough prisons, repression might bring on an insurrection, and, besides, "the least one could do for so many people suffering was to leave them the right to complain."

He kept in his employ officials he knew were active against the government. He failed to stop the posting of royalist propaganda, allowed small conspiring groups to meet under his eyes, and watched the dissident Faubourg-St.-Germain complacently. He considered himself far-seeing and clever, and was fooled by all. Particularly by Talleyrand.

Rovigo was aware there were quite enough dissident forces to form a party against Napoleon, but thought that since no party existed yet, all he had to do as minister of police was to keep his eyes open. He assumed Talleyrand was the man who would head the party against Napoleon, but did not consider him dangerous so long as there was no party for him to head. Except for a few exalted royalists, a vociferous but largely inactive aristocratic population in the Faubourg St.-Germain, and a handful of tenacious republicans, the disaffected had no banner to rally them. Divided into all shades of opinion, they were united only by the belief that Napoleon would fall and the desire to avoid going down with him. While more and more of Napoleon's administration joined the disaffected, all took care to keep a foothold in Napoleon's camp. What if the Allies never reached Paris? Or Napoleon returned breathing vengeance? He might even win the war, and if he did, his victory would carry all France with him as before. It was too early for open commitments.

"Nevertheless," Rovigo wrote, "while deploring the sad state of affairs, Napoleon's government was taking leave of him little by little."

In the meantime, Rovigo looked forward to Talleyrand's visits. He would show him the daily police bulletin, a sheaf of thick vellum papers tied with brown string, filled with handwritten entries covering arrivals in France, departures, arrests, and a hodgepodge of information ranging from the suicide of a horse trader to attacks on tax collectors by armed rebel bands. Rovigo and Talleyrand would discuss the progress of the French army, the morale of the country, the news brought by the latest courier.

Rovigo valued Talleyrand's comments and his contribution of bits of information picked up elsewhere, but most of all, he felt complimented that Talleyrand would spend time with him. Like the rest of Napoleon's officials, Rovigo was baffled and awed by Talleyrand, never quite at ease in his presence. They all sensed the contempt Talleyrand hid beneath his courtier's mask for dukes and princes ennobled by a commoner who had crowned himself. Their operatic titles sounded ridiculous to Talleyrand, who could trace his ancestors through eleven centuries to the Carolingian kings. When Savary became Duke of Rovigo; Marshal Ney, the cooper's son, became Prince de la Moscowa; Marshal Macdonald, the honest Scotsman, Duke of Tarentum; and vainglorious Marmont, the Duke of Ragusa, Talleyrand was highly amused. When he himself was first addressed as "Your Highness" after being made Prince of Bénévent by Napoleon, Talleyrand said, smiling, "I am less than that, yet perhaps much more."

The Duke of Rovigo was flattered that Talleyrand would deplore the sad state of France during their talks, shake his head over the army's impending defeat, and hint that it was time to look for an alternative.

"Well, what is one to do in such sorry circumstances?" said Talleyrand. "Not everyone chooses to stay in a burning house. You should look out for yourself."

Rovigo took such remarks as a sign of comradely concern, although for form's sake he pretended not to understand.

Talleyrand's next visit was to Pasquier in the prefecture. As chief of the city police, Pasquier was one of the few officials Napoleon had ordered to remain in Paris should the city be seriously threatened. Pasquier had consequently taken steps to ensure his own future in the event that Paris was not only threatened but taken. He avoided measures that might be held against him. By sending warnings he helped the Bourbon princes who entered French territory in the Allies' wake to avoid capture, and he persuaded Rovigo not to set a trap for one of them.

Though just as disconcerted by Talleyrand as Rovigo was, Pasquier would pretend to be at ease by lolling in his armchair or propping his feet on the fireplace grate while he listened to the statesman talk about the royalist movement. Like Rovigo, Pasquier was preoccupied by the question dominating so many men's thoughts: "Everything is coming to an end, but how should the end be arranged?" Like almost everyone, he looked to Talleyrand for the answer.

The police summary of March 24 that Pasquier showed Talleyrand told him public morale was worsening in Paris. Posters of a kind never seen before invited people to assemble and summon deputies from all parts of France to the capital to consult on how to negotiate with the enemy. Such treasonable initiative would have been unthinkable if Napoleon had been in Paris or his government had reflected his will. The stock market, index of the public pulse, had dropped again. There were rumors of an attack on Lyons, the second largest city in France. There were even rumors of an impending attack on Paris. The police report concluded, "The fear of seeing hopes for peace fade seems stronger than yesterday. . . ."

Talleyrand's next destination was de La Valette's office in the General Post Office on Rue Jean-Jacques Rousseau, a valuable source of news. It was the headquarters for couriers carrying dispatches between the army and the government. It was also where refugees of occupied areas flocked to try to get in touch with friends and relatives left behind, and where people exchanged news, stories, and rumors of what was happening outside Paris.

Another valuable visit was to the palace of Luxembourg, Paris residence of Napoleon's older brother Joseph, whom Napoleon had named lieutenant general during his absence. Joseph blamed his brother for the loss of his Spanish kingdom, and was tantalized by the hope that king-maker Talleyrand might help him to succeed Napoleon one day.

The door was always open to Talleyrand at the Ministry of Foreign Affairs, too, where his comments and advice were welcomed by the men who once worked under him. Even Napoleon's loyal servant, Caulaincourt, who hoped Talleyrand might help him force Napoleon to accept peace on the Allies' terms, had arranged to keep Talleyrand posted on peace negotiations by correspondence in code. Talleyrand was thus one of the first in Paris to be informed when the peace conference was broken off.

For Napoleon's administration to show government reports to Talleyrand was not odd, since, as Vice Grand Elector, Talleyrand was still a high-ranking official. His position was peculiar. For eleven years after they met, though they disagreed more and more, Talleyrand had been Napoleon's closest confidant. Probably no other man was ever so intimate with Napoleon. Napoleon was flattered by the association. He was impressed by the older statesman's brilliance, finesse, and impassivity, but, above all, by his aristocratic lineage. Napoleon used to boast that he had "picked up his emperor's crown from the gutter on the point of his sword." Blue blood, however, was something he could never acquire, which may explain why he stood in awe of it. After citing his faults, Napoleon once said of Talleyrand: "He is the scion of a great family and that makes up for everything. That is the advantage of noble birth."

At the beginning, Talleyrand was Napoleon's political conscience. His good sense checked Napoleon's imagination. As the man famous for the phrase "Above all, not too much zeal," Talleyrand saved Napoleon from many hasty decisions in their early years together, but Napoleon was not to be restrained easily or for long.

"I can give you anything but time," he used to say. "If I lose a moment, I could lose everything."

As Napoleon took over country after country, Talleyrand lamented, "If only he were a bit lazier," and complained that the most difficult person Napoleon's foreign minister had to deal with was Napoleon himself. While Napoleon dreamed of a Europe united by French military might, Talleyrand worked for a Europe united by French diplomacy. Conflict was inevitable.

When he failed to achieve his political aims through Napoleon, Talleyrand turned elsewhere. While still foreign minister, he forewarned other powers of Napoleon's designs and offered advice on how to thwart them. He stole and sold government papers, planted false information to mislead Napoleon's police, engaged in secret correspondence with foreign spies and heads of state, and for some time was in the pay of Austria and perhaps also Russia. It was while in Napoleon's diplomatic service that Talleyrand first ingratiated himself with Russian emperor Alexander in order to foil Napoleon's schemes of aggrandizement. Talleyrand's subsequent relations with the young Russian chancellor of embassy, Count de Nesselrode, became so suspect that Nesselrode left France hastily in 1811 to avoid public charges of espionage.

That Talleyrand was in touch with foreign powers did not mean he favored foreign causes. He was a Frenchman and a patriot, but he happened to believe the best interests of France were identical with the best interests of Europe. Throughout the empire, he continued to work toward his goal of a stable European peace based on a balance of power. Throughout, he continued to give Napoleon his best advice and hoped the Emperor would listen before it was too late.

"I'm attached to this empire of his," Talleyrand wrote a confidante. "I'd like it to last as my final achievement, and as long as I see some chance of success, I won't give up."

Napoleon was equally reluctant to give up Talleyrand. He insulted him, humiliated him publicly, stripped him of office, accused him of treachery, threatened to exile or hang him. In 1809 he called him a traitor, thief, and "shit in a silk stocking" before the assembled court. And yet, however consistently he might reject Talleyrand's advice, he could never bring himself to dispense with it altogether. He knew Talleyrand understood the society and courts of Europe far better than his imperial parvenus—those men who, as Talleyrand remarked, obviously did not know how to walk on parquet floors. The honeymoon was over in 1802, the rift open by 1809, but divorce was unthinkable.

"I can't help liking or consulting the man," Napoleon confessed between outbursts. Once, when Napoleon called him back after upbraiding him in public, Talleyrand said, "But you act as if we had never quarreled."

"Bah, let's get down to business," said the Emperor.

Unable to think of anyone more qualified to handle his diplomacy, Napoleon asked Talleyrand to take up the portfolio of minister of foreign affairs again as late as December of 1813. Talleyrand refused.

"I no longer know your affairs," he said.

"You plan to betray me then," said Napoleon.

Singling out Talleyrand in the government delegation that saw him off from Paris in January of 1814, Napoleon said, "I leave behind in Paris worse enemies than those I'm going to fight." Yet Talleyrand remained in Paris and at his post.

Why Napoleon vacillated between arresting and reappointing Talleyrand, and why he left him in a post entitling him to a seat on the Council of Regency in 1814, is difficult to understand. Perhaps he felt Talleyrand was less dangerous in prominence than behind closed doors. Perhaps he felt arresting him would crystallize opposition rather than quell it. Perhaps the most accurate explanation is Rovigo's: that Napoleon never completely abandoned a man with whom he had been satisfied even once. He scolded, said harsh things, but forgot them almost immediately, always preferring to keep the same men around him.

Talleyrand discharged the duties of Vice Grand Elector mainly by playing whist with the empress in the evenings in the Tuileries Palace and keeping in touch with top government officials in his daily visits. He cultivated lesser sources, too. What Napoleon's brother Joseph told him, he supplemented through his good friend Count de Jaucourt, a senator who had been first chamberlain to Joseph in Italy. An intimate in Joseph's Parisian household, de Jaucourt exploited as subsource Miot de Melito, equerry to Joseph. Loyal de Melito responded to de Jaucourt's concern about the progress of the French army by bringing him the latest news every time a courier arrived, news de Jaucourt promptly passed on to Talleyrand.

Through ladies-in-waiting in the Empress's household, Talleyrand learned some of the confidences the Empress made to her chief lady-in-waiting and favorite, the Duchess of Montebello. He got occasional information directly from the Allies through his German-born friend, the Duke of Dalberg, whom Napoleon had ennobled and made councillor of state. Through Dalberg and through various ex-mistresses and aristocratic female admirers, Talleyrand kept in touch with the royalist movement and took steps to ensure that his past would not be held against him should the Bourbons return to the throne. Those people it was unsuitable for him to seek out, he met at the houses of his adoring circle of women.

It was in the elegant and witty salons of his mistresses and ex-mistresses that Talleyrand carried on much of his political intrigue. When accused of bringing women into the conversation whenever politics were discussed, he said, "Women *are* politics."

For him, it was true. Women carried out delicate missions for him, wrote letters for him, brought people together for him, reconciled, persuaded, insinuated—in short, wielded on his behalf all their considerable influence over Paris society. Though he was far from handsome, his power to attract women was one of his great assets. He had a grotesque limp, a long nose, waxen face, and lizard's eyes. His detractors described him as half man, half snake, debauched and deformed. Yet even women who disliked him agreed his charm surpassed that of other men, and the many who fell in love with him remained devoted to him for life. His charm inspired his last mistress, the ravishing Duchess of Dino, to say after he died that the experience of having known Talleyrand made the rest of the world seem inadequate.

"The minds I encounter now," she said, "seem to me slow, diffused, too easily distracted. They were forever holding back, like people going downhill, while I have spent my life with the feeling we were urging the wheels to go faster, like people climbing a hill."

In 1814, Talleyrand completed the spectrum of his supporters with the help of the adoring ladies of the Faubourg St.-Germain. They persuaded even the ultrarightists to overcome their natural distaste for a renegade like Talleyrand. Gradually the most diehard royalist turned to Talleyrand in the belief that France could be won over to the Bourbons only with the help of men close to Napoleon, men Talleyrand alone could lead.

Publicly, Talleyrand remained uncommitted. In the power vacuum, dissidents fluttered around him like moths around a light, but Talleyrand shed the same light for all. He listened to everyone, gave an appearance of agreement without commmitting himself, and led people into divulging information without saying anything of importance himself. He was on good terms with all factions, informed about all and aligned with none, content to remain the undeclared prophet of an unnamed messiah. On March 24, 1814, he, like other Frenchmen, was waiting for the Allies to make a decisive move.

He was pleased that the Allies had broken off the peace conference at last. The Allies could not openly help overthrow the French government while negotiating with it. Now if they would only stop playing Napoleon's game, quit zigzagging back and forth across the Marne and the Seine, take matters in their own hands, and march on Paris, the tide would turn and Talleyrand could put his plans into action.

On March 24 he complained, in another note to the Duchess of Courlande, of Prince Schwarzenberg's inactivity: "He has 100,000 men. All that faces him is the corps of Marmont and Mortier, who can't possibly put up any resistance, and still he doesn't move. It's unbelievable! The proverbial Austrian slowness never deserved its reputation more."

A dramatic change was nevertheless about to take place, thanks largely to the intrigue Rovigo had dismissed as obscure and unimportant. As Rovigo and other prominent Parisians indulged in schemes, fears, and waiting, Talleyrand continued playing whist with Empress

Marie-Louise, going his daily and nightly rounds, and laying the foundation for the next government and the role he would play in it. Far away in the beautiful city of Nancy, an agent was conferring with Louis XVIII's brother after bringing the Allies a message from Talleyrand that was about to turn the tide. The agent, Baron de Vitrolles, alias M. St.-Georges, alias M. de Vincent, had not risked his life in vain. To borrow Talleyrand's words, it was the beginning of the end.

Talleyrand was not the only man chafing at Austrian torpor on March 24. When Prince Schwarzenberg and the King of Prussia rode off with Allied troops on Napoleon's trail at ten that morning, young and dissatisfied Emperor Alexander stayed behind at Sompuis. Paris had slipped through his grasp many times and seemed about to elude him once again. He so clearly saw himself riding across the Place de la Concorde before cheering crowds, who reached out to touch France's liberator, the liberal monarch, the greatest prince in Europe.

He heard the words he had used to Baron de Vitrolles: "When I reach Paris, the French people will be my only ally." He heard the baron urging the step he had longed to take for months. "Do you want to put an end to the dangers and terrible wrongs of war in one generous, courageous act? Abandon your complicated strategy, unite your forces, burn your bridges, and march straight on Paris without looking back."

The picture de Vitrolles had drawn recalled the pleasant illusions the Allies had enjoyed when they crossed the Rhine. They had expected a rapid march across France, their overwhelming forces almost unopposed by the military and welcomed by a population eager to be rescued from Napoleon's tyranny and constant wars.

"We come as liberators," Allied propaganda proclaimed. "We are the allies of the French people. We are fighting only the French government, or, rather, the overweening ambition of its leader, from whom the French have suffered along with all Europe. We come only to restore true peace to all."

The dream and reality were far apart. What Alexander liked to think of as a rescue mission was all too obviously a foreign invasion. Alexander realized the French peasant was not going to believe in the Allies' pacific intentions when he saw Allied soldiers plundering, robbing, and killing on French soil. Though the Allies continued to post proclamations of brotherly love, they found it increasingly necessary to threaten and punish inhabitants who did not cooperate. In confused semantics, Allied placards accused the French government of inciting *rebellion* and threatened to hang any *traitor* who aided Napoleon's troops. The longer the Allies fought in France, the more intense popular feeling against them became—and the more untenable the fiction of their having come as liberators.

Allied soldiers committed many atrocities. How could it be otherwise with multinational, multilingual troops under divided command, subjected to forced marches and obliged to pillage for food and fodder? The Prussians, who had suffered most from Napoleon's repeated invasions, sometimes indulged in personal revenge, and the Cossacks were worse. Bands of them, some not regular troops but mere hangers-on of the army, roamed the countryside raping, robbing, and burning. Eventually the invaders became so identified with the dreaded Cossacks that any enemy soldier was loosely called a Cossack. Wherever foreign troops spent much time, French apathy quickly turned into hostility. By March 24, when the Allies had been crossing and recrossing the area between the Marne and the Seine for over two and a half months, no isolated Allied soldier or unit was safe from ambush in that part of France.

As the morale of Allied troops sank, rifts among their leaders deepened. The alliance was shaky at best. "The enemy is, in my view, a source of danger much less to be dreaded than what arises among ourselves," wrote the English ambassador to Austria from Châtillon.

Bickering over the future partition of spoils had almost dissolved the peace conference before the Allies found a pretext to disband it, and the armed alliance was no more solid. All the little German states were jealous of one another. The Russians hated the Prussians; the Prussians mistrusted the Russians and each other. Both despised the Austrians and their hesitant commander-in-chief, Schwarzenberg, referred to in an official Russian dispatch as "that miserable Viennese garbage." Only the strong character of old Blücher, nicknamed Marshal Vorwärts ("Forward"), had kept the Army of Silesia together. Soon after he was forced by illness to delegate his command, one of his generals stormed off toward Belgium in a pique and was induced to return with difficulty. Blücher's senior officer, Langeron, was so frightened by the possibility of having to assume sole responsibility for the army that on leaving Blücher's sickroom one evening, he said, "Whatever happens, in God's name, let's carry this corpse along with us."

Alexander's lofty dream was dying in the midst of ugly realities. No wonder he thought back with pleasure to his talk with Baron de Vitrolles, who spoke the exalted language the Tsar liked to hear.

Baron de Vitrolles was not the sort of man Talleyrand would have chosen to send to the Allies, but he was the best one available. As Talleyrand once observed, although heroes in novels are always endowed with qualities fitting their roles, in real life, mediocre men are sometimes called upon to play important roles.

De Vitrolles was reliable, courageous, and eager to undertake a mission behind the Allied lines. He was also more vain than intelligent, more zealous than informed, bombastic, self-intoxicated, and ultraroyalist. None of this mattered to Talleyrand. If de Vitrolles' concept of his mission differed from Talleyrand's, that was of no importance either. He would accomplish Talleyrand's purposes just the same.

A royalist who had returned to France after years of exile, de Vitrolles had foreseen the collapse of the empire and had prayed for the return of the Bourbons ever since Napoleon's retreat from Moscow. For a year, there seemed little he could do but hope and talk with others of like sentiments in small, ingrown circles. That hardly anyone else in France had given the Bourbons a thought for two decades did not discourage de Vitrolles.

When he decided it was time to act, de Vitrolles, like many others, turned to Talleyrand. And like so many others, he thought he was using Talleyrand instead of being used. Perhaps the only opinion he shared with Talleyrand was the belief that governments are felled by defection within, not attack from without. (Luther could never have founded a Protestant sect, de Vitrolles wrote in his memoirs, had he not been a Catholic and a monk.) The only men who could launch the movement for restoration successfully, in de Vitrolles' view, were men of high position in Napoleon's empire. De Vitrolles picked Talleyrand as their potential leader, though he despised the man as a traitor to his class.

De Vitrolles did not know Talleyrand personally. A provincial baron who had led an obscure life, first in the country near Grenoble, then in the emigration, and, finally, as inspector of sheepherding for the imperial government, he did not move in high circles. However, he had known one of Talleyrand's intimates, the Duke of Dalberg, when they were young men in Germany almost twenty years earlier. In the fall of 1813, he asked Dalberg to sound out Talleyrand.

De Vitrolles was bursting with arguments for Dalberg to present to Talleyrand. Only the Bourbons could guarantee a stable future. As soon as their restoration became a concrete possibility, support would burst forth from Frenchmen seeking new hopes or yearning for old ties. Helping to restore the Bourbons would bring honor to Talleyrand's illustrious family name, de Vitrolles suggested. He had not yet learned that Talleyrand was no more susceptible to persuasion than Napoleon.

Dalberg reported back to de Vitrolles what Talleyrand wanted the baron to hear.

"I understood Talleyrand listened, but was afraid," de Vitrolles wrote. "The stakes were too high."

He urged Dalberg to press Talleyrand, who expressed hatred for Napoleon but made no commitment. As for the return of the Bourbons, de Vitrolles felt Talleyrand would never have chosen it had he found anything better. "At times he even seemed afraid of it. 'And then how will they act toward us?' he would say in a low voice."

After the peace conference at Châtillon opened in February, Dalberg told de Vitrolles that Talleyrand had spoken more openly.

"You see," he quoted Talleyrand as saying, "Europe knows nothing of your position. . . . She is opening negotiations with the man she should crush at the very moment she's in a position to crush him . . . and once peace is signed, what will become of us? He has guessed our desires, he'll never forgive us. . . . The Allied sovereigns must be informed at all costs of the state of affairs, told what they can safely undertake, and warned of the dangers of the negotiations they've let themselves be drawn into. But how?" Dalberg told the baron he answered Talleyrand: "By sending de Vitrolles."

De Vitrolles was delighted. Ever since the Count d'Artois had left England for Switzerland, de Vitrolles had wanted to dash behind the lines to kneel at his feet and offer his support. Dalberg had a hard time convincing the romantic baron that he would serve the Bourbons best by going to Allied headquarters first. In the end, de Vitrolles agreed.

So long as peace negotiations seemed likely to bring results, Dalberg kept his friend from leaving for fear he would be in great danger if Napoleon made peace. When the conference dragged on, as both the Allies and Napoleon kept changing their demands according to the results of the latest battle, Dalberg agreed it was best to try to influence the outcome. On March 6, the baron started his 150-mile journey to Allied headquarters at Châtillon.

It was a hazardous mission. To the risk of being captured or shot while traveling through battle zones was added the risk of being taken for a spy by either side. For the French, the baron had false papers under assumed names. His credentials for the Allies consisted of a cachet of Dalberg's German arms engraved on a cornelian; a note for the Austrian delegate to the peace conference, Stadion, written in secret ink and containing only the names of two women Dalberg and Stadion had courted at the same time in Vienna; and a few lines, also in secret ink, for the Russian diplomat, Count Nesselrode. For the Count d'Artois, de Vitrolles carried in his coat lining three lines written on a piece of silk by an aristocratic lady whose handwriting the count knew well. De Vitrolles had expected some credentials from Talleyrand, but the latter produced only a few phrases from which one might conclude that he knew and approved of the motives of the mission. Dalberg told de Vitrolles that Talleyrand insisted nothing more was necessary.

"You don't know that monkey," Dalberg said to the baron. "He wouldn't risk his paw in the fire if the chestnuts were all for him."

Dodging French authorities who wanted to stop all civilian travel, narrowly escaping roaming Cossack bands and battling armies, posing alternately as a Frenchman and a Swiss businessman, de Vitrolles reached Châtillon on March 10. Dalberg's note immediately gained him the confidence of Stadion, who sent him on to Allied army headquarters at Troyes the following day. At Troyes, he had a number of talks with Austrian Foreign Minister Metternich, and a lengthy audience with Tsar Alexander. Lastly, after accompanying the Allies on their retreat eastward, he was allowed to address an assembly of Allied diplomats that included those just returned from the peace conference disbanded at Châtillon on March 19.

De Vitrolles was not the first French emissary to reach the Allies. Frenchmen with illustrious names and extravagant claims for a mysterious organization known as the Chevaliers de la Foi had preceded him. The secret chivalric order, vaguely accredited by Louis XVIII, had made no impression on Allied leaders. De Vitrolles, on the other hand, was taken seriously because he came accredited, if indirectly, by Talleyrand. The unsigned note de Vitrolles brought for Nesselrode contained a message the Allies interpreted as coming from Talleyrand.

Receive the person I send you in all confidence. Listen to him and recognize me. It is time to be clearer. You are walking on crutches. Use your legs and will what is within your power.

Here was the first indication the Allies had received that Talleyrand would cooperate, the first hopeful sign they had had since entering France. Though his message was worded obscurely, Talleyrand was clearly urging the Allies to march on Paris, and everyone knew Talleyrand never associated himself with a venture unless it had a good chance of succeeding.

De Vitrolles added his own urging. Over and over he told the Allies, singly and jointly, that they could only learn what the country wanted by going to Paris.

"You will be welcomed with open arms," he said.

These were words Tsar Alexander liked to hear, but found difficult to believe.

"We brought war to France with regret and only in order to make peace," he said in his private interveiw with de Vitrolles. "But to our disappointment, instead of pacific intentions on the part of the inhabitants, we found France bristling with soldiers and enmity. If the sentiments you express exist, we have seen no sign of them."

"As long as the Allies continue to support Napoleon by negotiating with him, what Frenchman would dare declare himself openly?" de Vitrolles asked. "How could you expect the country to support you when all you bring is the evils of war?"

To de Vitrolles the solution was simple. If the Allies would stop dealing with Napoleon, denounce him, and come out in favor of a restoration, then France would declare herself wholeheartedly behind both the Bourbons and the Allies.

The Bourbons? No peace was possible with Napoleon, Alexander agreed, but the Bourbons were too inadequate, too embittered, and too unpopular to rule. In his eyes, the Bourbon cause was not only not a good one, it was dead: if the French were going to be inspired by royalists, they would have given some sign of it. For months, the Count d'Artois had been trying to spread his influence in eastern France. One of Louis XVIII's nephews, the Duke d'Angoulême, had joined Wellington in southwestern France, and another nephew, the Duke of Berry, was on the isle of Jersey trying to arouse support in nearby Normandy. Yet their presence had been ignored by all but a handful of ultrarightists.

The fact was that the Bourbons were, as the author Chateaubriand put it, as unknown in France of 1814 as the family of the Emperor of China. Even fanatics like de Vitrolles knew nothing about the Bourbons. The abstract concept the baron worshiped was unrelated to the middle-aged gouty gentleman claiming the crown of France from bourgeois obscurity in Hartwell, England. And for most of France, Louis XVIII was as much a ghost of the past as his decapitated brother, Louis XVI.

"Do you know the royal princes?" Alexander asked de Vitrolles with an expression of mixed displeasure and regret. "If you did, you'd realize the burden of such a crown would be too much for them. . . ."

He proceeded to shock de Vitrolles by listing other candidates he preferred "should the Emperor disappear," as he put it. There was Bernadotte, the French marshal adopted by the king of Sweden. There was ex-Empress Josephine's son, Eugène de Beauharnais, or—worse yet—a republic.

"Great god!" de Vitrolles wrote afterward. "I had had too little experience of royalty to be prepared to hear such ideas."

When Alexander assured him the Allies would follow the wishes of France, de Vitrolles assumed he had won them to the Bourbon cause.

In his mission of convincing the Allies to march on Paris, de Vitrolles was somewhat more successful. Talleyrand's note made the move appear less risky, but the Allies wanted to make specific plans with the oppositon in the capital before committing themselves.

"You say Paris will receive us with open arms," they said to de Vitrolles. "But who will prepare our reception? Not your Bourbon prince in Nancy or Louis XVIII in England. We need someone in Paris."

"You *have* no contact in Paris?" De Vitrolles was astonished to find that the Allies could think of no candidate more qualified than ex-republican Talleyrand, though he himself had no one else to propose.

"You must return to Paris to consult your friends and make arrangements for them to support us," said Metternich. "Then come back to us to work out the final plans."

De Vitrolles insisted he had to get approval first from the Count d'Artois, who had just moved his headquarters to Nancy.

"That's just time lost," Metternich said. "He's bound to approve since we're working in his favor. We don't need him to serve him. It's cooperation in Paris you promised us. It's there action is needed, and time is pressing."

De Vitrolles insisted he had to get approval first from the Count Paris in four," he said as he set off eastward to see the count.

The Allies were swayed but hesitant. If they marched on Paris, they had to be sure of taking it before Napoleon could come to the rescue—and sure of enough cooperation within to hold it. They hesitated to trust this lone indication of support when everything they had seen in three months in France contradicted it. They might march on Paris and find bitter hostility. Or a desperate resistance inspired by fear of the invaders if not love for Napoleon. Who would take such a risk without more evidence? Certainly not Commander-in-chief Schwarzenberg.

In addition to lacking the necessary determination, Schwarzenberg was handicapped by having to please the Austrian emperor without alienating the other powers. Under constant fire from the two Allied sovereigns who shared his headquarters at the front, Schwarzenberg agonized over each day's decisions and wrote long dispatches of self-justification to Emperor Francis in the rear. As a result, he always dictated the next day's marching orders so late that Allied units were never in position in time.

His indecisiveness was one of the traits that had made the Austrians insist on his being commander-in-cheif. They did not want a bold commander pursuing the war at all costs. They favored a partial victory, one that curbed Napoleon while keeping Marie-Louise on the throne, one that would not leave Austria's allies free to carve great slices for themselves off the French empire, and one that could be won without the loss of many Austrian soldiers.

With Schwarzenberg in command, there was no risk of a rash move risking Austrian lives, no danger of a sudden advance beyond the point Austria wished to go—and that point fell short of Paris. Schwarzenberg had strict orders from Emperor Francis not to go beyond the Seine. Since he himself believed such a move would be unwise, he was happy to observe the restriction. A march on Paris "was against every rule of military strategy" and "would lead to chaos, not peace," he wrote his wife.

From the beginning of the campaign, Prince Schwarzenberg had lived in dread of being forced into such a move by his allies. Tsar Alexander made no secret of wanting to get on with the war, march on

Paris, and get rid of Bonaparte. The Prussian King was of the same mind. So were the English, although with their usual concern for an appearance of fair play, they felt it would be embarrassing to overthrow Napoleon while negotiating with him. Alexander's disregard for such niceties alarmed them.

"He has a personal feeling about Paris," wrote the English Foreign Minister, "distinct from all political or military combinations. He seems to seek the occasion of entering with his magnificent guards the enemy's capital. . . ."

The Austrian Emperor was equally bent on preventing an attack on the French capital.

"If the Allies insist on marching on Paris in the face of all common sense," he instructed Schwarzenberg, "you are to call an immediate council of war at which I will fully support you."

Thus far, there had been no such occasion. As long as peace negotiations continued, Russia and Prussia had respected the scruples of England and Austria. When the peace conference at Châtillon broke up on March 19, they were relieved. With the possible exception of Austria, none of the countries represented had sincerely wanted to reach an agreement there because none believed peace made with Napoleon could last.

Now that Napoleon had refused their terms, they were free to hunt him down. As the English diplomat Sir Charles Stewart wrote a colleague from Bar-sur-Aube, "You will rejoice, I am persuaded, at the termination of the conference of Châtillon. . . . A higher game will be played now, and I have no doubt this will agree better with your blood."

Unfortunately there was no simple, obvious course for getting on with the war, any more than there had been one for pursuing peace. Austria's reluctance and the peace negotiations had not been the only obstacles to an attack on the capital. A host of military arguments against such a move made even Tsar Alexander hesitate. Aside from the problems of taking such a large city, there was the possibility Napoleon might simply sacrifice his capital to take up a stronger and better military position beyond. And the game of Moscow might then be played over again.

"Supposing," Sir Charles Stewart wrote, "while you are moving on Paris (which Bonaparte holds out as bait), he throws himself on our flank, collecting at Châlons, moving into the strong * country in our rear

* *Strong* used in the sense of strategically advantageous.

and pushing for his fortresses on the side of the Low Countries, or maneuvering on our left, relieving his fortresses of Besançon, Belfort, Huningen, and Strasbourg. Our predicament may be disagreeable—I do not say dangerous, for I am quite of opinion that unless by gross mismanagement this cannot happen—but we come into a dilemma and we do not arrive at our end of getting rid of the man."

Even with the peace conference out of the way, there were still political reasons for the Allies' hesitation. Fully united in the goal of beating Napoleon, they were not at all agreed as to what should happen once they won. The Austrians weren't saying, but were suspected of favoring Napoleon's continuing in power or abdicating on behalf of his son. Alexander was for Bernadotte, the English were for the Bourbons. The English wanted the question settled before risking a march on Paris. If the Allies couldn't agree beforehand, they would be less likely to once they had achieved the goal that bound them together. The English saw a dangerous trap in Alexander's assertion that the Allies must submit to the will of the French. Since there did not seem to be any strong national sentiment, there was a danger that thirty-six-year-old Alexander, increasingly dominant in the coalition, would impose his own will instead. To prevent that, the English wanted the Allies to announce some noble goal as the purpose of their invasion. Besides, it would look so much better that way: "A noble object excuses a rascally proceeding," Sir Charles Stewart wrote from Allied headquarters.

As Alexander pondered on March 24 in the room at Sompuis his elusive enemy had vacated forty-eight hours earlier, he reconsidered the risks of a march on Paris. So much had happened in the last few days while the Allies continued their retreat, far too much to absorb in the midst of rapid changes of headquarters, quick marches, and the writing and rewriting of orders. First there was the end of the peace conference—not that Alexander had felt much hampered by that. Nevertheless, things went more smoothly now that the Allies had stopped quarreling over the distribution of the French empire and set about conquering it. Other events had followed rapidly: the stalemate at Arcis, thanks to Schwarzenberg's ineptitude; the suspension of action afterward because of uncertainty regarding Napoleon's plans; the panic caused by reports of Napoleon's continued march eastward; the hurried Allied evacuation of reserve bases in eastern France in the face of growing harassment by the local population.

Not all the news was bad, however. The Allied sovereigns and their staffs had spent a good part of the night pouring over intercepted French dispatches with feverish curiosity and growing optimism. Some of the dispatches reached them on their march north from the Aube, some after they halted at Sompuis about 3 A.M. Alexander had been awakened several times during the night to read incoming information, but there was too much for him to grasp. In midmorning, sleepy but alone and able to concentrate, Alexander pored over the reports again.

News that advance units of the two Allied armies had met was followed by the extraordinary announcement that Bordeaux had declared itself in favor of Louis XVIII after Wellington's army entered the city on March 12. Alexander remembered de Vitrolles' insistence that anywhere the French people were freed from fear of Napoleon, royalist enthusiasm would overtake them, even where it had been completely unapparent before.

Next came a copy Blücher sent of the letter Napoleon had written Marie-Louise from the chateau of Plessis at 3 A.M. on the twenty-third, outlining his plans to trap the enemy.

"I decided to move toward the Marne against his communications to draw him farther from Paris and get closer to my strongholds. I'll be at St.-Dizier this evening." *

All Prince Schwarzenberg had seen in the intercepted letter was proof that his own plan to follow the emperor east was correct. As Alexander reread the letter the morning of the twenty-fourth, he saw clearly that Napoleon was warning Marie-Louise that he was heading away from Paris, warning her he might not be able to write for a time, warning her he was leaving the road to Paris open.

In addition, Napoleon's plans guaranteed the Allies a line of retreat toward Belgium from Paris. Since he was heading east, Napoleon would be in no position to cut off an Allied withdrawal to the north of Paris. If the Allies had to abandon their attack on the city, they would have Bernadotte's army north of Paris to assist them, and Belgium was certain to rise in revolt against the French at the Allies' approach. In other words, the Allies could count on getting out if they were unable to win or hold Paris.

Alexander turned to yet another stack of papers that had arrived during the night, a thick batch of dispatches found on two French couriers captured the evening of the twenty-third. They were the imperial couriers Caulaincourt had heard about during his journey to

* See page 32 for full text.

St.-Dizier. It was true, as Caulaincourt had been told, that one of the letters was from the Empress to Napoleon, but there were others of much greater interest to Alexander. A series of reports from imperial ministers in Paris warned Napoleon that there were few troops or arms left, that public opinion was opposed to resistance, and that it would be almost impossible to defend the city if the enemy approached. Here was confirmation of de Vitrolles' claims from high officials of the enemy's government.

With growing resolution, Alexander reread the Duke of Rovigo's dispatch to Napoleon.

> The treasury, arsenals, and powder stores are empty. We have no resources left. The population is discouraged and discontented. It wants peace at any price. Enemies of the imperial government are sustaining and fomenting popular agitation. Still latent, it will become impossible to suppress unless the Emperor succeeds in keeping the Allies away from Paris.

The road to Paris was open, Paris was unarmed, its inhabitants unwilling to defend themselves, and Talleyrand was waiting to welcome the Allies. Yet Schwarzenberg was following Napoleon east. Why?

According to the latest reports from scouts, Napoleon had moved east so fast that the Allies couldn't catch up with him in time to keep him from reaching his strongholds anyway. Communications with Germany and Switzerland were already lost. The speed of Napoleon's march made it unlikely that the Allies could recover them before being drawn out of France, which was just what Napoleon wanted. Wasn't a serious risk preferable to continuing this pointless, dangerous retreat? Was Alexander to continue dancing to Napoleon's tune with that fool Schwarzenberg, who hadn't won a fight in twenty years? Was he to see his dream turn into a nightmare, his glorious army trapped by a handful of ragged troops and hounded out of France by angry peasants? There were better things to do than to follow Napoleon's little army.

Alexander summoned the staff officers he trusted most for a hasty conference. Unrolling a large map showing the battle positions, he asked them, now that communications with Blücher had been established, whether the Allies should follow Napoleon to attack him with their superior forces or march directly on Paris. None of his officers wanted to be the first to answer. Impatient, Alexander questioned his senior staff officer, General Barclay de Tolly, with a toss of the head.

"We must unite our forces, follow the emperor and attack him resolutely," said Barclay.

Giving no sign of his displeasure, Alexander turned to Lieutenant General Diebitsch.

"And you?"

Diebitsch hesitated to contradict his superior officer. He suggested a compromise dividing the army in two, part to cross the Marne in pursuit of Napoleon and the other to march on Paris. He had barely finished when Lieutenant General Toll exploded with impatience.

"There is only one possible course. We must make a forced march on Paris with our entire army, leaving just 10,000 cavalry to follow Napoleon and mask our move from him."

"If Your Majesty wants to reestablish the Bourbons, in fact, the best thing would be to march on Paris with all our troops," Diebitsch said.

"Eh! The Bourbons have nothing to do with it," said Alexander. "The object is to overthrow Napoleon."

Barclay de Tolly was unconvinced. Did the Tsar believe the world's greatest general was going to be taken in by 10,000 cavalrymen? Napoleon would see through the hoax, turn right around, and march on Paris, where the people and garrisons would put up a desperate defense with barricades, street fighting, sniping. Even if the Allies took the capital, they would lose the war. Had everyone forgotten what happened in Moscow?

Alexander's other staff officers took up the argument against Barclay. Even if Napoleon discovered in twenty-four hours that the 10,000 cavalrymen were a phantom screen, the Allies would have gained at least a two-day advantage over him since they would have been heading west while he headed east. Two days' advance would give them ample margin to reach Paris without having to worry about an attack by Napoleon from the rear. Once masters of Paris, they would have two rivers, the Seine and the Marne, to shield them in the fight against Napoleon. The threat of serious resistance by Paris was slight. Imagine how demoralized Parisians would be, after an exclusive diet of Napoleon's intoxicating victory bulletins, when they saw the supposedly decimated Allied armies marching upon them 200,000 strong. French resistance would crumble, while Allied ranks took heart at the prospect of winning Paris and putting a quick end to the war.

The Allies would not be trapped or isolated in Paris. France was not Russia; Paris was not Moscow. The climate, the distance, and the spirit of the inhabitants could not be compared. Besides, the Allies could restore communications as quickly from Paris to the north as to the east, and by marching to Paris they would turn the tables on Napoleon by cutting off his contact with his government.

When Barclay de Tolly yielded to majority opinion, Alexander leaped on his horse and set off to intercept Schwarzenberg and the King of Prussia. He did not have far to go. Riding at the head of the cumbersome column of Allied troops, the pair had gotten only a few miles north of Sompuis. An open-air conference was held at once on a little hill at the side of the road overlooking the walled town of Vitry. There, at twelve noon, the Allies took the most momentous decision of the campaign, one that changed the course of events almost beyond recall for Napoleon.

Dismounting, General Toll unrolled the map while Alexander gave the reasons for his decision. The King of Prussia was only too happy to agree, but Schwarzenberg hesitated. Though fully aware of the weakness of his present course, he was afraid to assume responsibility for a decision that contravened his Emperor's orders. His staff was even more hesitant. Like everyone associated with Alexander, they were afraid of being led down the daisy path by the Tsar, whose fits of exaltation and illumination were a recognized hazard of the alliance. Nevertheless, the army's present course looked pointless and dangerous. The situation had changed since Emperor Francis issued his instructions, and there was no way of checking with him. Napoleon's sudden move east had isolated the Austrian Emperor from Allied headquarters.

Schwarzenberg gave in.

Brief disagreement on tactics followed. Finally, in the fear they might meet strong resistance in Paris after all, the leaders decided to keep all forces united, marching in two close parallel lines. The concentration of such numbers would encumber the roads, exhaust supplies, and slow down the march. What could have been covered in four days by dispersing forces was going to take much longer. Never mind, they would be heading for Paris at last.

Couriers would speed to halt Allied advance columns before they started eastward across the Marne. Blücher would be notified of the change of plan and instructed to reverse his course to head for Paris via Etoges and Montmirail. Schwarzenberg's army would march just south of Blücher's on the most direct route to Paris, via Fère-Champenoise and Sézanne. General Winzingerode would be given command of 10,000 cavalrymen to follow Napoleon, report on his moves, and make him believe the whole Allied army was still after him. The sovereigns would stop overnight in Vitry to draw up marching orders and reassemble all units for their army's grand departure for Paris on the twenty-fifth.

Alexander rolled up his map.

"Let us all march to Paris!" he said joyfully.

Schwarzenberg did not share Alexander's joy. He spent most of the afternoon at Vitry writing a timid, apologetic letter to Francis I in which he presented the march west as one of those unavoidable necessities forced upon the Allies by events. Napoleon had gone so far east so fast that there was not time enough for the Allied armies to join and pursue him effectively. In fact, Schwarzenberg wrote, "it is to complete that juncture that the armies are marching toward Paris." Hopefully, in their march west, they would manage to destroy the corps of Marmont and Mortier, thereby depriving the enemy of his principal reserves, he added. That done, "the Allies would begin considering the reestablishment of their communications." The army might be heading for Paris, but Schwarzenberg said nothing about its getting there.

It was late as usual when Schwarzenberg wrote his orders for the twenty-fifth. They did not go out until the night of the twenty-fourth, which made it impossible for the army to set off at 5 A.M. as planned. Because he was not certain that orders for Blücher would reach the general himself, Schwarzenberg dispatched individual instructions to the various corps of the Army of Silesia. Blücher's army was at Châlons. Was Blücher?

He had, in fact, reached Châlons on the twenty-fourth, still ill, but in command again. Napoleon's tactics had aroused as much concern and bewilderment in Silesian army headquarters at Châlons as they had among the staff of the Allied army. Blücher's chief of staff, Gneisenau, thought Napoleon was trying to reach the other side of the Rhine before his forces collapsed in defeat. The Allies should follow him there to crush him, Gneisenau said. Other officers thought Napoleon planned to swing north toward Belgium to defeat the Allied army under Prince Bernadotte, collect the garrisons bottled in France's northern strongholds, and return in force to attack the Allies. The thing to do, therefore, was to foil his plan by continuing to maneuver north of him. Only Marshal Blücher saw the situation clearly. Napoleon was simply making an effort to draw danger away from his capital, he said, and what the Allies must do is head for Paris.

Hours before receiving his new instructions, Blücher issued orders for his artillery, infantry, and cavalry to head for Paris on the morning of the twenty-fifth with Meaux, twenty-eight miles east of Paris, as their destination for the twenty-eighth. Having learned from prisoners of war that Marshals Marmont and Mortier were nearing Châlons on their way to join Napoleon, Blücher planned to intercept them en route.

When Schwarzenberg's orders finally arrived, Marshal Blücher found himself in accord with decisions at main headquarters for the first time since the beginning of the campaign.

"This is no longer the only place you hear the cry, *Forward!* It's everywhere now. I knew my good Schwarzenberg would join me. Now we'll get this over with in short order."

Paris, the target, was increasingly uneasy. Unrest mounted, stocks fell further, rumors multiplied. Royalist circles were animated by the news from Bordeaux, the collapse of peace negotiations, and the absence of news from Napoleon. Perhaps at this moment he was being defeated in a final battle far away? In the Faubourg St.-Germain, portraits of Louis XVIII and his brother the Count d'Artois were hung on salon walls, signatures of loyalty were collected, and talk of the return of the good old days lifted spirits.

"Anyone who has not lived before 1789," Talleyrand once said, "has never known the pleasures of living." Twenty-five years later, in March of 1814, French aristocrats were hoping the old era could be revived. Napoleon was a bore. He had ended the terrors of the Revolution, but he had also put an end to all the *douceur de vivre* of the old regime. His new aristocracy was ridiculous, his court pompous and duty-bound, his influence tasteless and stifling. If his marshals had earned stature by glorious feats, their wives remained impossible.

"Bonaparte's court knew neither relaxation nor pleasure," a Parisian aristocrat wrote, "filled as it was with people bent on duty, doing it well, taking risks, but always in deadly earnest. They never learned how to laugh or profit from every moment because they were so afraid of wasting one. This rigid way of living is unbearable to those who have savored the *savoir-vivre* of former times, composed of nuances and that gentle nonchalance that imbues life with gaiety, wit, and lightness of spirit."

The Faubourg St.-Germain dreamed of restoring those graces along with the Bourbon dynasty. The royalist victory in Bordeaux, where the

Chevaliers de la Foi had maneuvered the town into proclaiming Louis XVIII, made a like success in Paris seem more attainable. Royalists redoubled their propaganda, undermining loyalty to the empire by planting and spreading alarming rumors while painting the restoration as the only salvation. Young Viscount Sosthène de Larochefoucauld, the Duke of Fitz-James, and their high-born colleagues rolled posters and leaflets off their presses, threw them in doorways, pasted them on shops and houses. There would be no more conscription in France, no more confiscatory taxes. The tyrant would fall, the war would end, peace would reign, the old era would return.

At his palace of Luxembourg, King Joseph realized that the lack of news from Napoleon must mean the Emperor had moved so far behind Allied lines that the Allied army had cut off French troops from Paris. When that had happened before, Joseph had been able to count on Marshals Marmont and Mortier, but this time the marshals had been summoned east. For the first time, Joseph became seriously concerned about the defense of the capital.

"The Emperor's maneuvers might require Paris to defend itself for a few days against some units or even an army corps with cannon," he told the head of the Paris National Guard on the twenty-third. He ordered a review of the supply of guns, ordered cannon and howitzers placed on the heights, and drew up plans for building trenches and ramparts. He continued to postpone all construction, however, "until the Emperor approves the plans I've sent him."

Empress Marie-Louise was still holding her nightly receptions in the Tuileries Palace, but on the twenty-fourth, she failed to give the order to cut the envelope holding the playing cards. That was a sign: the usual whist game was not to take place. When general attention turned away from her, she talked to Rovigo of the Emperor. Rovigo felt she was seeking reassurance in the face of growing alarm.

"Have you had any letters from the Emperor?" she asked him.

"No."

"*Eh bien,*" she said, "I can give you news of him I got this morning."

Rovigo showed his surprise. No courier had arrived that day.

"That's true," she said, "and I'll surprise you even more if I tell you it's Marshal Blücher who sent me the Emperor's letter, which he tells me was among several the courier was carrying when captured by the enemy. I confess I'm much alarmed when I think of the possible consequences of this incident. The Emperor has always written me in code. All his encoded letters came through without trouble since he left, and now this one, which is not in code, had· to fall into enemy hands. What dreadful luck!"

Rovigo read the note Blücher had sent to French advance posts with Napoleon's letter of the twenty-third for Marie-Louise. The crusty old Prussian must have enjoyed writing it. "I am delighted that this circumstance gives me an opportunity to place my profound respect at Your Majesty's feet. . . ." Blücher's profound respect had not, however, kept him from reading the letter or from having copies rushed on to other Allied headquarters.

"What a horrid turn, it makes me so angry," the Empress wrote her confidante, Mme. de Montebello.

As March 24 drew to a close, Napoleon slept soundly at Doulevant, unaware that his letter had been intercepted, even as he was unaware of most of the important events of the past forty-eight hours. As Joseph had surmised, by going behind Allied lines to cut off Allied communications Napoleon had effectively cut off his own communications with Paris. It was Napoleon's own move that had made it possible for the Allies to intercept his couriers and estafettes; his own move that made it impossible for him to keep informed of the movements of his own and Blücher's forces to the west.

When Napoleon started his march east, Blücher had been immobilized for days at Laon, northeast of Paris. Napoleon had received no further news of Blücher, nor had he been in touch since the twentieth with the 27,000 men he had summoned east to support him in this final gamble. The bulk of these forces, some 17,000 men, were under the command of Marshals Marmont and Mortier. Orders of the twentieth instructed the marshals to march to Châlons, twenty miles north of the town of Vitry, at which Napoleon had originally planned to arrive the night of the 20th to regroup his forces. The marshals were to take the northern route in order to block Blücher from heading south to join Schwarzenberg's army.

Napoleon, having had no word since sending those orders, nonetheless never doubted that the marshals would soon arrive, no matter what difficulties they encountered. Calm, slow, and precise, Mortier was sometimes overcautious, but Marmont would stride through hell without hesitating. That was what had led Napoleon to give him tacit command over his senior, Mortier. Napoleon had a special fondness for Marmont, the swarthy, curly-headed, great-hearted man of lion-sized courage. Youngest of all his marshals in this campaign, Marmont was the one Napoleon had known longest. The two men had fought together as captains when Napoleon was twenty-four and Marmont was nineteen.

It was unfortunate that Marmont's jealousy and vanity were as remarkable as his courage. They had caused more than one disaster, leading Napoleon to distrust Marmont's judgment so much that he had hesitated to give Marmont his marshal's baton until years after others had gotten theirs. Marmont resented the slight without analyzing the reason for it, though Napoleon upbraided him time and again for lack of judgment.

"You maneuvered like an oyster," he told Marmont after one battle.

It had no effect. Criticism only led Marmont to the conclusion that he was misunderstood. Always cocksure, he continued to believe he could predict an enemy's moves better than any other general, and was so sure of his judgment that once he made up his mind, no opinion, no report, no evidence would induce him to change it.

Just two weeks earlier, Marmont's stubbornness had caused another disaster. Pressed by orders to advance on Laon, Marmont had managed to drive an enemy army of 100,000 before him with just 10,000 men. This extraordinary success made him so contemptuous of his enemy that he committed every error an incautious general could commit. He camped for the night in the middle of a huge plain in full view of the enemy with a narrow defile behind him as his only line of retreat. He failed to place his advance guard in a favorable position and allowed his inexperienced units to camp unsupervised in the positions they occupied at the end of the day. While his men carelessly lit fires and fell asleep, Marmont, who was called King Marmont by his troops because of his penchant for princely living, went off to a nearby chateau for the night.

He was not stupid; he certainly knew better. It was pride that led him to flaunt his disdain for the enemy. The result was disastrous. The enemy attacked after dark, took 40 cannon and 32 caissons, captured or killed 3000 men, and effectively knocked Napoleon's right wing out of action for days. It was a typical Marmont folly on such a grandiose scale that Marmont avoided Napoleon for some time after.

When the two came face to face on March 13 after the victory at Reims, Napoleon raked Marmont with insults in a violent scene before witnesses. Once his spleen was vented, Napoleon forgave the marshal and invited him to dinner.

There were three main roads between Paris and eastern France. The one to Châlons, which Napoleon had ordered Marmont and Mortier to take, was the most northerly. The center road, on a direct line from Paris to Vitry through Sézanne, he had assigned to the additional 10,000 men he had summoned east under other commanders. When he reached Doulevant on the twenty-fourth, he sent scouts to explore the third main road to Paris, the southern route through Bar, Troyes, and Nogent, along which he planned to reestablish his communications line while awaiting the Allies' return from their wild-goose chase over his false trail to the north.

As a glance at the map will show, he was thus covering Paris as well as possible by keeping all three main east-west roads between himself and Paris under observation while looking forward to regrouping his forces in a continuous north-south line that would bar the Allies from the capital.

The plans looked good. Encouraging news kept coming in from imperial garrisons in the east. Napoleon's scouts and advance cavalry in the eastern provinces reported that enemy movements seemed disturbed and uncertain. General Piré, operating against Allied depots around Chaumont, Joinville, and Châtillon, wrote of the continued retreat of Allied reserves toward the Rhine, and of the joyful anticipation of revenge aroused among Frenchmen liberated from Allied occupation.

Numerous reports confirmed the evacuation from Bar-sur-Aube of the Emperor of Austria and all Allied rear headquarters staff with some 10,000 infantrymen and 400 wagons of munitions.

Napoleon had reason to be optimistic as he retired early on March 24 in the low-ceilinged, modest, second-story bedroom of a row house belonging to a notary in the little town of Doulevant. Later that night perhaps he would have details on the Allies' moves and news of the arrival of his troops from the west. With one soldier at the foot of his bed, others in the room outside, and his traveling carriage harnessed and at the door, he was ready for instant action. What action, time and incoming information would decide.

III

—————

INDECISION

March 25, 26

WHEN NAPOLEON WAS awakened at his usual hour of midnight to read the incoming reports, he found little enlightenment. Panic and disorder on the enemy rear were spreading to the right bank of the Rhine, but there was still no substantial information on the main Allied army from anywhere. Many reports read, "No news, nothing has been heard." Others spoke of two infantry men, an isolated enemy patrol—trivia.

Macdonald, who had been pursued all the previous day by what he took to be the entire Allied army heading north, was observed by a few scouts on the twenty-fourth as he moved into position as rear guard at St.-Dizier. Ney, halfway between St.-Dizier and Doulevant, had been left in peace. The Allied move toward Vitry seemed stopped or slowed. Where was Schwarzenberg, and where was he heading? There were rumors of all sorts—of disagreements among the Allies, of Schwarzenberg in disgrace and relieved of command—but no facts.

Napoleon discounted the possibility that the Allies might have decided to head for Paris. It was not in keeping with their operations throughout the campaign or with Schwarzenberg's character. The Austrian commander had renounced marching on Paris twice at a mere threat to his line of retreat. Now that the French army had thrown his reserves and communications into confusion, was it likely he would decide to head for Paris?

Blücher had the determination to make that sort of decision, but not Schwarzenberg. It was more logical to believe the prince either was moving northeast on Napoleon's phantom trail or had paused to regroup his widely dispersed army and join forces with the Army of Silesia.

Nevertheless, not knowing left Napoleon in painful uncertainty. He would not admit guesswork. His own instructions stipulated that every officer "must set down nothing by hearsay, report only what he has seen, and when obliged to state something he has not seen, say he has not seen it." Napoleon followed these rules himself. He inspected, reviewed, and checked everything with his own eyes. With no concrete information coming in to reassure him that he should continue his plan—and nothing to indicate that he should change it—he suspended action.

At 3:30 A.M., Napoleon immobilized the main body of his army by sending orders to Marshal Macdonald, Marshal Ney, and cavalry general Sébastiani to halt in place. He sent scouts and light cavalry to reconnoiter farther north, south, and west. To units pursuing enemy reserves fleeing toward the Franco-German border, he sent orders to investigate the possibility of capturing the remaining Allied-occupied bases. To all, he sent encouraging news about French reoccupation of towns the Allies had fled.

"We have entered Bar-sur-Aube, Chaumont, and Troyes," he announced. "The Emperor of Austria retreated in haste with all reserves the Allies had at Chaumont and Bar. We are also masters of Brienne. I will have a clear idea of what the enemy is doing only four or five hours from now. It is essential that no one move."

At 4 A.M., Napoleon sent officers to set up a new message center and military post at Bar-sur-Aube. A staff officer was to try to reach Paris from Bar via Troyes and Nogent to open the new communications route, spread news of Napoleon's successes in the east, and send back reports on the enemy.

At 5 A.M. Macdonald, who had not yet gotten his orders to halt, left St.-Dizier. His rear guard was attacked as it hurried out of a narrow defile near Valcourt, two miles south of the town. The attackers had ten guns supported by 3000 cavalrymen on the north bank of the Marne, but did not pursue the French. At 10 A.M. Macdonald got Napoleon's order of 3:30 A.M. and halted.

"Nothing new on the enemy," he wrote. "Only a few scouts sighted."

At about the same hour, Ney wrote he had heard cannon fire from the direction of St.-Dizier. He assumed it was Schwarzenberg's advance guard firing on Macdonald's rear. At 11 A.M., the guns were quiet, but Macdonald reported having sighted from afar a column of 10,000 cavalrymen with some fifty or sixty guns on the Vitry-St.-Dizier road.

Distance and a fine rain kept him from seeing whether there was infantry too, but he concluded that the horsemen were an advance guard for the entire Allied army, which was probably marching east along both banks of the Marne. Incoming reports that afternoon supported his belief.

At 5:30 and 6 P.M. there was cannon fire to the rear of Macdonald's corps again. Ney reported that the 10,000 cavalrymen he had spotted earlier were crossing the Marne and entering St.-Dizier. This was puzzling. Since neither regrouping south of Vitry nor following Napoleon's false trail northeast would lead the Allies to St.-Dizier, they must have chosen a third course.

As Napoleon was mulling over this news, some Russian prisoners taken by patrols were brought in for interrogation. To his alarm, all of them insisted that the two Allied armies had joined and were marching on Paris, leaving General Winzingerode to follow Napoleon with his cavalry. Napoleon was sufficiently shaken by these reports to decide to take the road to Paris at once. Just then, a message came in from the mayor of St.-Dizier, at whose house Napoleon had stayed the previous night. Ney's report was confirmed: General Winzingerode, the mayor wrote, had entered the town with his cavalry at 6 P.M. The cavalry was obviously the advance guard of the Allied army after all, for as soon as Winzingerode arrived, he requisitioned and started preparing a suite of lodgings for Tsar Alexander, the King of Prussia, Prince Schwarzenberg, and their retinues.

Napoleon made his decision at nine that evening. With its back to the Marne River, Winzingerode's cavalry, whether an advance guard or something else, was imprudently exposed. It was a good moment to attack, retake St.-Dizier and see for certain what was behind that curtain of cavalry. Orders for the attack went out at 9:30 P.M. The army was to assemble at Wassy, halfway to St.-Dizier, by six-thirty the following morning.

"Everything points to a good day for us tomorrow," Napoleon's orders concluded.

Optimistic though he might sound in his orders, Napoleon backed his gamble by putting chips on another number. That evening he allowed a grateful Caulaincourt to take advantage of the Austrian emperor's isolation from his fellow sovereigns and initiate negotiations for a separate peace.

"The Emperor asks me to renew negotiations in the frankest and most positive manner," Caulaincourt wrote Metternich. "Do not leave to others, Prince, the task of restoring peace to the world. There is no reason why peace could not be concluded in four days. . . ."

In the meantime, it was on with the war.

March 26

At 2:30 A.M., the cry "To horse!" echoed from the Emperor's suite as Napoleon strode out. Caulaincourt rushed ahead to hold his left stirrup and hand him his crop and reins while Napoleon's staff scrambled onto their waiting horses. Within two minutes they were off at a gallop.

Reaching Wassy as March 26 dawned, Napoleon continued at once to the plain of Valcourt, a high plateau overlooking the Marne. It was a superb spring day. Through the tender green of spring, across the river, the helmets of thousands upon thousands of Russian cavalrymen glittered in the sun.

What a glorious sight it was! Uniforms were gallooned and festooned. Coats and trousers were white, cream, pink, scarlet, sky-blue, and green, braided in gold and red, embroidered in gold and silver, trimmed with fur. There were bearskin hats, cocked hats, gold helmets, shakos, and plumes of egrets, horsehair, and heron feathers. Swords and sabers gleamed in gold scabbards. Long lances held high-flying pennants. The horses had silk blankets, fur blankets, and gold studded bridles, but even without the handsome trappings the cavalry would have been impressive by sheer numbers.

"Never since the beginning of the war," Marshal Macdonald exclaimed, "had I had a chance to see so many horses in action."

Taking his spyglass from one of his pages, Napoleon scanned the mass of cavalry. He saw some supporting infantry and cannon. He searched for the familiar colors and uniforms of the enemy sovereigns and their retinues, but distance kept him from telling whether they were there or not. Impatient, he gave the order to charge.

Napoleon led on his white mare with Oudinot at his side. Close behind the familiar plain black hat and baggy gray coat of Napoleon came his mamelukes in oriental splendor, turbaned, with broad scimitars, astride richly caparisoned Arab horses. Napoleon's cannon opened fire to provide cover for the four divisions of guard cavalry that trotted out ahead. In two hundred yards, the horsemen broke into a fast trot. In another two hundred, as they came into enemy musket range, they surged into a gallop, and for the last fifty, still in close formation, dashed at the enemy across the Marne at a dead run, their short, straight thrusting swords leveled. Instantly wheeling and re-forming ranks after they broke against the enemy, they withdrew to charge again.

Hoofbeats, shouts, and cannon drowned the birdsongs; smoke from artillery and burning farms clouded the sun. The enemy was routed, but rallied, retook the heights, retreated, and regrouped in front of St.-Dizier. For hours, the Allies held out in the town itself, then in the woods and surrounding villages. It was almost two in the afternoon before they were dispersed.

As the Russian cavalry scattered, barrels of tobacco rolled across the highroad from Russian supply wagons. Strongboxes broke open, littering the ground with packets of multicolored Russian banknotes. Disputing the value of the various colors, French soldiers scrambled to scoop up the money. White was favored for some reason, and those who gathered it reportedly did well later selling it in Paris. The French snuffed the strong Russian troop tobacco, coughing and sputtering, while Russian prisoners snatched at it with pleasure. Riderless horses capered and whinied; French peasants and soldiers captured them with glee.

At 2 P.M., Napoleon reentered St.-Dizier at the head of his troops to trumpets' blare and cries of *Vive l'Empereur!* The affair was a brilliant success. The French had killed or captured over 2000 enemy cavalrymen and taken nine cannon, some bridge equipment, and a great many supplies. The survivors had scattered in opposite directions. Oudinot was detached to pursue and annihilate those fleeing northeast toward Bar-le-Duc, while Napoleon remounted his horse to dislodge enemy troops that had taken refuge in the woods south and west of St.-Dizier.

His joy at victory was short-lived. Interrogations of captured enemy officers revealed that it was not Schwarzenberg's advance guard he had fought. All he had defeated was a Russian cavalry unit detached from the Army of Silesia. Napoleon walked over the battlefield alone, somber and preoccupied. How could Blücher be here when, at last report, he was far to the northwest and totally immobilized? And where was Schwarzenberg, who had been marching on Vitry just two days earlier?

Napoleon was reluctant to conclude that the enemy had marched on Paris, reluctant to proceed east without greater certainty. Before returning to St.-Dizier, he rode through his troops' bivouacs. It was dark when he reached the units camping on the road the enemy had taken toward Bar-le-Duc. The campfires lining the narrow road rising steeply behind the town looked like a lighted staircase climbing the sky, shedding light on the countryside below.

As he rode past, Napoleon was saluted by his men, all quite content with this day. For them, a battle won was a victory, and that was enough. The officers were more perceptive. As one captain wrote home after going to look over the Russian horse that was his prize for the day, "I was pleased to see he was a good, handsome animal with a bottle of champagne for my supper in the saddle, but then my heart sank at the thought the Russians were in Champagne and we were no longer dating our bulletins from Vienna, Dresden, Berlin, Madrid, Moscow, Lisbon. . . ."

Napoleon got back to St.-Dizier at eight-thirty that night to closet himself in his study with his maps, just as he had in the same room two nights earlier before leaving for Doulevant. He still had the same reasons to doubt that the Allies would be bold enough to march on Paris. Besides, it seemed unlikely that the Emperor of Austria would have fled east unless the other Allied sovereigns planned to follow. Nothing could make sense until he had a reply to the unanswered question: Where was Schwarzenberg's army?

Napoleon wrestled with the dilemma for hours. If the Allies had headed for Paris, he could still beat them there by making a forced march at once. Yet if he guessed wrong, he would have abandoned for nothing his plan of rallying his forces in the east. The plan was going so well that it could win him the war in a few days.

Guided by his contempt for other men and his faith in himself, he concluded that he could keep all the options open a little longer. Even if the Allies were marching on Paris, they always moved so slowly that, with Marmont and Mortier in their path to delay them, he would have time later to rush west and pin them between his own and the marshals' forces. The decision could still be postponed.

He would keep Piré's indefatigable light cavalry operating on the Allied rear, let Oudinot continue to Bar-le-Duc to destroy the remains of Winzingerode's cavalry and join the troops being led out of the Metz garrison. That way his plan to arouse the population and rally his garrisons would move forward, while he himself prepared for a possible race to Paris by taking the fort at Vitry the next morning. The enemy force occupying it would probably yield promptly if still there. With the key passage over the Marne at Vitry in his grasp, Napoleon would control the roads north to Châlons and west to Paris. Backed by the additional forces being assembled to his rear, he would be ready to push on to encounter the Allies wherever they had gone.

At 5 A.M. on the twenty-seventh, Napoleon's orders went out. The town stirred as the army prepared to move again.

When Napoleon issued his orders, he was unaware that Marmont had just committed a series of follies surpassing his blunders at Laon. The last imperial courier to reach Marmont and Mortier had brought them Napoleon's orders of the twentieth to march east in all haste. The marshals had set off at once, encountering numerous hardships and forced to make long detours. Nevertheless, on the morning of the twenty-fifth, the end of the hard trail was in sight. They were just a dozen miles west of Vitry, where Napoleon had said he would be. Relaxing over breakfast at Soudé Ste.-Croix, they were looking forward to joining him that day. Local inhabitants assured them Napoleon was heading up the Marne with the Allies in pursuit.

They had been unable to adhere to the itinerary in his orders. They were to have followed the northernmost route east through Reims or Epernay to Châlons both to keep Blücher from moving south to join Schwarzenberg and to keep a retreat open to Paris for themselves. Before those orders arrived, Marmont had already jeopardized the march and aroused Napoleon's anger by retreating toward Paris and calling on Mortier to evacuate Reims and join him, all because Marmont anticipated a threat to Paris that never materialized.

Napoleon fired a reproach to Marmont at once, but it was too late. The enemy lost no time in moving into the territory left open by the marshals' ill-advised retreat. Blücher's advance cavalry under Winzingerode reoccupied Reims, and an additional force of some 3000 horsemen spread out, scouting and skirmishing between Reims, Epernay, and Châlons. With Reims barred to them, the marshals swung south in hopes of passing through Epernay, but it, too, fell to Blücher's army before they reached it. Pursued by two enemy corps under Generals Yorck and Kleist, the marshals turned still further south to seek a way east. Mortier's progress was slowed by having 3000 to 4000 infantrymen and a strong artillery firing fourteen cannon constantly on his heels. He had to stop to take up defensive positions several times during the day before catching up to Marmont at Château-Thierry the evening of the twenty-first. Destroying the city's bridges over the Marne and leaving a feeble rear guard to delay their pursuers, the marshals set off the following morning on separate roads heading diagonally southeast toward Vitry.

That the marshals' move south left Paris open to the northeast had not passed unnoticed at Blücher's headquarters, but it was Blücher's chief of staff, Gneisenau, not the ailing marshal, who was responsible for making decisions. If Blücher had been in command then, he would probably have marched on Paris at once, since he had been seeking that opportunity since the beginning of the campaign. As temporary commander, Gneisenau shrank from taking on such grave responsibility, particularly since it had been made clear to him that what mattered most to the King of Prussia was having a large and splendid army left when peace was signed.

On the evening of the twenty-second, Gneisenau wrote a dispatch in which he noted that the direction taken by Marshals Marmont and Mortier left the way to Paris open, and that Napoleon seemed to be "abandoning Paris to its own forces and leaving its defense to the National Guard." He concluded:

> Since the rule is never to do what the enemy wants, we should not head for Paris. More than ever, our goal is to annihilate Napoleon's forces. We must therefore cross the Marne ... hasten to support the Grand Army, and try to fall upon the flanks and rear of the enemy while the Grand Army occupies it from the front.

Gneisenau's dispatch started the move east of the Army of Silesia along the very route Napoleon had ordered Marmont and Mortier to take. Blücher, still feverish, weak, in pain, and half blinded by ophthalmia, had until then refused any sort of eyeshade. Presented with a lady's elegant, wide brimmed, green silk bonnet someone found in a closet in his quarters, he clapped it on his head without a word and rode out with his troops on the twenty-third. Still in this attire, he reached Reims that day and Châlons on the twenty-fourth, while his cavalry marched on a parallel line south of him, bivouacking on the twenty-third at Vatry and

Soudé Ste.-Croix, the same towns in which Marshals Mortier and Marmont slept twenty-four hours later.

It was Marmont who had insisted on taking the short-cut through these towns to reach Vitry. Mortier and his cavalry commander, Belliard, had argued strenuously in favor of going directly south from Château-Thierry to join the central road from Paris to Vitry through Sézanne and Fère-Champenoise. Heading south first was longer, but much safer, they felt. It would allow them to keep open a retreat to Paris and to avoid venturing out on a vast plain that offered no cover and had not been reconnoitered. Had Mortier's argument prevailed, history might have been rewritten. The marshals would have joined forces at Fère-Champenoise with the additional units Napoleon had ordered east under Generals Pacthod and Amey. Even if they had encountered the Allies head on, they would have had greater numbers and a better position.

Marmont was too cocksure and stubborn to listen. He would take the short-cut to Soudé alone if necessary. There was no danger of an attack, he claimed, except from the two corps pursuing them under Yorck and Kleist, who would be delayed repairing the bridges at Château-Thierry. Marmont marched on without bothering to scout ahead, without taking routine precautions, without making any effort to assemble or even keep in touch with the various other units he knew Napoleon had summoned east.

Marmont was behaving like a fool. Yet if Napoleon had been able to mark the positions of his marshals' and the enemy's armies on his map on the morning of the twenty-fourth, he would have been satisfied on the whole. The marshals' move south had facilitated the juncture of the two Allied armies, but Napoleon's overall strategy was a success just the same. Paris was exposed, but Napoleon had succeeded in drawing the Allies away from it. Except for the Allied commander Bülow, left behind to besiege Soissons, northeast of Paris, and Generals Yorck and Kleist, who were following the marshals (and therefore moving east too), all the Allies were duly pursuing Napoleon toward the frontier just as he had intended.

Imprudent as Marmont's procedure was, he was right in believing the enemy was ahead and marching east—right, that is, until the afternoon of the twenty-fourth. Throughout the twenty-fourth, local inhabitants continued to assure both Marmont and Mortier that the

Grand Allied Army was following Napoleon up the Marne, and the Silesian army was moving east just in front of the marshals themselves.

The night of the twenty-fourth, the marshals camped seven or eight miles apart, at Vatry and Soudé Ste.-Croix respectively. Mortier wrote Marmont from his headquarters to the north, at Vatry, that a Russian cavalry general commanding what local inhabitants estimated at 15,000 horsemen had slept in that town the night before. It was Winzingerode, he suspected from the description. Other Allied cavalry units had moved on toward Vitry from Soudé the morning of the twenty-fourth, informants told Marmont. There was no one in sight on the open plain when Marmont arrived at Soudé late in the afternoon to stop for the night.

"At nightfall, I saw an immense horizon covered with fires, extending for several leagues," Marmont wrote. "Were they all enemy fires? Or were there French bivouacs too, and where? To answer these three questions, I chose four very intelligent officers who spoke German and Polish, and sent them in four directions, each with an escort of four men, to approach and evaluate the situation. . . ."

Had they found Napoleon at last? Alas, no.

"Before the night ended, all four had reported it was the enemy, the Emperor having crossed the Marne, heading for St.-Dizier."

Marmont was undismayed. It might be the enemy, but it was not a threat, just a rear guard following the Allies east on Napoleon's trail, he said. He stuck to that view no matter what his scouts reported. He called one of his generals gullible for believing the fires were lit by Allied troops heading west, not east. He threatened one of his reconnaissance officers with his saber. (The man, he said, was scared into seeing double.) He dismissed interrogations of enemy prisoners on the grounds that the prisoners were stupid or scheming, not to be believed.

A Polish officer under Marmont's command crept into the midst of the Russian troops, counted their regiments, eavesdropped on their plans, and even captured and brought back one of their scouts to corroborate his story. This evidence also failed to shake the marshal. The only precaution he took was to send word to Mortier to join him as quickly as possible so that the two armies could march on together. He then retired comfortably to bed in the little chateau of Soudé Ste.-Croix, saying he knew more about his position than anyone else. He was quite unaware that 200,000 Allied troops lay between himself and Napoleon, and that all 200,000 were about to march in his direction.

The town of Vitry was stirring by daybreak on the twenty-fifth. Late as usual, Allied units scheduled to get underway at 3 and 4 A.M. broke camp from the half circle around the west side of Vitry at dawn. Thick columns formed in Vitry itself and poured out, heading for Paris and for the chateau where Marmont slept.

The weather was dry, the roads much improved, and the men in high spirits over advancing at last on the capital. A broad, seemingly endless mass of men marched in the magnificent, multicolored uniforms of dozens of nations, overrunning the narrow road to Soudé Ste.-Croix. The artillery occupied the road proper, flanked right and left by infantry, while cavalry rode ahead and guards and reserves detoured cross-country.

When Mortier, riding on ahead of his troops, reached the chateau of Soudé at 7 A.M., he found Marmont leisurely studying his maps. Mortier had missed Marmont's message en route. His troops were exhausted, he told his colleague. They had covered sixty miles in as many hours across a treeless, icy plain with Cossacks sniping at their heels, but they would be getting underway at once. Marmont invited Mortier to join him at breakfast while waiting. The two sat down to a peaceful meal in a large room on the ground floor of the castle. Mortier's aide-de-camp, Baron de Bourgoing, who was seated at a larger breakfast table in the same room with Marmont's entire general staff, described the scene.

We had been at table for some time when we heard rifle fire. Marshal Marmont sent an aide to find out what was happening. The officer returned shortly to say it was just some soldiers firing at doves on the roof of the chateau. Hardly had he said that when two enemy cannonballs shattered the slate roof over our heads. . . . It was the light artillery of the Allied army's advance guard attacking us.

Everyone rushed out. The narrow courtyard of the chateau was instantly jammed in the inevitable confusion of a surprise attack. The marshals' packhorses disputed the passageway with the two marshals and their staffs, struggling to get to the head of their troops. We finally managed to get out and gallop to the top of the heights surrounding the plateau of Soudé. From there we could see countless masses of Russian, Prussian, and Wurtemberger cavalry. Marshal Mortier dispatched me to speed the arrival of his army. Leaving behind my orderly lancer, who would have made me more conspicuous, I set off at a full gallop.

Where there were sunken roads bordered with hedges, I had cover, but from time to time the protecting curtain of leaves disappeared as the terrain changed, and I had to cross completely open fields. The Cossacks finally spotted the lone rider galloping full speed toward a French army corps. A pack of swift horsemen hurled themselves after me with loud cries, while others drove their horses ahead to cut me off. In the daily vicissitudes of an aide-de-camp's life, everything depends on the speed of his horse. Sometimes these cross-country steeplechases determine the outcome of a battle. . . . I was lucky to have a fine Polish horse that beat my pursuers to the head of General Charpentier's column.

"The marshals are being attacked by what they believe to be the Grand Allied Army," I said.

"They'd better believe it," the general replied. "Cannon fire like that can't come from an advance guard."

Marmont, who until that moment had clung to the illusion he had only a curtain of token forces to pierce before joining Napoleon, was aghast when he saw enemy cavalry fill the plain. Where was Napoleon? What was the whole Allied army doing here, heading west? His rashness came home to him in a rush. Nothing behind him but endless plains and two difficult defiles; nothing in front but a tiny stream—if only Mortier's troops were meeting him at the defile instead of marching into this trap. Under heavy fire, Marmont hurried his 10,000 men into defensive positions as the Allied army advanced upon him.

The all-day battle was a disaster in heroic proportions. Alternately fighting and retreating, Marmont held out alone for three hours. After Mortier's troops arrived, the marshals continued fighting and retreating together through plains, defiles, and more plains, through a hailstorm followed by torrents of rain and wind so violent that it blinded the soldiers. Friend and foe were indistinguishable at three paces. Cannon bogged down, waterlogged muskets became useless, men and animals slipped or sank in the viscous mud. Occasionally panic overcame the ranks. Often an incredible courage distinguished the raw recruits.

One battalion, formed only two months earlier, could not be gotten into symmetrical squares for defense. The recruits had not had enough training. The Old Guard leader in command herded them together facing outward.

"All right, my friends," he said. "Just huddle together like a flock of sheep. Fire only from close range, aim low, and that cavalry won't be able to touch you." They resisted charge after charge.

Fighting and retreating, the marshals' troops halted in midafternoon near Fère-Champenoise during a brief lull, but were attacked almost at once by fresh arrivals, 12,000 cavalrymen under the Prince Royal of Wurtemberg. The French halted to make a stand, returning fire staunchly in the face of repeated charges. But new bodies of enemy cavalry kept appearing on their flanks, while hard rain driving in their faces blinded them. They had fallen into a disorderly rout when a fierce cannonade burst from somewhere to the rear.

"The Emperor!" the men shouted. Rallying, demanding to be led in an attack, they hurled themselves on the foe so violently that the enemy cavalry fell back despite its heavy superiority.

The gunfire was not the Emperor's. The enemy re-formed and the French attack lost force, though the firing to the rear created enough of a diversion to allow the French to escape massacre and continue their retreat. Fortunately for the marshals, the Prince Royal decided it was wiser not to pursue the battle. His men had been in action almost twelve hours, his infantry was too far behind to catch up before dusk, the fire he heard to the rear made him fear being caught between two French forces, and he was not certain of the size of the column he was attacking. The fury of the Frenchmen's last rally led him to suspect it might be larger than he had first guessed.

The Wurtemburgers, content from then on to follow, observe, and snipe at stragglers, trailed the French for another five hours without renewing the fight. About 9 P.M., with enemy campfires and scouts all around them, the marshals halted at Allemant, five miles north of Sézanne, to rest troops that had been marching and fighting for most of the last fourteen hours. They could congratulate themselves on their escape, but it had been earned at the price of a battle lost by other French forces heading east under General Pacthod to join Napoleon. The cannon fire they had heard to their rear had marked the slaughter of more than half of the general's 5500 men before the eyes of the Allied sovereigns.

General Pacthod, escorting 4500 national guardsmen, had joined General Amey with his thousand men at Sézanne. Taking under their charge a large convoy of cannon, munitions, and 200,000 rations of bread and *eau de vie,* the two generals continued east together. When they stopped for the night a dozen miles northwest of Mortier's headquarters at Vatry, Pacthod learned Mortier was nearby and sent an orderly for instructions. For unexplained reasons, the orderly was badly received when he reached Vatry at 3 A. M. He was instructed to tell Pacthod to join the two marshals early on the twenty-fifth, but was not warned of the horizon covered with campfires Marmont had seen at nightfall. He was refused a horse for his return, though his own had dropped dead of exhaustion. He got back to Pacthod's camp on foot too late to speed up the general's march.

By ill luck, as Pacthod headed southeast with Amey to join Marmont and Mortier, he halted to rest his weary men around 10 A.M., confident that all danger was behind him. While stopped, he was attacked head on by Blücher's advance cavalry of 5000 that had set out for Paris from Châlons that morning. Grouping his inexperienced troops in squares around the convoy, Pacthod and Amey put up a gallant fight for two hours. When 4000 more Allied cavalrymen arrived, the French no longer had a chance. Pacthod abandoned some of the cumbersome supply wagons, hitched the freed horse teams to the cannon in order to move faster, and started retreating cross-country with the hope of meeting the marshals en route.

It was not the marshals he met, though he came within earshot of them. In midafternoon, when he was about five miles from Fère-Champenoise, he came upon an enemy cavalry unit blocking the road. While he was trying to force a path through, he was suddenly attacked on both sides by clouds of enemy horsemen. Retreating, he rallied his troops to head for a swamp to the north, but the enemy kept him from reaching it. More Allied units continued to arrive.

Emperor Napoleon had been defeated, Pacthod concluded, and he and his few thousand guardsmen were all that stood between the enemy and the capital. He could not stop the enemy, but he would make him pay, show him what Frenchmen were.

"Who would want to live if France is lost?" he harangued his men. "Let us swear to die for her!" He formed his men into little squares, bayonets facing out, cannon placed at the angles. With raised swords, the soldiers swore to die. The enemy cavalry charged.

The Allied sovereigns arrived at the height of the battle when 14,000 enemy soldiers surrounded Pacthod, Amey, and their diminishing squares in the middle of the plain. Tsar Alexander, the King of Prussia, and Prince Schwarzenberg watched in horrified admiration. The tiny French army formed a living wall against repeated cavalry charges. As men fell, lines reformed instantly, never wavering, but the squares shrank with each assault. The Tsar sent parliamentaries to plead with Pacthod to surrender. One parliamentary was killed, the other taken prisoner. Military law forbids negotiations under fire, General Pacthod said.

The Tsar advanced his infantry. The French held their ground. Allied guns moved in close. The French fought back with bayonets. Only when Pacthod and five of his generals were wounded and 3000 of his men were killed or wounded did he agree to surrender. Eyewitnesses say Tsar Alexander himself went into the midst of the last remaining French square calling, "I want to save them!"

Pacthod's gallant stand was not for nothing. Not only had the gunfire created the diversion that allowed Marshals Marmont and Mortier to escape, his troops' desperate heroism convinced the Russian Tsar that the French army was still fanatically loyal to the empire. Alexander greeted Pacthod and the other generals personally and had their horses and swords returned to them.

"Men who use swords so well should never be separated from them," he said.

The indelible impression this battle made on the Tsar greatly influenced his course in the following days. The army was tired of war, de Vitrolles had said? The country eager to lay down arms? Ready to welcome the invaders? Yet here were conscripts just two months away from the plow who were ready to die defying the whole Allied army!

If the Tsar was subject to doubts at that moment, others were not. *On to Paris!* was the cry. From Fère-Champenoise, Prince Schwarzenberg wrote Marshal Blücher with unaccustomed enthusiasm:

> The army's advance was crowned with success. The enemy was repulsed all along the line and routed despite his resistance. We took over thirty cannon, a large number of caissons and wagons, five generals, and several thousand men. The advance guard is already at the level of Allemant....

Pacthod and the marshals lost a total of 9000 men and forty-six cannon to the Allies on March 25. The remaining men who had been heading east to join Napoleon raced for Paris with the Allies in close pursuit. All the French could hope to do was delay the enemy attack. Their immediate goal was to rally at the fortified town of Meaux, which protected the bridges over the Marne and the approach to Paris. If they reached Meaux before the enemy did, they could make a stand, perhaps keep the Allies from crossing the Marne until Napoleon could come to the rescue.

Only a small number of the troops hurrying back toward Paris made it to Meaux. Fighting every step, Generals Vincent and Compans, with 2500 men between them, outdistanced the Allies by a few hours to join forces with the garrison at Meaux early on the twenty-seventh. Marshals Marmont and Mortier never arrived. Their 11,000 men, straggling with fatigue, fell farther behind each day. Finding town after town in their path taken by the enemy ahead of them, they kept having to detour farther south.

They were resting men and horses at Provins, over forty miles away, when the Allies' advance column reached Meaux at four on the afternoon of the twenty-seventh.

IV

THE RACE FOR PARIS
March 27, 28, 29

NAPOLEON WAS 100 MILES to the east when the gateway to Paris was attacked. The evening of the twenty-seventh found him still at St.-Dizier, still hesitating.

That morning, his map pinpointing Allied units had remained blank. Again he sent scouts in all directions. Couriers went to query the proprietor of the nearby chateau of Plessis, where Napoleon had slept the night of the twenty-third. Other couriers left to query the mayors of all local towns. Macdonald advanced to Vitry to size up the strength of the enemy garrison. Napoleon followed in person at 10 A.M. to take the fort.

Macdonald was dismayed to find that the main Allied army had just left Vitry. Where had it gone?

"It was easy to guess," he wrote afterward, "for since it had not followed us and since it left a strong garrison in the town, it had obviously faced about and was advancing, unopposed, on Paris."

It was a dark moment.

"We had marched through pouring rain that scarcely let up," Macdonald said, describing the scene in front of Vitry. "My men were utterly exhausted. The ground was so soaked neither cavalry nor artillery could budge. Emperor Napoleon turned to me and said, 'Storm the town.'

" 'What? In the state the troops are in? Don't you see the size of the garrison on the ramparts? I grant you the ramparts are only dirt, but they're reinforced with fraises and palisades,* surrounded by trenches filled with water. How are we supposed to get across?'

* Fraises and palisades: fortifications consisting of stakes. Palisades are vertical, fraises horizontal.

101

" 'Have bundles of straw gathered and thrown in.'

" 'Where are we to get straw? There isn't any left in the villages around. Besides, how could we make a solid bridge out of a few bundles of straw? And how can you hope for success, trying a *coup de main* with men in the shape mine are?' "

Napoleon insisted.

"Try it with your own Guard if you will, sire, my men aren't fit now," Macdonald said as he walked away. This from Macdonald, who himself said just six months earlier that everyone around Napoleon trembled at a sigh.

While Napoleon awaited the return of a reconnaissance party scaling the hilltop town, one of the scouts brought Macdonald a little bulletin he had found. Apparently printed by the enemy commander occupying the fort, it read:

Colonel and Commander de

Schwichow

Vitry, March 29

announces an Allied victory at Fère-Champenoise

5000 p.isoners including

6 generals and

40 cannon taken

We are pursuing the enemy. The defeated corps

will probably be completely destroyed.

Another bulletin listed generals and commissioned and noncommissioned officers taken prisoner at Fère-Champenoise. Macdonald recognized the names of officers in General Amey's division, which was part of his own corps. He hurried to Berthier to beg him to take the bulletins to the Emperor at once.

Berthier refused.

"The news is too disastrous," he said in his nasal voice. "Take it yourself."

"You're our go-between, it's your obligation."

A heated argument ensued. Realizing that the knowledge of these events would change the Emperor's plans, and aware there was no time to lose, Macdonald gave in. He found the Emperor sitting alone by a campfire.

"You look worried," said Napoleon. "What's wrong?"

Macdonald handed him Colonel Schwichow's bulletin. "Read this." Napoleon read it and smiled.

"It's not true," he said. "That's the sort of trick the Allies play all the time."

"Not true! But all the details are there. I recognize the names and positions, and our heavy artillery should have just gotten to Fère-Champenoise about now."

"What day is it today?"

"The twenty-seventh."

"Have a look," said Napoleon. "This is dated the twenty-ninth, which is day after tomorrow."

Macdonald was nonplussed; he had not noticed the date.

"It must be a mistake," he said. "This unfortunate affair must have taken place yesterday at the spot named."

Taking back the sheet in confusion, Macdonald returned to Berthier's bivouac, where the chief of staff sat with his red-trousered officers and the Emperor's aides-de-camp, looking up at the fort bristling with enemy guns.

"Well?"

"He won't believe it's authentic."

"May I have a look?" asked General Drouot, one of Napoleon's four principal aides on the campaign. Drouot studied the bulletin closely and handed it back.

"You're only too right, *Monsieur le Maréchal.* It's a misprint. That's a 6 upside down."

Macdonald went back to the Emperor.

"The devil! That changes everything." Napoleon paced up and down a few moments in silence. "So you don't think we can carry Vitry by force?"

"I thought you were convinced," Macdonald answered.

"Quite true. Very well, let us leave."

"Where will you go?"

"I don't know yet. For the present, to St.-Dizier. Stay here as rear guard. Keep check on the enemy, don't let him leave. I'll be sending you orders. I'm sure to have news waiting for me at St.-Dizier."

"Whatever news you have, Paris, undefended, will have fallen before you can get there—if you're going there, that is—no matter how fast you march. In your place, I'd go into Lorraine and Alsace, gather up the garrisons, declare a fight to the death on the enemy's rear, cut him off, intercept his supplies. Then he'd have to retreat and you'd have the support of our strongholds."

"I've ordered General Durutte to assemble 10,000 men around Metz," Napoleon said, "but I have to see the latest reports before I decide anything."

If Napoleon wanted further confirmation of the Allies' move, he had it soon enough, right there in front of Vitry. Local peasants brought in other Allied bulletins that corroborated the first. Enemy prisoners and French soldiers who had escaped the enemy reported that the Allies had joined forces and started east toward Paris two days before.

There was additional confirmation in the enemy's own words in an intercepted dispatch from Allied general Barclay de Tolly. Written in Russian near Vitry at 8 P.M. on the twenty-fourth, the dispatch ordered all supplies, artillery, and munitions at Chaumont sent at once to Fère-Champenoise, where the Allied army was to be the night of the twenty-fifth.

Fère-Champenoise was thirty miles west of Vitry and over a quarter of the way to Paris. If the Allies had gotten that far on the twenty-fifth, they would be far ahead of Napoleon by the twenty-seventh. They had already dispersed the forces Napoleon had counted on to delay them. Was there any point in his trying to reach Paris now? He was not only over 100 miles away, his army was widely scattered. The rear guard was at St.-Dizier, some units were still strung out between St.-Dizier and Doulevant, and Oudinot and Piré were far to the east. It was unlike Napoleon to hesitate, unlike him to consult his staff, but he did both.

Macdonald and Baron Fain pleaded with him to continue east.

"Leave the capital to its fate and let the enemy find his tomb there," said Fain.

Ney, his face as red as his hair, argued for marching on Paris at once. Berthier and Caulaincourt seconded Ney. Paris would be destroyed if Napoleon persisted in heading east, they said. The Allies would burn it to the ground in revenge for Moscow. Most of Napoleon's top men agreed. They did not relish the thought of abandoning their possessions and positions in Paris to go off in the mountains to head a peasant revolt. They pictured other men taking over their positions under a new government while they themselves turned into penniless outlaws. March straight on Paris from Vitry, they urged, but though Napoleon consulted them, it was alone in his study at St.-Dizier that he would make the decision he was later to regret.

Napoleon mounted his horse. Taking all but Macdonald with him, he retraced his steps, withdrawing eighteen miles to hesitate for almost twenty-four hours at St.-Dizier. The war had moved out of his reach at a decisive moment. Two hundred thousand enemy soldiers moving across the open plain to Paris with almost no one to oppose them! The sweet taste of yesterday's triumph had soured quickly.

Napoleon's choice was essentially between the same two alternatives he had been contemplating for days. He could leave Paris to its fate and continue east as Macdonald urged. He could race west in the hope that Paris would hold out until he arrived, and that his arrival would inspire a defense vigorous enough to drive out the enemy. The morning's news changed the situation only in that his prospects for success were greatly darkened, whichever choice he made. And the time for decision had not only come, it had perhaps passed.

The Allies' sudden march on Paris took him by surprise. Though the possibility had loomed every time Napoleon headed east on the Allied rear, he always hoped it would not materialize. In his declining fortunes, he was increasingly reluctant to believe what did not suit him. He had been eager to reject the assertions of the Russian prisoners and believe Winzingerode's ruse in preparing quarters for the Allied sovereigns at St.-Dizier.

His error is clear in retrospect, but his conclusions were logical enough at the time. The Allies had been doing the wrong thing consistently. Napoleon had every reason to expect them to continue to do the wrong thing, and they would have, but for a series of coincidences. For them to decide to march on Paris, it had taken Talleyrand's invitation, followed by the intercepted letter telling them Napoleon was leaving the city exposed, followed by the intercepted dispatches that assured them Parisians would put up little resistance. And even then, if Emperor Francis had not happened to be isolated by Napoleon's moves, the decision might never have been made. Napoleon can hardly be blamed for failing to anticipate such a run of bad luck, nor could he have foreseen that the combined Allied armies would blunder full strength onto the forces he had counted on to delay any advance on the capital.

While Napoleon was sure he could keep the city with his vastly inferior forces if he got there first, he was not certain of being able to recapture it. With nothing to stop them and a three-day head start, the Allies might well take the city before he reached it. Then he would find he had rushed to the rescue only to lose both the capital and the chance to win the war with his successful operations in the east.

Impassioned pleas to continue action in the east were pouring in from Marshal Oudinot in his native town of Bar-le-Duc. He had been a local hero since the age of twenty, when he galloped his horse up eighty stone steps to attempt the singlehanded rescue of a man about to be hanged by a mob. His mission of arousing popular resistance was a spectacular success, he wrote Napoleon on March 27, 1814. At first stunned to find themselves under enemy occupation when they had believed Napoleon invincible, the population was now ready for vengeance. The people of the Meuse, Moselle, and Vosges were already partly armed and awaiting only a signal to rise up in mass. Enthusiasm was spreading rapidly.... He had only to give the word to let loose a full-scale partisan war, Oudinot assured the Emperor.

The story was the same in the south.

"All I ask for is orders and bullets," General Piré wrote from Chaumont. "French blood courses through every vein, every head is on fire. I think the moment has come when the Emperor can rely on the nation and use the army only to guide and assist.... I am besieged by peasants demanding arms and ammunition to march against the enemy. I propose the Emperor have the tocsin sounded throughout the area on a fixed day and hour.... We'll march on Langres and Vesoul. We don't have many weapons now, but we'll get what we need from the enemy."

Between March 25 and 28, peasants combing the area around Chaumont with hunting rifles, pitchforks, and sticks brought in 1000 prisoners plus munitions, horses, and cannon. Enemy cadavers were piled in wells, strung from trees, thrown in ditches. Partisan bands formed spontaneously in villages. National guardsmen organized companies. Volunteer armies of 1000 to 1500 men were reported here and there, and in one province, 6000 peasants responded to the tolling of the tocsin.

In addition, the garrisons Napoleon had summoned to join him were about to add sizable reinforcements to his small army. General Durutte had reached Luxembourg with 4000 men on the twenty-seventh. General Broussier had forced his way out of Strasbourg with 5000. Another 2000 from the Verdun garrison were marching on Châlons, and still others were getting ready to break out of Allied blockades. Napoleon's plan was working—but what if Paris fell? Napoleon returned to St.-Dizier to weigh the questions he had contemplated over and over.

He sometimes dismissed Paris as unimportant. "Paris isn't the capital of France," he said. "The capital is wherever I make my headquarters." Usually he said exactly the opposite: "Paris will never be occupied so long as I live. . . . Paris must not be abandoned. We will bury ourselves under its ruins. . . . If the enemy ever reaches the gates of Paris, the empire is finished. . . ."

The French, Napoleon said, were not Russians or Germans.

"With the French, as with women, one must never be absent too long. No one knows what might happen if there were no news from me for a long time."

When Napoleon and his army had been incommunicado in Russia for some time in 1812, a conspiracy by a half-mad general named Malet had almost succeeded in taking over the government. Now on March 27, 1814, Paris was once again without news of Napoleon and his army. No word had reached the city since the twenty-first of March. Another conspiracy like that of 1812 could easily flower, the conspirators could connive with the enemy, and the empire might be lost without a battle when all it would have taken to save it was Napoleon's timely reappearance.

The fall of Paris was a greater threat to Napoleon than the occupation of Vienna, Berlin, and Moscow had been to the hereditary Allied kings. Emperor Francis and his fellow sovereigns could lose their capitals and keep their crowns, but Napoleon's crown was a prize of war. The crown he boasted of picking up from the gutter with his sword could be lost by the sword. Napoleon suspected that the day his capital and government fell, even if he headed a huge army off in the mountainous east of France, he would find himself a mere adventurer again. And yet, perhaps to take that risk was his only chance to win.

Napoleon reached his decision late in the evening of the twenty-seventh. Unfortunately, he did not reach it alone. Clausewitz and other military experts agree that Napoleon had a good chance of succeeding had he followed his inclination to head east.

"I lacked character," Napoleon wrote afterward at Ste.-Hélène. "I should have pursued my idea imperturbably, continuing to the Rhine. . . . I would soon have had a huge army . . . the enemy would have trembled at the dangerous course he had undertaken, and the sovereigns would have been grateful to me for allowing them to retreat . . . peace would have followed . . . and we would have enjoyed happy days again."

While Napoleon blamed himself later for having listened to his generals, on March 27, 1814, he was convinced he could not carry off the gamble of abandoning Paris to its fate and heading east unless he had their enthusiasm and confidence. Perhaps he returned to St.-Dizier from Vitry partly in hopes that the news coming in from the eastern provinces would inspire them, that the fire Piré and Oudinot predicted would spread over the countryside would touch them too.

Instead, as the day wore on at St.-Dizier, their rebellious mutterings grew louder. In the end, Napoleon gave in. He not only agreed to march on Paris, he accepted his staff's choice of routes. Though he favored taking the fastest way to Paris, the central road through Sézanne, he gave it up when Berthier and others insisted that the army would starve on the way after the Allies' passage over this already ravaged territory, and would be unable to get across the Marne at the logical crossing point of Meaux because the Allies would already occupy the town.

At 11 P.M., Napoleon's orders went out. The army would about-face to head back to Doulevant and, from there, to Paris by the southern route Napoleon had taken care to open in the last few days. Whatever advance the enemy made along his shorter central route, Napoleon hoped to march fast enough to rally his forces at the city gates before Paris fell. Piré and Oudinot would abandon their missions and head west at once. Macdonald would form a rear guard with Piré at St.-Dizier. Oudinot sent a last, exasperated protest before leaving to join Napoleon. "It is incomprehensible not to profit from the enthusiasm of the peasants of Lorraine and Barrois." But the decision was made.

Optimism reigned in the dispatches Napoleon sent out through the night. Winzingerode's force was severely crippled, masses of prisoners were being brought in from Troyes and Langres, and Schwarzenberg was now totally cut off from his artillery and munitions reserves, "which must worry him greatly."

The race of the tortoise and the hare was on. After the rapid advance of the twenty-fifth, which had won him such great advantages,

Schwarzenberg had relapsed into his usual torpor. Conducting his march like a parade, watchful that no unit, no wagon stuck out of the ranks to which it was assigned, he made a bloody battle under the walls of Paris inevitable.

All his fears had been revived. While Napoleon was wondering how far the Allies had gotten, Schwarzenberg was still wondering where Napoleon was. The only news the Allies had received since leaving Vitry came from light cavalry units scouting along the southern road to Paris. From Winzingerode, who was supposed to be following and reporting on Napoleon, there was total silence.

The Allies got their first news of Napoleon the evening of the twenty-seventh, and it was shattering. They were camped across the Marne from Meaux, about to start crossing the combined forces of both armies, when they heard from their light cavalry that Napoleon was at Bar-sur-Aube and French troops had entered Troyes. In the time the news had taken to reach them, Napoleon might already be at Troyes with no obstacles in his path. Given his capacity for speedy marches, he might get to Paris before they did, the Allies calculated, or he might arrive on their rear while they were in the midst of what promised to be a slow and cumbersome crossing.

Meaux is a difficult place to cross the Marne. The river takes such a sharp bend there that troops assembling to cross from the south are bottled in a cul-de-sac with the river on three sides and the fortified town facing them across the water. Napoleon's arrival on the Allied rear would close the noose, leaving no possibility of retreat. The Allies felt that the mere announcement that Napoleon was approaching might send their troops into panic.

No longer elated at being close to Paris, Tsar Alexander, the King of Prussia, and Prince Schwarzenberg wondered whether they had not made a fatal move. Their fears of an attack from the rear redoubled when a report came from fortress commander Colonel von Schwichow of Napoleon's move against Vitry. If Napoleon had continued on the central road through Sézanne, he would be closer yet.

Then, and for the following two days, the Allies discounted prisoner reports to the contrary and continued to be guided by the belief that Napoleon was approaching via Sézanne and might attack at any moment. In a worried council on the evening of the twenty-seventh, they decided to spend another twenty-four hours reorganizing the crossing, establishing a strong defense to the rear, and staging small units into the crossing site at irregular intervals. Had Napoleon insisted on marching to Paris by the central road, he might have arrived in time to rout the Allies despite their enormous numerical superiority, a feat that would certainly have aroused an elated France to rally behind him once again.

Instead, having given in to his generals in the choice of roads, Napoleon was much farther from Paris than the Allies imagined. Early on the morning of the twenty-eighth, the imperial army set off once again from St.-Dizier to Doulevant. The weather continued to be miserable. The mud was so deep on the road that sixty caissons had to be unhitched and burned to release enough horses to pull the remaining vehicles. The men lacked food, shoes, and clothes. Long, painful marches had exhausted them. Retracing their steps over these abominable roads was demoralizing. Incoming news was bad. Yet Napoleon's soldiers marched stolidly, without a murmur, while the generals grumbled.

Knowing he could not count on his generals much longer, Napoleon seized upon a chance opportunity to send another personal appeal to Papa François before joining the march that morning. Just as Napoleon was sitting down to breakfast, some peasants arrived in great excitement, escorting important prisoners taken in a popular uprising between Langres and Nancy. The peasants hoped they had captured the Count d'Artois, but the party proved to consist largely of foreign diplomats. Among them was the former Austrian ambassador to London, Baron von Wessenberg. By a curious coincidence, Baron de Vitrolles had been traveling from Nancy with the captured dignitaries on his way to royalists in Paris with credentials, instructions, and encouragement from the Count d'Artois. Posing as von Wessenberg's servant and getting rid of his most compromising secret papers by the simple if distasteful expedient of eating them, the baron was still a captive, but had escaped being taken by the peasants to Emperor Napoleon's headquarters.

Napoleon invited von Wessenberg to breakfast and postponed his departure for a long conversation. With few exceptions, he was willing to accept the conditions the Allies had offered at Châtillon, he told the baron. In any event, Austria could have whatever she wanted and more than she had ever had. Thus only Prussia and Russia would benefit from continuing the war to unconditional surrender. Emperor Francis would be showing a lack of judgment if he refused this offer. He would also be showing a lack of paternal feeling for Marie-Louise. Napoleon praised her as his cleverest, most industrious and most faithful minister, adding, "Your Kaiser does not seem to love his daughter."

To make certain the diplomat reached the Austrian Emperor safely with this appeal, Napoleon took von Wessenberg along as far as Doulevant. Von Wessenberg spent the night there, at Napoleon's headquarters in the notary's modest house, while the hungry, tired, wet, muddy French army bivouacked at various points north. In the baron's words, while everyone else at imperial headquarters spent an anxious night, Napoleon could be seen through a doorway "lying on the ground on a mattress and sunk in deep sleep like a man without a care in the world."

The situation in Paris was worse than Napoleon could have imagined. Knowledge of the approaching crisis, far from electrifying all spirits, immobilized them. In the face of growing certainty that the Allies were heading for Paris—and mounting conviction that the Emperor would not return in time to rescue it—Parisians debated whether the city should resist at all. No one was sure what would happen when Allied soldiers appeared outside the city walls.

The government was as inactive, querulous, and ineffective as ever. Responsible officials were paralyzed, some because they felt unable to make a move unless commanded by the Emperor, others because events seemed to have gone beyond any human power to influence them. The same dependence on Napoleon that fired men with enthusiasm in his presence made them apathetic in his absence.

The government was not entirely to blame. Napoleon did not trust the Parisians when he was there, and less when he wasn't. He had seen the Paris Guard and the rabble in action in the Revolution. He was reluctant to mobilize and arm them until the last moment for fear they might rise up against his government. When he decided the moment had come to take that risk, his orders met no response in Paris. Afraid to face the consequences of arming the people in Napoleon's absence, Parisian officials procrastinated. They did not disobey outright. They questioned, delayed, and discussed, while volunteers grew discouraged and many men in the National Guard decided that, given the hopelessness of defending Paris under the circumstances, the best way to protect their property was not to try.

As the Allies neared Paris and town after town fell in their path, little or nothing was done to organize the city's defense. Although he had known for three days that the enemy was marching on Paris, Napoleon's brother Joseph continued to see his role as that of receiving and transmitting reports. Minister of War Clarke postponed decisions by burying himself in paperwork, from which he emerged only to issue contradictory orders. Plans for defense works were still pending funds, or Napoleon's approval, or both. In a half-hearted effort, the government mobilized 12,000 of the 30,000 national guardsmen by the twenty-ninth, but balked at arming them all. Three hundred cannon were still sitting in the city arsenal on the Champs de Mars, where they remained. Of the seventy put in place, many were provided with balls of the wrong caliber or exercise balls made of cinders. While both army and Guard lacked arms, there were 20,000 rifles in storage, along with five million infantry bullets and large stores of powder, cartridges, and shrapnel charges.

Men available and ready to fight were not summoned. There were an estimated 20,000 in depots within two days' march of Paris, but none were called in. Seven thousand men were left south of Paris on the Yonne River. The military police made no effort to round up the soldiers absent without leave who filled Parisian cafés and restaurants. Ten thousand civilian volunteers could have been raised easily, but the government was so reluctant to issue arms to the populace that it was still turning volunteers away the morning of the battle. All troops arriving in Paris were sent east at once, as Joseph continued to dream of stopping the enemy before he reached the capital. In any case, surely Napoleon would come soon.

"We've been awaiting news of your approach to the capital from moment to moment," Joseph wrote his brother on the twenty-seventh. There was no answer.

At Joseph's urging, Minister of War Clarke multiplied the number of couriers dispatched to Napoleon. Minister of Police Rovigo repeated his dismal litany in one report after another: morale had collapsed, Paris had no interest in resisting. Postmaster General de La Valette sent out "swift and clever couriers" on the twenty-seventh and twenty-eighth carrying ciphered letters of his own to Napoleon. "I begged him to come back at all costs, told him the police were not strong enough to contain the royalists, that only his presence could stop the coming disaster, that if the enemy took Paris, he was lost." Some of these dispatches were enjoyed by the Allied leaders when they intercepted French couriers the morning of the twenty-eighth, but Napoleon's government knew only that no word came back. Whether Napoleon was aware of the plight of Paris or not, no one could tell.

If Napoleon did not arrive before the Allies did, his top officials were ready to give up Paris quickly and flee. Talleyrand had made certain of that by systematically spreading fear and defeatism. His means were vast, his methods original.

One evening at nightfall, he called on an aristocratic lady who had remained staunchly royalist, though marriage to a man active in the empire brought her in close contact with high imperial officials.

"I come to ask you to render a service important to me, but much more so to the men you love," Talleyrand said. He asked her simply to read Rovigo a letter from her brother, a royalist émigré fighting with the Allied army.

She was surprised that Talleyrand had such a letter in his possession. The writing resembled her brother's. The words were vindictive. "We're coming, determined to purge France of the assassins of the royal family. I've sworn to tie the murderers to the tail of my horse. . . . All my friends feel the same way. Pity the wretch who falls into our hands. . . ."

"Why should I show this to the Duke of Rovigo?" the lady asked.

"Because it will serve the cause of our legitimate kings," said Talleyrand. "It's essential that the Empress leave Paris. If the Allies find her here when they enter, all is lost. Emperor Alexander, who is more knight-errant than politician, will rush to lay his sword on Marie-Louise's lap and pronounce her regent."

"But how will the letter help?"

"By frightening the Duke of Rovigo, who will frighten Marie-Louise, her brothers-in-law, the archchancellor, and others."

"Frighten the Duke of Rovigo? Do you think you can? He's a brave man."

"On the battlefield, yes. In his office, not at all . . . Don't worry, I know my world . . . "

Talleyrand was right, although, when the Duke of Rovigo read the letter, he protested that Napoleon was on his way with an aroused countryside behind him and a redoubled army.

"Please, spare me an official bulletin," the lady replied. "There's no army or resistance left. Your emperor is finished. The Allies will be in Paris in three days, and woe to those here to face their anger."

When Rovigo left, she was certain he would be far from Paris when the Allies arrived. The success of Talleyrand's ruse led her to try it on old Archchancellor Cambacérès, who went so far as to beg her to recommend him to the Bourbons if they returned to power.

When Parisian officials learned the full extent of the losses Marmont,

Mortier, and Pacthod had suffered at Fère-Champenoise, they realized there were no forces left to delay the Allies' descent on the city. It was unlikely that Napoleon would get there first.

"There's no counting on the Emperor anymore, we're on our own," said Police Chief Pasquier.

When word at last arrived from Napoleon, it was hardly reassuring. The *Moniteur* of the twenty-eighth printed the latest imperial bulletin, dated the twenty-fifth:

> The Emperor's headquarters is at Doulevant. The army occupies Doulevant, Chaumont, Brienne. It is in communication with Troyes, and patrols are maneuvering as far as Langres. Prisoners are being brought in from all sides. His Majesty's health is excellent.

What was the Emperor doing, maneuvering between Langres and Doulevant, both over 130 miles from Paris? Furthermore, the fact that the bulletin was three days old indicated that the courier had been forced to take a roundabout route to reach Paris. In that case, the Allies must have been closer to Paris than Napoleon was when he wrote on the twenty-fifth. By the twenty-eighth, the Allies must be closer still. What difference did it make if the French reoccupied Brienne, when the enemy was about to occupy Paris? Napoleon must be ignoring or ignorant of the Allies' threat to the capital. Parisians complained of having been abandoned without adequate defenses. They condemned the Senate for stripping Paris to give the Emperor all the power and means for defense. Napoleon's enemies in Paris played this theme to advantage.

In the virtual absence of news of any kind, rumors flourished. There were tales of rebellion, of plots to remove Napoleon from power, to restore the Bourbons with the help of the invaders, to force Napoleon to abdicate in favor of his son. Some said Napoleon was at St.-Dizier, some said he was heading for Metz, others said he was near Lyons.

Official news was nonexistent. One of the front-page items in the *Moniteur* was that the Queen of England had a bad cold. Even the best informed man in Paris, Talleyrand, knew little of what was happening.

"Nothing new this morning to my knowledge at least," he had written the Duchess of Courlande on the twenty-fifth, the day the forces of Marmont, Mortier, and Pacthod were decimated. On the twenty-seventh, he was able to inform the duchess that the Allies were threatening Toulouse, and that what little news there was, was all bad. "The empire is crumbling," he wrote. "No one obeys and no one as yet dares take command. . . . I see only a nation in ruins."

In Paris, people were amusing themselves as usual. Theaters and the circus played nightly from 6 or 6:30 to 10 P.M. There were crowds everywhere, larger than ever. During the day, people wandered about the streets, squares, and boulevards, and went up to the heights around the city to scan the countryside. Because trade was slack, there were plenty of idle people to swell the crowds. Many workers were jobless, many businesses closed, many shops shut for lack of customers. Those still open sold items below cost.

The situation disintegrated daily. Collection of taxes dropped to almost zero. Many were reluctant to pay and many couldn't if they had wanted to. Money was so scarce that people were sending their silver to the treasury for cash, and the government offered a bonus for gold francs.

There were so many unemployed that the police tolerated the gatherings of idle workers that would normally have been promptly dispersed. Every morning the jobless crowded in front of the gate of St.-Martin at the edge of the workers' quarters on the northeast side of Paris. There they would watch the arrival of prisoners, refugees, and wounded, and the departure of couriers on missions and detachments joining the imperial army. More and more wounded arrived daily, passing through the gates to the broad exterior boulevards, which were lined with chairs for the wealthier spectators. One of the spectators described the scene on one of the last days of March:

> There were straw-filled carts, sometimes driven by women, containing six to eight wounded, barely clothed. There were cavalrymen, some wrapped in their coats, others in remnants of uniforms, most wearing bandages that almost hid their faces under their helmets. Some rode lame or wounded horses, others led their exhausted beasts by the reins. We saw fresh blood everywhere, and many cavalry or infantry soldiers had to walk despite foot and leg wounds. They leaned on their swords or guns or a stick, while carts followed with arms, casks, supplies, saddles, reins. The dead had been left on the field.

Terrified refugees poured through the gates in increasing numbers. The boulevards were crowded with carts piled with hay, corn, and household goods, surrounded by women, the aged, the infirm, children, cats, dogs, and livestock. Many of these wretched people had to sell part of their livestock at the barriers in order to pay the duty still levied on all goods entering the city. Customs was one of the few services remaining rigidly in force.

As the poor crowded in from the country, many of the bourgeois in the city joined the rich in fleeing south or west. There were signs of the Allies' approach. Blood on the soldiers' wounds was a brighter red, refugees came from towns nearer. Unsure at first whether it was an enemy column, a corps, or an army that was descending upon them, Parisians, by the twenty-eighth, had reason to expect the entire Grand Allied Army. Refugees from Coulommiers, just thirty miles away, reported that Emperor Alexander and the King of Prussia slept there the night of the twenty-seventh. Despite government silence, the public gradually learned of the ·defeats of Fère-Champenoise from the wounded arriving in Paris. For all their air of insouciance, Parisians felt an undercurrent of panic. What would the Allies do if they took Paris? Pillage and burn the city? Partition France? The thought of the Cossacks let loose on Paris terrified everyone.

On Sunday, March 27, crowds watched the review of troops in the courtyard of the Tuileries in splendid spring sunshine. Wearing handsome, clean uniforms and carrying arms borrowed for the occasion, 12,000 national guardsmen assembled in the courtyard at 9 A.M. to parade until mid-afternoon. Men, horses, and guns filled streets and squares for blocks around—the Place du Carrousel, the Quai du Louvre, the Place Vendôme, the Rue de Castiglione, the Rue de Rivoli. The spectators were thrilled by the sight of so many new uniforms. They had no idea that the Allies were starting to cross the Marne at Meaux, twenty-eight miles from Paris, or that 2000 of the guns the handsomely uniformed soldiers carried had to be returned to the Imperial Guard the next day.

It was at Meaux that Joseph had hoped to stem the enemy approach. On the twenty-fifth, he sent 600 men there. On the twenty-sixth, he added three squadrons of Polish scouts, and on Sunday night, some of the men from the afternoon parade. As usual, it was too little, too late. Defense works at Meaux had been started only on the 26th. The garrison consisted of a mere 3340 conscripts and national guardsmen, badly trained and badly equipped. Many lacked guns and many were unable to handle them anyway. Including some five or six hundred men who had escaped from the battle of Fère-Champenoise and the 2500 under Generals Vincent and Compans, there were fewer than 7000 at Meaux to hold off the combined Allied armies. It was not much of a fight.

The advance column of the Silesian Army came in sight at 4 P.M. on the twenty-seventh. Taking advantage of some barges the French had forgotten or not had time to destroy, they started crossing the Marne at once under heavy protective fire. In short order, enough men had crossed to threaten surrounding the cavalry General Vincent had stationed on the north bank to defend the approach to Meaux. When Vincent's veterans were driven back to the town, the raw recruits in Meaux panicked.

"For heaven's sake, hold out," Joseph wrote the garrison commander at Meaux that evening, but Meaux fell quickly. The commander's despairing note of 9 P.M. crossed Joseph's dispatch.

> My troops fell into the greatest disorder. There was no holding them back. Cavalry, artillery, and infantry threw down their arms and rushed pell-mell into the square. Worse soldiers are not to be had. . . . Unable to defend Meaux with troops that don't want to fight, General Compans has issued orders to withdraw to Claye.

Parisians heard the sounds of distant artillery fire throughout the day and evening. At 3 A.M. on the twenty-eighth, they heard an explosion. It was the French rear guard blowing up the munitions dump at Meaux just before Prussian troops entered the town, but Parisians were still unaware a battle had been fought. To forestall panic, the French government had announced that National Guard artillerymen would be exercising daily just east of Paris at Vincennes. "News from Meaux is not at all disquieting," Talleyrand wrote the duchess the morning of the 28th.

Later that day, Parisians could no longer entertain any illusions. The enemy was almost upon them. Inhabitants arrived from Claye with tales of a morning-long combat in the town followed by battles for woods and hamlets further along the road. By 8 P.M., French troops had been forced back to Bondy, eight miles northeast of the city gates. Joseph sent Compans 2400 more men, again with orders to hold out, gain time.

In Paris, the Emperor's archivist burned the archives, the head of museums requested permission to remove the treasures to safety, ministers destroyed compromising papers and sent their wives and families out of the city. Even the chambermaids were leaving the Tuileries. At the whist table of the Empress and Talleyrand, there were jokes about the enemy taking over the city, but the Empress knew the danger was real. The night of the twenty-seventh, she wrote to advise her dear friend and confidante, the Duchess of Montebello, to send her children outside Paris. The Empress was anxious to know what plans the government had for her own person. "I am sure these *messieurs* are planning something concerning my departure that they don't want to tell me. I count on you to tell me anything said to you in secret. I see I'm taken to be a loose-tongued, weak woman. . . ." Thus wrote Napoleon's "cleverest and most dependable" minister in Paris.

King Joseph had little time left to take the measures Napoleon had ordered in the event Paris was seriously threatened. The first of these concerned the safety of Napoleon's wife and son, who represented the future of the empire. On March 28, Joseph summoned the Regency Council to an evening meeting at the Tuileries Palace.

Chairman only in name, Marie-Louise came prepared to learn her fate. There were some twenty-five people present in the room at 8:30 P.M., ministers with portfolios, ministers of state, the president of the Senate, King Joseph, and the four grand dignitaries (Vice Grand Elector Talleyrand, Archchancellor Cambacérès, Archtreasurer Lebrun, and Grand Judge Molé).

As minister of war, Clarke took the floor first to describe the situation as he saw it. The Emperor was too far away, the Allies too close; he saw no possibility of resisting. Everything he said was factual, but he omitted anything that might have tended to reassure. No one listening could help being overcome by a feeling of foreboding, thought Rovigo. Clarke's speech was such a peculiar mixture of adulation, independence, prudence, and professions of loyalty that it was impossible to make head or tail of it. What Clarke seemed to be saying was, in essence, "I warned you about everything, I wash my hands of the rest."

Things were bad, but why make them look worse? Rovigo asked himself. If the Minister of War sees no possibility of resisting, who is going to contradict him? Clarke's gloomy introduction made the departure of the Empress the first subject for discussion, since he depicted her as surrounded by imminent danger.

Everyone agreed: Parisians would interpret her departure as proof that the government considered resistance hopeless. If the Empress remained, they argued, her presence might inspire Parisians to fight, and only if they fought could the city be saved, since its military force was completely inadequate. Recalling how Marie-Louise's grandmother, Maria Theresa, had roused the Hungarians to resist the Prussians, Councillor of State Boulay de la Meurthe proposed that the Empress move to city hall at the moment of danger.

"Madame, you must make the Hôtel de Ville your headquarters and parade the streets with your son in your arms. All Paris will precede you to the advance posts. Let the Allied sovereigns know you are staying in the capital with your faithful subjects, sharing their dangers. Let the Allies know that to remove you from power, they would have to tear you from the throne you mounted to the applause of the very nations and kings now besieging you."

Talleyrand carried the argument a step further. Only the presence of the Empress could ensure them against the danger of a popular revolt in the city, he said.

Rovigo insisted that the empress should stay. He read a letter from Chief of Police Pasquier to support his view that her departure would have a disastrous effect, while if she stayed, the huge lower class would be inspired to make unlimited sacrifices.

After a moment of silence, the archchancellor took the votes. All except Clarke and King Joseph agreed that Marie-Louise should remain. Clarke took the floor again for a long speech that was to have a serious effect on the future. The strength of the empire should not be so quickly discounted, he said, citing historical examples of sovereigns forced to leave their capitals. It was a mistake to regard Paris as the center of Napoleon's power. Power followed him wherever he went. So long as he had a single village in which he or his son was recognized as sovereign of France, that would be the true capital.

"I do not understand how men who have been professing their devotion to the Emperor for so long could suggest exposing his son to the risk of falling into enemy hands. His son is all that binds Austria to our interests. France would have no resource left if we allowed ourselves to be led into delivering Hector's son to the Greeks."

Clarke was very emotional, constantly stressing his devotion to the Emperor. The council members countered his arguments one by one. When a new vote was taken, again only Clarke and Joseph favored the departure of Marie-Louise.

Next Joseph introduced a bombshell. The Empress had to leave because Napoleon himself had ordered it, he said, producing two letters Napoleon had written. The letters were out of date but unequivocal. Clarke's speech had followed their contents closely, even to the example of Hector's son, Astyanax. Napoleon wanted at all costs to avoid his son's becoming a pawn.

"I've answered you on the fate of Paris. You don't have to raise the subject again," Napoleon wrote Joseph on the eighth of February. "I've given you orders regarding the Empress, the King of Rome, and Our family.... If the battle is lost or you get news of my death ... send the Empress and the King of Rome to Rambouillet. Order the Senate, the Council of State, and all the troops to assemble on the Loire. Leave the prefect or a mayor or an imperial commissary in Paris. ...

"If I die, for the honor of the French, my son and the Empress must not let themselves be taken. They must retreat to the last village with our last soldiers. There's nothing the Allies would like better than taking them to Vienna as prisoners. I'm surprised you haven't thought of that.... Once the Empress and the King of Rome are in Vienna or in enemy hands, you and anyone who wants to defend our country would be considered rebels.

"I would rather see my son's throat slit than see him brought up as an Austrian prince in Vienna, and I have a good enough opinion of the Empress to be certain she is of the same mind, insofar as a woman and a mother can be. I've never seen *Andromache* presented without deploring the fate of Astyanax. ..."

Napoleon's letter of March 16 was still more explicit, ordering the Empress, his son, the grand dignitaries, ministers, officers of the Senate, Council of State, grand officers of the crown, treasurer, and treasury sent to the Loire "if the enemy should advance on Paris with such force that all resistance becomes impossible."

The Regency Council was dismayed by the letters, but most of its members still held that neither Empress nor government should leave the capital. If Napoleon's letters of the past were to prevail at present, there was no point in having convened the council. Since Joseph had convened it, it must be up to the members to judge whether the moment Napoleon had designated as the time for the government to leave had, in fact, arrived. That was the question at stake, not one of obeying or disobeying Napoleon's will, for no one would think of disobeying.

Boulay de la Meurthe insisted the letters were written for other circumstances, and that it was in Napoleon's interest for the Empress and King of Rome to remain. She would be a safeguard for the capital, he said, and if worse came to worst, she would obtain better conditions from her father and the other Allied sovereigns if she were in Paris than if she were fifty leagues away.

"If the government leaves Paris, all is lost," said Talleyrand.

Several of the men who had been swayed by the reading of Napoleon's letters were again persuaded that the Empress should stay.

Then someone brought up the problems disobeying Napoleon's orders might present. What if Napoleon had to retreat and the Allies recognized the King of Rome with Marie-Louise as regent? Napoleon would then become an exile at the hands of his wife and well-wishers. In the end, the council voted that the Empress leave early the next day, March 29.

Joseph may have been so insistent because of a portion of Napoleon's letter of February 8 that was not read aloud at the council meeting. "I tell you frankly," Napoleon had written him, "that if Talleyrand supports the view that the Empress should stay in Paris if our forces evacuate it, it will be because of some treachery afoot. I repeat, do not trust this man. I've known him for sixteen years. I've even felt affection for him, but he is definitely the worst enemy our house has now that fortune has abandoned it. Follow my advice. I know more about it than those other people."

By 2 A.M., details were settled. King Joseph would stay in Paris. The archchancellor would accompany the Empress and King of Rome out of Paris at 8:30 A.M. All the other dignitaries and ministers would remain until Joseph sent them individual orders to leave through Grand Judge Molé. The president of the Senate would accompany the Empress, and before leaving would advise each member of the Senate in writing to hold no meetings except under conditions provided for in the constitution. The morning of the twenty-ninth, Joseph would reconnoiter the enemy forces. If he found them so large that all resistance was out of question, he would follow the government to the Loire.

Late as it was when the council adjourned, the members lingered in the antechambers to deplore the resolution.

"I felt as if we were taking a last leave of each other," Rovigo said later.

Several officials told Rovigo: "If I were minister of police, Paris would be in arms tomorrow and the Empress would not leave."

"Would any of you be willing to take responsibility for what happened afterward?" he asked them. "Especially after you yourselves decided we had to follow the Emperor's orders? . . . Besides, what do I know of the Emperor's plans? How can I be sure such a move wouldn't interfere with them? If I failed, I'd have brought on the killing, pillage, and disorder arousing the populace leads to for nothing . . . How would I answer Napoleon's reproaches then? Or the reproaches of some 100,000 families who'd lost their breadwinners, houses, and fortunes thanks to me? That's too many victims, too many tears. . . . Even if I had the strength to do it, my instructions forbid it. . . . Only a fool would flatter himself into believing he could control the consequences of that sort of violence. In wanting to serve the Emperor, I might destroy his last chance. . . . All I can do is comply. I deplore this fatal resolution as much as everyone else, but I can't take it upon myself to do alone what you don't dare do together."

As Rovigo walked down the stone steps of the palace, Talleyrand sidled up.

"*Eh bien!* It's all over now, don't you agree? That's throwing in the game with good cards in your hand! That's what giving these fools a say has brought us to. Good God! The Emperor's to be pitied, but I don't feel sorry for him. There's no excuse for his obstinacy in keeping these men around him. . . . What a colossal comedown! To go down in history as an adventurer instead of giving his name to his century— Well, what next? Not everyone wants to wait and be buried in the ruins. . . ."

Regrets at the decision were being voiced in the inner chambers of the palace as well. There, too, each tried to get someone else to assume the responsibility of countermanding Napoleon's instructions. The Empress begged Cambacérès and Joseph to advise her on interpreting Napoleon's wishes. They, in turn, tried to persuade Marie-Louise to take the decision upon herself.

"You're my advisers," she said. She insisted that she needed their signed opinions before she could give orders contrary to the Emperor's instructions and the vote of the Privy Council.

"I would have been quite brave enough to stay, and I'm very angry that they wouldn't let me," Marie-Louise wrote Napoleon that night, "especially when the Parisians were showing such eagerness to defend themselves, but my opinion carries no weight at all in this matter, and the archchancellor told me it was absolutely essential for me to leave. I'm sure you won't like it and the enemy will be in Paris tomorrow."

The departure remained set for 8:30 A.M., although Joseph asked his sister-in-law to delay until he had completed his daybreak inspection of the positions outside Paris and gotten news of Marmont and Mortier.

The Empress spent the night packing.

All through the twenty-eighth and twenty-ninth, there were more people in the streets of Paris than ever, observing, guessing, exchanging conclusions on the impending battle. Bread wagons crossed the city heading north—aha! the French troops must be to the north. Cannon were dragged to the southeastern gates—aha! The enemy would close in from north and south simultaneously. Soldiers wounded fighting the Allies at Meaux, at Claye, and at Bondy arrived in Paris with wild estimates of the size of enemy forces. There were 15,000, 25,000, 40,000, 125,000! Gendarmes on continuous patrol found it impossible to break up the crowds. Workers, refugees, shopkeepers, aristocrats—the Parisians were there to see what could be seen.

"Paris is all up in the air," Chateaubriand's sister, the Countess de Marigny, wrote in her diary on the twenty-eighth. "You can't get across the Rue St.-Martin or St.-Denis, they're so jammed with troops leaving, wounded arriving, and entire villages seeking safety in Paris with their households and animals. Women carrying children run around crying for husbands they can't find, men search for wives lost in the crowd. . . . There are shouts, tears, and moans, with Parisian idlers adding to the chaos in their eagerness to see the novel spectacle, for in the midst of this disaster, the French spirit remains unchanged."

Toward the end of the twenty-eighth, there were false reports that the Cossacks had set fire to Meaux and were advancing rapidly on Paris, but even these rumors failed to arouse the Parisians from their passivity. Thomas Underwood, an English prisoner of war with nothing to do but wander freely about Paris, wrote at length in his diary about the mood and events of those days. On the morning of the twenty-ninth, he was among the crowds out before dawn on the streets. Everyone was claiming a spot along the boulevards to watch as soon as it got light. Even peasants seeking refuge in Paris came to line the boulevards with the rest as soon as they found a place to leave their belongings. No one was sure yet of the position or strength of the enemy, but no one seemed much alarmed about it.

"I went to the Louvre museum this morning," Underwood wrote in his diary, "and found about the usual number of artists, some peacefully copying pictures while others watched the preparations for the Empress's departure through windows overlooking the court of the Tuileries. The disorder that had reigned in the palace all night was exposed to public view. I could see candles sputtering out in the candelabra, ladies-in-waiting and servants, some crying and all very upset, running from room to room. About 8 A.M., the traveling carriages were brought up in front of the palace. . . . A little before nine, an officer ordered them back to the stables. A quarter of an hour later, Archchancellor Cambacérès drove up.

Almost at once, a servant ran to the stables to fetch the carriages back. Loading was completed as soon as they arrived. At ten-thirty, the Empress appeared in a brown riding habit and climbed with her son into her carriage. . . . The procession of carriages loaded with baggage continued leaving the Tuileries until the next day, but as soon as the Empress had gone, visitors were ordered out of the museum and the doors were closed. . . ."

If Underwood had had a view into the Empress's drawing room, he would have seen her dressed and ready to go at 7 A.M., seated with her son and ladies-in-waiting, anxious and filled with foreboding. Silence replaced the bustle of the night's packing. Any sudden noise, the opening of a door, was enough to startle the ladies as they waited for Joseph's return from his inspection.

A group of officers of the National Guard on duty at the Tuileries burst in to promise to defend the Empress and beg her not to leave. Marie-Louise was moved to tears, but said it was the Emperor's order. Nevertheless, she kept hoping something would happen to prevent her leaving. As news of the enemy became more and more alarming, Clarke sent officers intermittently to urge her to leave at once. At one point, the Empress stalked into her bedroom, threw her hat on the bed, sat in an armchair, head in hands, and cried.

"My God! Let them make up their minds and put an end to this agony."

At ten o'clock, Clarke sent an officer to insist that if she didn't start at once, she would risk falling into Cossack hands. The road out of Paris would probably be cut off by two that afternoon, he said. Though Joseph had not come back, the Empress left. Protesting, struggling in the arms of the equerry carrying him, the King of Rome clung to the balustrade, the curtains, the doors. He was carried out, soothed by the Duchess of Montebello.

The door of the heavy green berline with its coat of imperial arms closed. As a small group of onlookers watched in dull silence, the procession of ten identical carriages drove out slowly like a funeral convoy, followed by an escort of 1200 horsemen and the infantry of the Old Guard. The Empress stared straight ahead. She would never see Paris again.

When King Joseph returned to the Tuileries, it was almost noon and the Empress was far away. He could wash his hands of responsibility for that as he had done for almost everything else. The most energetic step he had taken thus far on his last full day in Paris was to write a proclamation designed to stir and reassure the city. He had read it to Count Miot de Melito, his chief equerry, early that morning before leaving on his reconnaissance.

Citizens of Paris, an enemy column has headed for Meaux. It is advancing along the road from Germany, but the Emperor is close behind at the head of a victorious army. The Council of Regency has taken steps to assure the safety of the Empress and the King of Rome. I am staying with you. Let us arm to defend our city. . . . The Emperor is marching to the rescue. Let us support him by a brief and vigorous resistance, and preserve French honor.

"I found it a bit too emphatic," Miot de Melito said. "I regretted its minimizing the danger and arousing hopes one could not count on, but, generally speaking, it had fine sentiments and there was no time to lose. It was posted. The initial effect was favorable, but as soon as the public learned the Empress and her son had left, excitement cooled down and confidence fell."

As Underwood continued wandering around Paris on the twenty-ninth, he saw people reading Joseph's proclamation near the Faubourg St.-Martin or buying copies for one sou each. There were murmurs. People objected to being asked to defend themselves while being deprived of the means. There was general discontent over the Empress's departure, and dissatisfaction with the government for sending 1200 veterans out of the city to escort her. Her presence would have saved Paris from Allied vengeance, some said. The National Guard should have stopped her from going.

"For the first time," Underwood noted, "I heard people blame the Emperor for their misfortunes, but I saw no inclination to fight the enemy back."

When the barrier at the Faubourg St.-Martin closed to all traffic at 2 P.M., Underwood left Paris by the northern gate of Poissonière to climb the heights of Montmartre. There was not a soldier to be seen on the whole plain of St.-Denis, though cannon smoke rose thick and black over the forest of Bondy to the northeast. At four-fifteen, to Underwood's astonishment, three cannon went off close to La Villette, almost at the gates of Paris. He later learned it was the French firing on an enemy reconnaissance patrol. The two dozen people watching from Montmartre hurried back inside the city for fear the barrier might be closed.

The populace in the workers' quarters along the northern and eastern limits of the city milled excitedly. The workers asked for nothing better than a chance to fight, according to Postmaster General de La Valette. Loyal to Napoleon or not, they were indignant at the thought of foreigners taking over Paris. They talked of tearing up paving stones, crenellating houses near the barriers, and throwing furniture and boiling water from their windows on the enemy if he dared enter the city. The government would not listen. Rovigo played billiards, concerned himself only with keeping order, and said the city could not be asked to resist. It was not a matter of planning for victory, but one of gaining time in order to avoid fighting inside the gates.

"You can't reach Charenton too soon," Clarke wrote Marmont. "The Emperor may arrive on the rear of the approaching enemy within three days at the latest. The future of the empire may depend on our resisting for those three days." To Compans at Bondy, he wrote, "Gaining time, that's what we need most to give the Emperor a chance to arrive to rescue the capital."

But there were no forces capable of delaying the enemy's approach. Generals Compans and Vincent were forced to leave Bondy without making a stand the afternoon of the twenty-ninth in order to avoid being surrounded and annihilated by the oncoming masses. The garrisons on the outskirts of Paris boasted a mere 1200 men. The 11,000 survivors of the corps of Marmont and Mortier "in a pitiful state of fatigue and desperate need of food and care" only reached the suburbs of Paris at nightfall after a last forced march of thirty-odd miles.

Taking stock at noon on the twenty-ninth after his reconnaissance, King Joseph concluded Paris could not hold out more than twenty-four hours with the means at hand. From the beginning, his plan in case of an attack on Paris had been to put up a brief resistance and then enter into negotiations to save the city from assault, pillage, and burning. Clinging to the hope of keeping the fighting well outside the walls, he sent all the troops he could lay hands on to the outskirts, to St.-Denis, Vincennes, and the bridges of Charenton, St.-Maur, and Neuilly. By the evening of the twenty-ninth, the only combatants left inside the barriers were the 12,000 men of the partly mobilized National Guard under sixty-year-old Marshal Moncey and some students of the Polytechnical and

Veterinary Schools, whose heroism at the barriers the following day won them lasting fame.

As Napoleon's lieutenant general, King Joseph was the only man who had the authority to coordinate the defense, responsibility for which was divided among six commanders inside and outside Paris. He seems to have cared barely enough to bother. Inexperienced and indecisive, he was inactive as well. Though he had been anxiously awaiting the arrival of the troops of Marmont and Mortier the evening of the twenty-ninth, he made no preparations for them. When Marmont's aide-de-camp, Fabvier, called at the Luxembourg Palace the morning of the twenty-ninth to coordinate plans for the defense of Paris and arrange provisions and billets for Marmont's men, he was turned away. King Joseph was in bed, he was told: "Why disturb his sleep?" Fabvier poured out his indignation to de La Valette, whom he met in the antechamber of the Minister of War's office later the same day. When every moment counted, he had been kept waiting three hours to see King Joseph, he complained.

"You'll be no better satisfied this time," de La Valette told him. De La Valette was still in the antechamber when Fabvier left Clarke's office.

"Good God, what have we come to!" said Fabvier. "All we can do now is get ourselves killed."

Late that afternoon, Marshal Marmont himself arrived in Paris in advance of his troops to get an idea of the terrain and work out details of the defense. He was unable to see Joseph at all and only got through to Clarke about 10 P.M. Worse yet, he found neither food for the men nor fodder for the horses when his troops and Mortier's reached Charenton. Three hundred of his men fought barefoot the following day.

The night of the twenty-ninth was spent in hasty organization of the defense. Because there wasn't enough time to move the troops into position, the Allies were able to occupy some strategic hills overlooking the city. Had the Allies attacked that night, the French would have been overwhelmed at once. They had only 5600 cavalrymen to hold off the enemy along a seven-mile front north and northeast of Paris.

The future of Paris was uncertain. Now the streets were deserted, theaters played to mere handfuls. The populace gathered around the barriers through which they hoped to see couriers arrive announcing Napoleon's approach. Surely the Emperor would not let them down.

The center of the city was strangely silent. At midnight the silence was broken by a knocking on doors to summon the guardsmen. The general alarm was beaten on drums through the rest of the night. No one knew yet whether Paris would defend itself, not even Talleyrand, who was busy laying the groundwork for all eventualities.

"I have hardly slept. I love you," he wrote the Duchess.

There was little sleep in the Allied camp either. The army was jubilant. That afternoon, a clear, windy spring day, the Allies had caught their first glimpse of Paris from one of the heights near Bondy. At their feet lay the plain occupied by the French, while the towers of Notre Dame rose in the distance, lit by the setting sun.

"Paris, Paris!" the soldiers cried, forgetting fatigue and privations, breaking ranks to press forward.

Their leaders' elation at seeing Paris quickly gave way to sober thoughts. Holding council that night in the chateau of Bondy, from which they had just forced General Compans to retreat, they made plans for the attack. Paris had to be taken before another sun set. Though his offer of a cease-fire had been rejected by the French that morning, Tsar Alexander gave orders that any opportunity to negotiate a capitulation should be seized. The Allies were running out of food. They were almost out of ammunition. Deep in enemy territory, they were about to attack a city of 700,000. Alexander dreaded a long fight at the barriers and was even more afraid of being drawn into street fighting, in which the Allies' numerical superiority would lose much of its advantage.

He had no idea where Marmont and Mortier were: what he dreaded most was the return of Napoleon, which he still anticipated at any moment. He sent orders to Meaux, where the last of the Allied armies had not yet crossed, for the two corps of Wrède and Sacken to remain as rear guard on the south bank of the Marne with their 30,000 men to guard against a surprise attack by the Emperor. Other troops were detached to keep open the roads north to the Netherlands in case Napoleon's appearance forced an Allied retreat. A price of 500,000 roubles was put on Napoleon's head.

Long after the lights went out in Paris, Tsar Alexander lay awake worrying. He was so afraid Napoleon might be closing in that he had ordered the attack on Paris launched at 5 A.M. Allied commanders would not have time to investigate the enemy's positions or form their own troops into line, but, ready or not, they were to strike simultaneously from the north, northeast, and southeast. Blücher's army, camped north of Paris in what was then the village of Le Bourget, was "to attack the heights of Montmartre at 5 A.M. and take them." Barclay de Tolly was to storm the heights of Belleville and Romainville northeast of Paris, while the cavalry of Prince Wurtemberg took the bridges at Charenton and St.-Maur and cleared the forest of Vincennes for an assault on Paris from the southeast. The Allies hoped to force a quick surrender by taking these dominating positions rapidly and ringing Paris from north to south.

No one in the Allied camp knew what would happen the next day. It was a restless night for the exalted Allied soldiers, the worried chiefs of staff, and the officer corps.

> I was unable to sleep that night though I needed rest badly [Prince Boris Galitzin wrote]. One had to reassure oneself one was not dreaming to believe one was really at the gates of Paris, whose name alone evokes so much, to believe that after campaign life and all the dangers, privations, and emotions we had gone through, we were about to plunge into the delights of that modern Babylon. Then I suddenly remembered the French had lulled themselves with similar thoughts on approaching Moscow, and my dreams gave way to worries.
>
> All the same, I told myself, the French aren't capable of sacrificing their capital like the Russians. And we're not the French, we don't want to subjugate France as they did our country. Such thoughts kept me awake all night. The next morning, everyone put on his most brilliant uniform, on the assumption that the gates of Paris would open to allow us to make our triumphal entry. But we had to buy the glory of conquering Paris in a last sacrifice.

The Allies would have been greatly relieved had they known Napoleon spent the night of the twenty-ninth 130 miles away at Doulevant. He slept peacefully, as Baron von Wessenberg observed, but he did not sleep long. By 3 A.M. he was again on horseback, surrounded by his guard, after having sent off a series of orders covering supplies, food, shoes, horses, and carts, as well as the movements of army units. His exasperation shows through those predawn dispatches.

"Why can't the peasants furnish horses and vehicles? Why haven't the supplies arrived as ordered?"

At Bar-sur-Aube, he stopped long enough to send a message to his good Louise to tell her he was on his way.

"No news for five or six days, thanks to those nasty Cossacks," he wrote, "but I am drawing nearer to you and hope to have news from you tomorrow. All my love. N."

News came from Paris, not the next day, but early that same afternoon. Just five miles down the road from Bar, at the tree-shaded stone bridge of Dolancourt over the Aube, an estafette was waiting for Napoleon with dispatches from the capital. Napoleon read them, standing in the open meadow by the bridge, while his officers watched him from a few steps away. Napoleon's face was usually transparent. When irritated, his eyes shone, dark and penetrating; when pleased, they had a gentle look, and his smile was fascinating, amiable. The officers saw no trace of emotion on his face as he read. After a few words to Marshal Berthier and Colonel Gourgaud, an orderly, he remounted his horse and set off at a gallop.

The news was bad, Napoleon's officers concluded, though there was as yet no general presentiment of real disaster. Recent successes and good news arriving from the Rhine area about peasant revolts and growing partisan warfare had persuaded the junior officers that the enemy would soon be driven out of France. The marshals and senior staff officers had fewer illusions. Those they had were dispelled when they read the orders Napoleon had Berthier issue from Dolancourt:

> We have just received our dispatches from Paris. The city's morale is good. Marmont and Mortier are fighting a large concentration of artillery near Claye. Blücher probably entered Meaux today. The Emperor will be at Troyes tonight, at Nogent tomorrow. You must march day and night, taking only indispensable intervals for rest. . . . Stop only long enough to feed the horses,

he added for cavalry general Piré.

Napoleon's generals would have been even more disheartened had they read the Paris dispatches with him. There was old news that was bad: the loss of Lyons, the double disaster of Fère-Champenoise, the evacuation of Sézanne and of Coulommiers. There was new news that was worse. Not only had Meaux fallen, but the Allies were about to attack the capital, undefended from without and betrayed within. One of de La Valette's messages reached Napoleon at last:

"Men in league with the foreigners, encouraged by what happened in Bordeaux, are raising their heads, supported by secret intrigue. The Emperor's presence is vital if he wants to keep his capital from being handed over to the enemy. There is not a moment to lose."

Napoleon had underestimated the speed of the enemy advance.

Time was running out. His army was still scattered, with Oudinot and Piré far to the east and the main body not yet at Doulevant. He hesitated briefly before deciding to try to reach Paris nevertheless. The army would assemble at Troyes. He himself would risk capture by galloping ahead of his troops to Paris to inspire the city to hold out. Hopefully Paris would resist until he got there. Before leaving Dolancourt, he gave Gourgaud orders to precede him to bring word he was coming:

> Go to the head of the column, pick the three least exhausted squadrons of Poles, and get to Troyes fast to keep enemy scouts from cutting the bridges. As soon as you get there, send a courier to the Empress to tell her to hold out, I am coming.

Napoleon sped toward Paris in growing anxiety. Gourgaud reached a peaceful Troyes, arranged for the protection of depots, hospitals, and bridges, and was about to send Napoleon's message off to Paris with the only post horse he had found when another of Napoleon's aides arrived. Because General Dejean's mission in Paris seemed even more urgent, Gourgaud turned the horse over to him and set about finding another to send off his own dispatch. Hardly had he laid hands on one when a carriage escorted by four or five *chasseurs* of the Guard appeared. It was the Emperor himself, followed by the Imperial Guard, who had covered fifty-four miles that day. The rest of the columns were behind him, Napoleon assured Gourgaud, who was alarmed to see the Emperor traveling virtually without escort.

Some columns arrived that night, others had to stop en route. Napoleon ordered Berthier to stay at Troyes to expedite the army's advance and then join him. Sending ahead still another aide, General de Girardin, to announce his arrival and tell the Parisians to hold out, Napoleon took a brief rest and galloped on toward Paris.

V

FOUR HOURS TOO LATE
March 30

PARIS OF 1814 covered a far smaller area than it does today. The city limits coincided almost exactly with the exterior boulevards that still ring the heart of the city. Most of the boulevards were there in 1814. A customs wall ran along them, enclosing Paris to facilitate the collection of duty on incoming goods. Fifty-two openings, or barriers, pierced the customs wall, some of them marked by monuments still standing today, like the elaborate stone archway known as the Porte St.-Denis.

Paris of 1814 stopped in the west at the Place de l'Etoile, to the north just short of Montmartre, to the east just short of the Butte Chaumont and the famous cemetery of Père Lachaise, and to the south, just before the cemetery of Montparnasse. The countryside began at the barriers, where today urban sprawl continues farther than the eye can see. In 1814, Parisians could look out on fields, hills, woods, windmills, and farms. Narrow roads led to outlying villages such as La Chapelle, La Villette, Passy, and Vaugirard, today part of the city itself.

One of the best views to the north of the city was from the windmill-covered hill of Montmartre. From there, you could see over the flat plain of St.-Denis, bisected by the canals of Ourcq and St.-Denis, to the villages of Aubervilliers, Le Bourget, and St.-Denis itself. From the heights of the Butte Chaumont, farther east, you could see the forest of Bondy on the road from Meaux in the distance, and, closer by, the hilltop towns of Belleville, Pantin, and Romainville. In the flatter section to the south, the stone columns of the Barrière du Trône, still standing today in the middle of the busy Place de la Nation, then marked a broad, bucolic avenue leading east from the city to the fortified chateau of Vincennes. In the extreme southeast corner, the Pont d'Austerlitz guarded an approach that was further protected, a short distance from the city, by the bridges of St.-Maur and Charenton over the Seine and Marne Rivers.

It was along this semicircle, girding Paris from southeast to northwest, that the Allied attack was expected. Years ago, Napoleon had planned to make Paris into a stronghold with redoubts, barricades, crenellation, and trenches, but he always hesitated to start defense works that might arouse the Parisians' fear of becoming pawns in a siege. Keeping them in line in times of peace and prosperity was hard enough. Perhaps de La Valette hit on the truth when he said Napoleon felt that if his army could not defeat the enemy, there was little point in contemplating the defense of a city that had so few means for resisting and so many resources for rebelling.

When Napoleon decided in favor of fortifying Paris in early March 1814, his vacillating government, lacking the decision, energy, and initiative needed to fulfill such tardy orders, did almost nothing. Gaps in the customs wall around the city were shored up with masonry or wood palisades. The road circling the city inside the wall was completed. A handful of strategically placed taller buildings were crenellated. Some wood defenses were put up at a few of the more important barriers and the bridges of St.-Maur, Charenton, and Neuilly, but these wood structures were designed only to repel a cavalry charge. No trenches were dug. Aside from the Ourcq and St.-Denis canals north of Paris—formidable obstacles, particularly for Allied heavy artillery—the best and almost the only physical defense was the natural terrain around Paris, the high hills with their ravines, terraces, and woods in which defending troops could take cover.

The morning of the thirtieth, King Joseph did not know both Allied armies were present in full force, but the knowledge would not have affected his plans. He never anticipated doing more than holding the enemy back briefly, whether there was half an army or two of them. That the battle was fought so hard, so heroically, and so desperately was no credit to Napoleon's brother or the rest of his government.

With the goal of keeping the enemy away from the city as long as possible, the plans devised hastily the night before the battle placed almost all the available forces at some distance from the walls. The top half of the threatened semicircle, from Clichy to the foot of Romainville and Belleville, was assigned to Mortier, commanding the 600-man garrison of St.-Denis and a mixed batch of cavalry and infantry totaling about 11,000 men. Marmont, with less than 12,000 men, was responsible for the lower half from the heights of Romainville and Belleville to the bridge of Charenton. To his own decimated Sixth Corps were added what remained of the troops of Generals Compans and Vincent plus a few hundred veterans, three generals recuperating from war wounds who happened to be in Paris, some 1200 volunteers, the student recruits from the Polytechnical School and the Veterinary School of Alfort, and the 400-man garrison of the chateau of Vincennes.

Inside Paris, the National Guard manned the barriers, concentrating on those along the expected line of attack. A few hundred guardsmen were sent to cover the bridges of Neuilly, St.-Cloud, and Sèvres to the southwest, while a few more volunteered to join some army veterans guarding the bridges at St.-Maur and Charenton to the southeast. Four thousand additional rifles were issued the Guard the morning of the attack, but many still had to fight with lances or with muskets that were downright dangerous to fire.

While the drums beat the alert through the night, Marmont and Mortier slept in their own houses in Paris. It was one of the few occasions they had in their lives to do so. About five in the morning, they left to join their troops. Desperate as the fight promised to be, they were determined to make the enemy pay for every foot of ground. As Marshal Mortier left his mansion on the Rue de Lille before dawn that morning, one of his aides met him crossing the bridge over the Seine. Mortier was absorbed by anxious thoughts.

"We don't have enough men to resist the masses we've been fighting these last few days for long, and we're going to see them grow every minute," he said. "But we're fighting for our honor today more than ever before. Let us think of the city of Paris first of all and not expose it to being burned down by enemy fire. Let us take our position as far from the city as possible, fight in the plain, far from the walls, and resist as long as we can."

A violent cannonade shook Paris awake just before 6 A.M. As the sun of a clear day began to lift the blue-gray mist over the chimneys, nightcaps appeared in windows and necks craned as men and women searched the sky. The blast sounded so close that they thought the enemy was at the barriers, but the fire was from Marmont's troops rushing into position on the heights of Romainville—where, to the marshal's surprise, the enemy had established himself during the night. Believing Marmont's little column to be as strong as it was bold, the Russians on Romainville withdrew. The unequal and desperately heroic battle for Paris was joined.

If the French army was ready to fight that morning whatever the odds, the French populace was ready to watch. Parisians hurried to get a good view of the action. Crowding the barriers, climbing hills and walls, deafened by cannon fire, they watched the battle while a street seller with *eau de vie* passed back and forth as if at a fair with his cry, *"Prenez la goutte, cassez la croute!"*

One of the interested spectators of the day, King Joseph, heard the battle but saw nothing. He had established his headquarters before dawn in a pavilion on the heights of Montmartre overlooking the road to the village of Clignancourt, north of Paris. King Jérôme was there along with Paris-based Generals Ornano and Hulin, Marshal Moncey of the National Guard, an admiral, a number of generals without assignments who happened to be in Paris, and a staff of numerous aides. The members of the Defense Council joined the group one by one.

One of the first to arrive was Rovigo, who was astonished to find Montmartre almost unarmed and unmanned. Montmartre was one of the city's best natural strongholds, an abrupt height so steep, so pitted with quarries and covered with rocks, woods, and gullies, that only one side was open to attack. Given sufficient firepower, the army could have dominated the entire plain of St.-Denis from Montmartre. Rovigo found not a single platform mounted for a gun on Montmartre, just six cannon and two howitzers in place, and no troops. There was only a large staff engaging in lively discussion without issuing a single order.

Though firing continued to be heard from the right, and black smoke rose from behind the hills that blocked the view in that direction, there was no movement on the plain.

"My dear, we've been shooting at each other for two hours," Joseph wrote his wife at 8 A.M. "Nothing serious yet, but we're at the beginning of the day."

Shortly after, he sent an officer of the National Guard on horseback to find out from Marshals Mortier and Marmont what was happening behind the hill.

Fortunately for King Joseph and the French, the Allies were far behind schedule. Their forces were not in position for the simultaneous attack on the entire semicircle until about 2 P.M., nine hours later than planned. Prince Wurtemberg's corps got under way so late in the assault on southeast Paris that its efforts did not affect the outcome of the battle. The plain in front of Joseph was empty because Blücher's Army of Silesia, which was to have started across the plain in time to take Montmartre at 5 A.M., got its orders so late that it was unable to join in the attack until after midday. Barclay de Tolly's attack on the French center, where Marmont was sustaining the brunt of the battle in the early morning, did not reach full strength until noon. In fact, the Allies were so little prepared for the day's battle that they had only 2000 men to oppose Marmont during the first exchanges. Soon there were 13,000 Allied soldiers attacking the French center, but, though hard pressed and outnumbered, for a few hours Marmont's men were still able to entertain the hope that they were not, after all, facing Schwarzenberg's entire army, much less both Allied armies united.

Again and again, against ever-growing forces, the French took, lost, and recaptured the strategic heights and woods northeast of Paris. By 11 A.M., unable to make headway, Barclay de Tolly paid the French the compliment of calling up his élite reserves. Marmont was forced back from Romainville to the heights of Belleville. Additional Allied troops moved into position to spread the attack north and south. When the national guardsman sent by King Joseph arrived to find out what the shooting was about, Belleville and neighboring towns were about to be engulfed by the enemy.

Guardsman Hocquet had found Marshal Mortier in fairly good shape between the Ourcq Canal and the road to Le Bourget, where the Allies had not yet launched a strong attack. When Hocquet reached Marmont farther along the line, he reminded the marshal that they had met once long ago.

"Ah, *mon ami*, we renew acquaintance in one hell of an hour," Marmont said, pointing to the advancing hordes that outnumbered him five to one. "I can't hold out much longer without reinforcements."

It was one hell of an hour, but Count de Ségur, one of Napoleon's generals, who wrote an account of this last campaign, called it Marmont's finest day, "the most splendid in a life of so many days of glory."

When Hocquet got back to Joseph's headquarters on Montmartre to tell him Marmont needed reinforcements, Joseph said, "Where the devil does he expect me to get them?" Marshal Mortier, hearing heavy fighting in Marmont's direction, had sent part of his troops to the very southern tip of his sector to sustain Marmont in midmorning, but was himself soon attacked from the north.

Marmont was unshakable. With Colonel Fabvier and a handful of brave men, he renewed the attack against Romainville. Barclay de Tolly fell back in astonishment. His élite troops suffered terrible losses. The firing stopped abruptly. There were anxious conferences in Allied headquarters, where hopes of taking Paris that day were fading. Between noon and 1 P.M., the Allies decided to renew the assault simultaneously on the whole line. If unsuccessful, they would retreat by the road north to Compiègne as soon as night fell. Before attacking, Barclay de Tolly waited for Blücher and Prince Wurtemberg to come into position on his right and left.

While Marmont took advantage of the lull to realign his troops, Mortier's position rapidly grew desperate. After sending aid to the sector nearest Marmont, he had only a thin line to cover his wide front. As the Allies moved into position at last, the line was threatened at several points at once. Aubervilliers, La Villette, and La Chapelle were attacked almost simultaneously while additional Allied forces gathered on the banks of the Ourcq Canal and still others massed in front of St.-Denis.

Back on Montmartre, at the very hour the Allies had begun to worry about their chances for success, Joseph had begun to doubt the usefulness of resisting. Just before noon, a French captain in the Engineering Corps had presented himself on Montmartre with an extraordinary story to tell and a message directly from the Russian Tsar.

Captain Peyre's adventures had begun the night before with a mission behind enemy lines. Though some said he was sent on reconnaissance, his own version was that General Hulin (the same general who had concealed firearms to avoid issuing them to the National Guard) had sent him to try to find out what terms the Russians had offered the day before when their parliamentary was turned back at French advance posts. Whatever Captain Peyre's mission actually was, the Cossacks who captured him considered him fair game as a prisoner and not a parliamentary since he was not accompanied by the customary trumpeter.

It is hardly surprising that they did not believe his story. Why would General Hulin pick an engineer rather than someone from his own corps and send him behind enemy lines to look for an enemy parliamentary at night? Be that as it may, Peyre somehow got himself brought before Tsar Alexander early the morning of the thirtieth before the battle began. The Tsar told Peyre he had decided to wait for Paris to propose negotiations, since his initiative of the twenty-ninth had been scorned. He asked Peyre a number of questions. He was glad to have rumors of Empress Marie-Louise's departure confirmed, but became visibly anxious when Peyre assured him that Paris would defend herself.

"You can see the size of our army for yourself," Alexander said. "This isn't a division confronting you as you've been told, it's the army of all Europe. Any resistance would mean useless bloodshed.... How many men are there to defend Paris?"

That question Captain Peyre refused to answer.

The Tsar summoned one of his aides, twenty-eight-year-old Count Orlov, and two trumpeters to accompany Peyre to French headquarters to urge King Joseph to surrender. To the background of sounds of the battle beginning in the distance, Alexander mounted his horse in the courtyard of the chateau of Bondy.

"Since Paris chooses to defend itself, tell the French we'll be ready to negotiate even when we've fought our way to the wall," Alexander told Peyre, "but once we're obliged to force the wall and fight our way in, we won't be able to stop the troops or prevent pillage. Go, Monsieur, the survival of your city is in your hands." Alexander turned to Colonel Orlov with an air of sudden inspiration and continued. "I authorize you to agree to a cease-fire when you think fit and without being responsible for the consequences. You have my authorization to suspend the most crucial attack, even one about to bring us certain victory, in order to spare Paris. When God gave me power and success at arms, He wanted me to assure the peace of the world. If we can achieve that without bloodshed, we can congratulate ourselves. If not, we'll fight to the end.... Europe must sleep in Paris tonight, whether in its palaces or camped on its ruins."

Reaching King Joseph was easier said than done. When Captain Peyre, Colonel Orlov, and the two trumpeters got to Pantin, the battle was lively. Firing stopped for a moment when the parliamentaries came in view, but the French suddenly resumed shooting once the party was between the two lines. Peyre made a dash for Paris while Orlov and the Russian trumpeters, charged by French cavalrymen, headed back to Pantin at full gallop. Peyre went first to General Staff Headquarters in the Place Vendôme to find General Hulin. There he was directed to Montmartre, where he made his report to King Joseph, handed him copies of an Allied proclamation Tsar Alexander had asked him to take, and repeated the Tsar's words.

Until then, Joseph had refused to believe reports that Paris was being attacked by the combined Allied armies. He could no longer cling to this illusion. Not only was Captain Peyre an eyewitness from behind the lines, immediate proof lay before him. As Peyre finished speaking, Joseph's chief of staff handed him a long spyglass with an exclamation. Far to the west of Mortier's troops, a huge army was descending the plain of St.-Denis, half of it heading for Montmartre itself, the other half branching off toward the west side of Paris, no doubt to take the heights of the Etoile and Chaillot. For the enemy to have such forces at his disposal in addition to those already engaged could only mean that both armies were present.

Before Joseph's eyes, the numbers grew, the plain filled. No French forces were available to oppose them. Every unit was already engaged, there were no reserves, and it was only noon. Before sundown stopped the fighting, the enemy would be battering the walls of the city and the battle would be fought out at the barriers and in the streets by the Parisians. Joseph had never had any confidence in that sort of stand; he had even less after reading the Allied proclamation Peyre brought. Containing an appeal to Parisians to bring about peace by following the example of Bordeaux, the wording indicated the Allies were counting on cooperation inside the city to overthrow the government.

In few words, Joseph authorized the surrender of Paris:

> If Marshal Mortier and Marshal Marmont can no longer hold their positions, they are authorized to enter into negotiations with Prince Schwarzenberg and the Emperor of Russia facing them.
> They will withdraw to the Loire.
> Montmartre, 12:15 noon.
>
> Joseph

He sent off hasty notes to Grand Judge Molé and the Archtreasurer to advise the high dignitaries, ministers, and councillors of state to leave Paris and join the Empress. Only the prefects of the Department of the Seine and of the police were to stay in Paris to keep public order. Joseph, Jérôme, Minister of War Clarke, and their staffs then left Montmartre hurriedly on horseback, taking the shortest route to the Bois de Boulogne in order to get out of the city before the enemy column they had seen crossing the plain of St.-Denis closed the western exit at the Etoile. Some of Joseph's staff thought he was heading for the bridge at

Neuilly to defend it from attack by that column. They learned he was leaving Paris only when he turned left instead of right at the barrier of the Etoile to follow the alley of the Bois de Boulogne. The defenders of Paris no longer had a commander-in-chief; the city had no administrative head. The popular lampoon inspired by Joseph's proud proclamation of the day before, in which he announced, "I am staying with you," had proved prophetic:

> Great King Joseph, ashen pale
> Is staying here to save us all.
> But rest assured, if he should fail
> To save our heads, his own won't fall.

Marshal Marmont, who got Joseph's authorization to surrender during the brief respite in his sector, read it with surprise and indignation. He hoped to gain a day by sustaining the defense until nightfall, and sent Colonel Fabvier to Montmartre at once to tell Joseph matters were going somewhat better. If the rest of the line was no worse off, he saw no need to think of capitulating yet.

When Fabvier reached Montmartre, there was no one left to tell. King Joseph, King Jérôme, the Minister of War, the staffs the generals —all were gone. On the height Fabvier found only a few hundred veterans, some volunteers, and some firemen, determined to make the enemy earn his victory. Their commander, Marshal Moncey, planned to end the military career he had begun at sixteen by defending the walls of Paris to the end. Mortier's cavalry general, Belliard, with his tiny group of horsemen covering the approach to Montmartre against the horde descending from the north; Mortier, fighting in three towns at once; and Marmont, once again heavily engaged on the slopes of Belleville, were all ready to fight on.

Of them all, Marmont was in the greatest peril. His Sixth Corps, fighting its sixty-seventh battle of the campaign, was riddled after seven hours of hard fighting. Because no courier from Joseph reached Mortier, Marmont alone had the authority to capitulate, but he did not use it.

As his companion-at-arms, Count de Ségur said of him: "The pride and nobility of Marmont went beyond comprehension. He was one of the Great Captain's oldest companions. It was the last battle of the remainder of the Grand Army, the last moment of independence of the capital of the great nation. Because he understood all these grandeurs, he

could not just succumb like many others. There must be greater sacrifices, bloodier burial rites. He dedicated himself. He did more: he knew
how to make all his men share his heroic dedication, for not one
abandoned him."

It was because of him that the fight continued for five hours after he
got authorization to capitulate; because of him that the French made an
effort so desperate that, as de Ségur said, no matter what Marmont did
after, Paris should never forget what he did that day.

When Fabvier returned from his futile mission to Montmartre, he
found his unit undergoing the heaviest Allied attack yet. Marmont, his
right arm still in a sling from a previous wound, his sword in his
mutilated left hand, his clothes torn and black with gunpowder, was in
the thick of the fight. Forced back from Belleville, he had reestablished
himself, but as Fabvier arrived, the enemy was attacking simultaneously
from left, right, and front. Marmont charged with Fabvier and his best
generals at his side. Step by step, house by house, the French were
successfully repelling the enemy down the main street of Belleville, when
Marmont turned to find enemy troops had cut him off from the rear.
Completely encircled, he rallied the handful of men around him and
hurled himself back down the street at bayonet point with such violence
that the vastly superior enemy forces gave way.

Marmont's horse was killed under him, his clothes were riddled with
bullets. A dozen men fell at his side and three of his generals were
wounded, but he won a path for his soldiers' retreat. With only 5000
men left, Marmont took up his last position, spreading south of Belleville
and north of it to Mortier's southern wing. With the aid of Mortier's
closest troops and a battery of twelve guns, he managed to keep forcing
the enemy back to Pantin for shelter every time he ventured to approach
Paris. Elsewhere, wherever Marmont looked, he saw the enemy gaining.
The hilltops left and right were in enemy hands. Mortier was being
slowly pushed back from La Villette and La Chapelle to the northeast
gate of Paris, the Barrier of St.-Martin. The enemy advance guard was
fighting a handful of students and national guardsmen at the Barrière du
Trône.

It was then that Mortier received a courier from Napoleon. General
Dejean, to whom Colonel Gourgaud had yielded the only post-horse
available in Troyes, had reached Paris about 1 P.M. after a hard night's
ride. He found the Palace of Luxembourg deserted. Joseph, he was told,
was at Montmartre. Dejean got a fresh horse at his father's Paris house

and headed for Montmartre, only to find that King Joseph had already left. Galloping to the Bois de Boulogne in pursuit, he overtook Joseph in the middle of the forest. Napoleon was racing to the rescue, he announced. The Emperor would probably reach Fontainebleau with part of his Guard that day, and if he did not get to Paris before nightfall, the city must hold out. He would be under its walls without fail the following day to defend it. There was another reason for Paris to hold out, Napoleon's messenger continued: new peace negotiations were under way. Colonel Galbois, the emissary Napoleon had sent Emperor Francis from Doulevant the night of the twenty-fifth, had returned with word that Austria looked with favor upon working out a peace agreement based on Napoleon's last concessions. Furthermore, she claimed authority to enter into negotiations on behalf of her allies.

Joseph would neither listen nor turn back. It was too late, he said. Marmont and Mortier could not hold out. He had already authorized them to capitulate. As the Emperor's brother, he did not want to risk being taken hostage. Telling Dejean to inform the marshals of Napoleon's message, Joseph turned to hurry away from Paris.

Pressed against the walls of the city, Mortier listened to General Dejean's story with growing hope. Perhaps it would be possible to gain a few hours and save the capital from occupation while the details of these new overtures to the Allies were worked out. It was unfortunate that General Dejean had nothing in writing. Galbois apparently had requested written instructions at Austrian headquarters but had been urged to start out and gain time while instructions were prepared and sent after him. Rovigo claims in his memoirs that written instructions were sent off with a party of negotiators, who were attacked and carried off by Cossacks en route. Whether that is true or not, Dejean had no proof of his story to show.

In a hail of bullets, resting his paper on a drum, Mortier wrote Prince Schwarzenberg:

> Negotiations have been reopened. Caulaincourt has gone to see His Majesty the Emperor of Austria. Prince Metternich must at this moment be with Emperor Napoleon. Under these circumstances, when matters may be worked out, let us spare human blood, Prince. I have sufficient authority to propose conditions. I therefore have the honor, Prince, to propose a suspension of arms for twenty-four hours during which we could negotiate to avoid inflicting the horrors of a siege on the city we are resolved to defend to the end.

Not unnaturally, Schwarzenberg thought Mortier's proposal a ruse to gain time, though he probably did not think Mortier was the instigator. The silent marshal had the reputation of being "a thorough-going gentleman." Joining to his reply a copy of the Allied coalition's agreement to refuse separate negotiations with the common enemy, Schwarzenberg wrote:

> The close and indivisible union among the Allied sovereigns assures me that the negotiations you assume have begun in isolation between Austria and France have not taken place, and that your information to that effect is without foundation.
>
> The declaration I have the honor to send you herewith constitutes incontestable proof.
>
> It is up to you alone, *Monsieur le Maréchal,* and to the authorities of the city of Paris, to spare the city the disaster about to overtake her.

Just before Mortier's aide returned to his chief with this reply, Tsar Alexander's aide, Count Orlov, arrived on a completely independent mission to ask Mortier to surrender. Mortier replied proudly that Paris was not taken yet.

"The army," he said, "will bury itself under the ruins of the city before it accepts a shameful surrender."

Marshal Marmont was by then of another opinion. The decision was his to make. He had been given the authority. Napoleon was not there. Joseph was not there, and Mortier was unaware of Joseph's authorization. Paris would soon be reduced to defending itself at the barriers and in the streets, and Marmont felt he could not take the responsibility for a defense within the walls.

"From the heights of Belleville," Marmont wrote afterward, "I saw new, formidable columns directed against all points of the line from the Barrière du Trône to La Villette, while other enemy troops were crossing the canals and heading for Montmartre. We were about to be attacked on all sides. It was three-thirty, time to use the authorization to capitulate that I had had in my hands since noon."

Marmont sent his aides to Prince Schwarzenberg to arrange a two-hour suspension of arms on two conditions. French troops were to be allowed to retire within the city walls at once, and the subsequent agreement would allow them to evacuate the capital. Once again, Orlov galloped through the lines, bringing the Tsar's consent. A cease-fire and a meeting at the gate of Pantin were set. Mortier, though reluctant, had to agree. Fabvier, who condemned Marmont for subsequent acts, praised his chief's decision to surrender.

"He yielded to cruel necessity as a loyal soldier without reproach. The honor of our arms was safe; his own, intact. Would to God for his glory he had died at that moment."

The war was not over, only the battle for Paris. Even there, fighting went on because word of the cease-fire either did not travel fast enough or was overlooked. The Prussians under Generals Yorck and Kleist continued attacking and took the village of La Chapelle. The Russians, under the French émigré general Count Langeron, continued their assault on Montmartre, where Marshal Moncey made a last stand against thirty or more enemy guns with his 400 men and the two cannon still in working order. The volunteers fighting under him were so inspired that they refused to obey orders to take cover to fire at the enemy. "We're not afraid, we don't want to hide," they said. They were only persuaded when Moncey's chief of staff pointed out that the senior marshal of France would hardly order them to take any cowardly action.

When word of the cease-fire got through about 6 P.M., Moncey was rounding up his troops outside one of the barriers while men, women, and children were building barricades out of carts and boards inside it. All the fighting was over then, except at the bridge of Neuilly, where fifty members of the Old Guard defied 200 Russians until the following morning.

The battle for Paris, a heroic challenge to many, a novel spectacle to others, was over. Fifteen thousand men had died. Under skies that turned somber gray during the day, Parisians who had never seen an army except in parade formation and brilliant uniform had followed the combat with unflagging interest. Throughout the day-long battle, the Boulevard des Italiens and the famous Café Tortoni were filled with men and women seated on chairs to watch the passing of wounded French and Allied soldiers. The curious crowded the avenues leading to Montmartre like people going to a premiere. Elegant dowagers in carriages, young ladies and gentlemen on horseback, dressed for a Sunday promenade in the Bois de Boulogne, joined the spectators. Nothing, not even the falling of a few stray cannonballs inside the city, discouraged or diminished the crowds.

At the close of the day, spectators gravitated to the Barrier of Clichy to watch the Allies take the village of Clichy and advance on Montmartre. Thomas Underwood was in the crowd, which he observed with as much interest as the battle.

"The Parisians seemed as blind to the significance of events as they were to the immediate dangers around them," he wrote in his diary. "The novelty, the roar of cannon on all sides, the falling cannonballs and shrapnel, the obvious progress of the Allies and the total confidence of all the people around me, so blinded by national vanity that they spoke of the battle as of something of little import—everything combined to make the scene one of the most singular and interesting of my life."

The spectators were as intrepid as they were curious. One of the members of the National Guard tells of being engaged in fighting behind the cover of a wall when his unit was joined by a group of Parisians undeterred by enemy bullets:

Cane in hand, they leaned over the wall to see farther. It's true the view was superb from there, but if they saw the enemy plainly, the enemy saw them equally well. We got the message instantly in the form of bullets and shrapnel. Our imperturbable bourgeois paid no attention. They seemed to think it was no concern of theirs. Our warnings having proved useless, our commanding general sent us orders to make them get down from the wall willy-nilly. We were setting about it when a shell carried off a man sitting on the wall, cutting him in two before he had time to say *merci*.

Three or four next to him jumped down and took off. The rest will follow suit, we told ourselves as we turned to other business. Believe it or not, a moment later I looked up to see the old occupants holding firm while a bunch of new ones fought for the vacancies. If those aren't heroes, I don't know one when I see one.

Then things got so hot and the bullets rained so thick that the Guard itself moved from its position. The spectators decided to do the same and it's well they did, because a quarter of an hour later when the smoke and powder cleared, I saw the wall moving, and in a moment there was no wall left.

After the fight was over, we had to walk back to the city over the bodies of dead and wounded that covered the plain. We were literally wading through blood. The sight was horrible and the danger not yet over—a few stray bullets interrupted the order of the march from time to time. *Eh bien!* Will you believe it? We had to drive in front of us women, ladies, yes—ladies in hats, who had come to see the battle and

were indignantly calling us brutes because we had forced them to turn
back. That's what I saw that day. They tell us Parisians aren't brave?
Heroes here have no sex.

The military leaders still had work to do. Negotiations were slow
and balky. Sometimes it looked as if the fight would be resumed.

Marmont met the Allied representatives, Russian Secretary of State
Count Nesselrode, Count Orlov, and two subordinates at the Barrier of
Pantin at 5 P.M. Marshal Mortier, missing, was found after a brief delay
near the Barrier of La Chapelle, and negotiations began in a nearby inn,
the Auberge du Petit Jardinet, which afterward put up a plaque to
commemorate the occasion.

The first round was brief. "Never," the marshals said to Allied
demands that the army be surrendered with Paris. No Allied argument
had any effect. The marshals were taking on a heavy responsibility,
Orlov said; they should think of sparing Paris. They should take into
consideration, he hinted, that Napoleon must be checked if France was
to be saved. They would die fighting first, Marmont said as a burst of
heavy gunfire close by interrupted their talk. It was the attack on
Montmartre by Langeron, who later claimed to have been unaware of
the cease-fire. The marshals remained undismayed and firm. Lacking
authority, Nesselrode left to get new instructions.

When he returned to the waiting marshals at the inn, it was 7 P.M.
The Allies agreed to allow the French army to leave Paris, but only in the
direction the Allies chose.

Paris is not blockaded, Marmont told the Allies, and the French
should be free to take any road open. Nevertheless, he asked what
destination the Allies had in mind. Brittany?

"In that case, we shall defend Paris foot by foot, and when we're
driven back to the Faubourg St.-Germain we'll take the road to Fontainebleau. I cannot agree to an armistice that is incompatible with the
honor of an old soldier, and grants the Allies an advantage they would be
unable to obtain by force.

"Fortune has smiled on you. Your victory today is indisputable, its
consequences are incalculable. Be moderate and generous, don't push us
to desperate resolutions. Sometimes there's more to be gained by chivalry
than force."

Again the Allied negotiators were unable to yield for lack of authority. As soldiers, said Orlov, we would have agreed with Marmont,

but our aim was to disperse the power of Napoleon for the good of France and all Europe.

There were heated words, prolonged arguments. It was eight o'clock. Negotiations were at an impasse after three hours of talk. At last, Mortier stood up, his tall figure commanding.

"I leave further negotiations to Marshal Marmont," he said. "I must go now to take the necessary measures to assure the continued defense of the capital."

A hundred Allied guns were trained on Paris. Over 150,000 soldiers would be at her gates by daybreak, but the Allied commanders did not feel confident. They worried about running out of ammunition, and were in constant fear that Napoleon might inflame the country's resistance simply by arriving in Paris. Moreover, they were reluctant to antagonize by shelling and street fighting a population they hoped to win over, and in no case did they intend to attack at night.

While these considerations persuaded Nesselrode that he should give in to the marshals, he could not contradict the Tsar's instructions. It was Orlov who suggested a solution. If they didn't improvise something, they would have to break off talks, he whispered to Nesselrode, and the French troops would do what they wanted anyway under cover of darkness. A compromise was offered. Since it was impossible for the Allies to prevent the army from withdrawing that night along whatever route the marshals chose, they would suspend negotiations and leave Count Orlov as guarantor of good faith until either an armistice was signed or hostilities were resumed. The Allies, Nesselrode said, would not renew hostilities until Orlov had returned to Russian advance posts. Marmont agreed. Nesselrode and the two aides went back to Tsar Alexander's headquarters at the chateau of Bondy while Marmont left for Paris with Orlov.

Marmont and Orlov rode slowly and silently through dark streets without seeing anyone except an occasional curious face that would appear at a window, then vanish. Both men were deep in thought. Once Marmont gave an order to his adjutant. There was a rumble of heavy guns on the move. The city was being evacuated.

The soldiers who had been leaving Paris since that afternoon were sad, though not discouraged. Some were angry with the Parisians for not having taken up arms and joined them. Soldiers sent to fight with guns that did not fire or cartridges filled with coal dust instead of gunpowder muttered of betrayal. Many were angry with their leaders for capitulating. One officer saw veterans of the Russian campaign bite their sabers with rage and swear they would die under the walls of Paris before they surrendered. "That's treason," General Chastel had called out at Belleville in Marmont's hearing when he learned of the armistice.

In Paris, soldiers bivouacked in the streets or filed to their billets in silence. Downcast, lacking everything, they asked for nothing and accepted nothing, as if they had no right to anything from the people they had failed to defend. There was a splendid dignity in their reserve, epitomized by a wounded dragoon who sat his horse stoically near the deserted Tuileries Palace. One hand on the pommel, the other holding his pipe, he smiled as he smoked though one eye hung from its orbit and his cheek was slashed to the bone.

Most Parisians knew only that the firing had stopped, without knowing why. They saw French soldiers camped in the street and others marching past, heading south. As darkness fell, they saw the hills north and east of the city covered with enemy campfires. The sky was clear, the moon brilliant, the silence broken only by the far-off music of the Allies. Many Parisians slept with their bags packed. Some feared the arrival of Napoleon. Some feared the arrival of the Allies. Some simply feared the unknown, but all were quiet in the emptiness that followed the tumult of the day. The Archbishop of Malînes wrote that a stranger arriving in the city at that moment would never have believed the city was no longer its own master. Never had Paris known such silence, such order.

Outside Paris, on the road to Versailles, there was confusion and noise all night. By midafternoon, the roads heading south of Paris on the west side were so jammed that it was almost impossible to move. Among the many who left that afternoon was the wife of Marshal Oudinot, who had followed the Empress out of Paris. Sleeping that night at an inn in Versailles, she heard the continuous noise of men, horses, and carriages passing. At daylight, she was up to see what was happening. It was an astonishing sight, she wrote.

"We stood motionless at our windows. What we saw passing was the empire! The empire, departing in all its pomp and splendor. The ministers, all in their coaches and six, taking with them portfolio, wife, children, jewels, livery. The entire Council of State, the archives, the crown diamonds, the administrations. And all this power and magnificence fought for space on the road with humble householders who had heaped up on barrows all they could carry away...."

The empire had left Paris, but not all of it. Remaining, among others, was Prince Talleyrand, Vice Grand Elector of the empire.

Napoleon was 100 miles away on the morning of the battle for Paris, galloping west with an escort of 1000 of his mounted Guard. Bad news greeted him at each halt. He had planned to sleep at Villeneuve l'Archevêque, just twenty-five miles beyond Troyes, to give the infantry columns that had reached Troyes during the night a chance to catch up. Impatience and anxiety drove him on. Reaching Villeneuve long before noon, he left his escort behind in order to make better time. Three four-horse carriages raced on. Napoleon shared one with Caulaincourt. General Drouot, General Flahaut, and another aide were in the second, followed by Napoleon's orderly, Gourgaud, and old Marshal Lefebvre. All along the way, Marshal Lefebvre talked excitedly to Gourgaud of what could be done to inspire Parisians to defend themselves. A miller's son who had enlisted as private at eighteen, he was one of the marshals who had come up through the ranks. He was delighted that Napoleon had chosen him to organize resistance in the workers' quarters, where he was known and loved by the many who had fought under his command.

On reaching Sens at 1 P.M., the Emperor ordered Gourgaud to man the gates and prevent anyone from leaving. Mayor Lorne was admitted promptly to Napoleon's headquarters on the first floor of the Hôtel de l'Ecu, overlooking the main square.

Lorne found two short, stocky men in the room, General Berthier and Napoleon. Napoleon looked anxious, preoccupied.

"Who are you, what do you want?"

Lorne identified himself.

"My army is following," said Napoleon. "I'll need 50,000 rations when it gets here. Can I count on you?"

At that moment, the Emperor's dinner was placed on a small table next to the fire. Napoleon served himself, Berthier followed suit. Napoleon ate so fast that he finished the second course of beef before Berthier had eaten the soup. In the meantime, Lorne was expressing his loyalty and desire to do the impossible, though pillage and destruction had left Sens with few resources. Unaware of the gravity of the situation, he seized the occasion to protest the heavy taxes the prefect had imposed on the richest inhabitants.

"Very well!" Napoleon said. "They'll pay only what they can. The city can count on my help, but I count on the city and on your zeal and energy to get the necessary food for my army."

Encouraged by this reply, Lorne said as he left the room, "We need peace badly!"

"Food for my army first," Napoleon said.

A bare half hour had passed when Napoleon noticed the horses standing ready in the square below. He left at once. To the crowds who watched him leave, he appeared calm and untroubled.

The pace quickened. The bleak countryside with stumps of trees, stumps of houses, sped by in gray monotony. News awaiting Napoleon worsened at each posting station. The Empress and the King of Rome had fled Paris. There was fighting in sight of the walls. Faster! Faster! The only stops were the brief ones necessary to change horses.

Throughout his life, Napoleon had felt driven by lack of time. Now all he asked for was a few hours, just time enough to reach Paris before the enemy did, to arouse the population, and to hold the enemy off for forty-eight hours and give his army time to arrive.

He passed Fontainebleau. He would not stop before Paris. He calculated. Paris ought to be able to hold out for forty-eight hours. Twenty thousand national guardsmen could be mobilized easily. Add the depots of regular troops nearby and you had an army of 40,000 to defend the city's strong natural position on the right bank of the Seine. With 200 or more well-placed guns, the occupation of the capital was not an affair of a day. Faster! Faster! At Corbeil-Essonnes, twenty-two miles south of Paris, he learned that there had been fighting around Paris all day. Onward! Between 10 and 11 p.m., his carriage rattled into the stone courtyard of the post inn at Juvisy, ten miles south of Paris, for a change of horses.

Another man had arrived just before him: General Belliard, commander of the cavalry that had fought at the foot of Montmartre that afternoon. Mortier had sent Belliard on with his troops to keep the road to Fontainebleau open.

Through the shadows and the crowd that immediately flocked around his carriage, Napoleon caught sight of the general's uniform.

"Who is that?" he asked.

"General Belliard, Sire."

Belliard ran to Napoleon's carriage door. Napoleon jumped out and led Belliard along the highway.

"*Eh bien*, Belliard, what's up? What are you doing here with your cavalry? Where is the enemy?"

"At the gates of Paris, Sire."

"And the army?"

"Following me."

"Then who is protecting Paris?"

"It has been evacuated. The enemy is to enter tomorrow at 9 A.M. The National Guard is manning the barriers—"

"And my wife? My son? Where are they? Where is Mortier? Where is Marmont?"

"The Empress, your son, and the entire court left for Rambouillet day before yesterday. I think they're to go on to Orléans from there. The marshals must be still in Paris completing arrangements."

"What arrangements?"

Belliard poured out the story of events since March 19, culminating in the heroic stand of the vastly outnumbered French army at Paris that day. Caulaincourt and Berthier came up. Napoleon turned to them.

"What cowardice! ... Capitulating! ... Joseph has lost everything ... Four hours too late! ... If I'd gotten here four hours sooner, everything would have been saved." He paced the road. *"Eh bien,* you heard what Belliard said, *Messieurs.* Four hours compromised our cause. My good, loyal Parisians can still save it in a few hours of courage. Caulaincourt, my carriage! I'll put myself at the head of our National Guard and our troops. We'll save the situation yet ... General Belliard, order the troops to turn back."

Napoleon had gone fairly far down the road, his quickening steps followed by a sad-faced group. Belliard pointed out to Napoleon that he could no longer go to Paris because there were no troops left there ...

"The National Guard is there, your troops will join me, we'll gain a delay, and the whole army will be with us in thirty-six hours. We can set things right."

Napoleon risked being captured at the gates, Belliard protested. Napoleon was adamant. He would sound the tocsin, illuminate the town, call the populace to arms.

"Bring up my carriage! Follow me with your cavalry."

"But, Sire, Your Majesty is exposing himself to being taken and exposing Paris to being sacked. I repeat, the enemy is at the gates with over 120,000 men. He holds all the strong positions ... Besides, I can't go back to Paris because I left it under a convention—"

"What convention? Who made it? Who gave the order? What have they done with my wife, my son? What is Joseph doing? Where is the Minister of War?"

"I don't know the details of the convention, Sire. Marshal Mortier sent me word of its existence and ordered me to march toward Fontainebleau. I've heard the convention was made by Marshals Mortier and Marmont. As for orders, we didn't get a single order all day. Each marshal acted on his own. I don't know where Prince Joseph and the Minister of War went. The army didn't see them all day, at least Marshal Mortier's corps didn't. And, as I've already had the honor of informing Your Majesty, the Empress, the King of Rome, and the court left for Rambouillet."

"Why were they sent out of Paris?"

"There I can tell Your Majesty nothing except that people say it was on Your Majesty's orders."

"We must go to Paris. When I'm not there, people bungle everything."

Berthier and Caulaincourt joined Belliard in trying to dissuade the Emperor. Napoleon demanded his carriage again. Caulaincourt signaled for it, but it did not come. Napoleon strode on down the road, reproaching everyone for failing to hold out until the army arrived.

"Paris had ten times what was needed to meet the storm if anyone had shown a little initiative," he said. "Nothing was done right."

"I believe, Sire, more was done today than it was possible to do or hope to do," Belliard said. "The active army of some 15,000 to 16,000 men fought off 120,000 with such courage that it held the enemy in check until the suspension of arms at four o'clock.

"We kept hoping for Your Majesty's arrival. When a rumor you were there reached the army, cries of *Vive l'Empereur!* burst out everywhere. The men had such a surge of ardor that the enemy, already nervous about approaching such a large city, slowed down its advance.

"The enemy spread to St.-Denis, attacked it to support his right, then took the Route de la Révolte leading to Paris, leaving part of his center wide open. We could have decimated the center if we had only had 20,000 more men in front of La Villette to make a flank attack. The National Guard manned the barriers, which were barricaded by palisades and crenellated, but had no trenches in front. There was one battalion of national guardsmen on Montmartre, covering the roads to St.-Denis and Neuilly. The few that engaged in combat did well. They were so eager we had to make them turn back because they kept going ahead of our riflemen. As for fortifications, I didn't see any, at least not where I was."

"What! Montmartre wasn't fortified? Where were the heavy cannon? Where were the men?"

"There were just a few palisades at the barriers, 1,800 horsemen in the plain, and six cannon on Montmartre, not all of which had ammunition."

"Clarke's a numbskull or a traitor . . . Montmartre should have been fortified and equipped with big-caliber guns for a vigorous defense."

"Fortunately the enemy assumed, as you do, Sire, that Montmartre would be fortified. I think they were afraid of it because they approached with great caution and not until three in the afternoon. Unfortunately no preparations had been made and there were only six six-caliber guns."

"What happened to all my cannon then? I had at least 200 in Paris and over 200,000 charges. Why wasn't it put in place along your front?"

"I don't know, Sire," Belliard answered, adding that not only were there few cannon in position, but that by 2 P.M., ammunition was running out for the few they had.

"I see. Everyone lost his head. Yet everyone knew I was coming on the enemy's heels, and that this was bound to influence him. With me so close, the Allies would have lost courage if you had just held out. It would have been easy to gain a day. Joseph is a *con* and Clarke's an ignoramus, a little man who should never be pulled out of his office routine. Ah, where was I, Belliard?"

"Much too far away, Sire. If you'd been at Paris with the army, we would have won. Your Majesty would have crushed the Allies. They were asking for defeat the way they'd been feeling their way and maneuvering all day. France would have been saved."

"If I'd been there—but I can't be everywhere. What were Clarke and Joseph doing? Why weren't my brave Parisians called into action?"

"We do not know, Sire. We were alone and we did our best."

"There's some intrigue behind this . . ." Napoleon said, still walking toward Paris. He had gone almost two miles from the post inn at Juvisy. The sky, dark at the inn, turned red as he neared the enemy campfires across the Seine. An infantry column came in sight on the road from Paris.

"Whose troops are those?" Napoleon asked.

"Marshal Mortier's."

"Send for him."

Mortier, however, was still in Paris.

Caulaincourt, Berthier, and a handful of officers following approached to renew their arguments against Napoleon's going to Paris. The risk of capture was too great. With the infantry already this far from the city, it was too late. Besides, the Parisians were relieved that the battle was over and had lost all desire to fight.

"What a great rush everyone was in!" said Napoleon. "Joseph lost me Spain, now he's losing me Paris, and that means losing France, Caulaincourt. Four hours too late! What a fatal blow! . . . If only I had my troops at hand to attack tomorrow when the enemy's drunk with the triumph of entering Paris. But I need at least three days to rally my forces . . . We shall fight, Caulaincourt. Better die sword in hand than be humiliated by foreigners . . ."

Napoleon's officers were silent.

"It's not over yet. If I'm supported, the retaking of Paris will launch our victory . . . The enemy will pay dearly for having dared steal three marches on us.

"Flahaut," he said to one of his aides, "go see Marshal Marmont. Order him to break off the talks and resume the battle with his corps and the National Guard."

For two hours, Napoleon had been walking, denouncing, and planning. He turned back to Juvisy, where he sat a moment by the two fountains at the side of the road across from the inn, La Cour de France. "Four hours too late," he kept repeating to himself. Belliard looked closely at the Emperor's face in the light of the inn's lanterns. It was unchanged. The conversation of the last two hours had left no mark. He looked very tired, that was all, after the day's journey of over sixty miles on horseback and by carriage.

As he went into the inn, word spread through the workers' quarters in Paris that Caulaincourt was there and Napoleon was about to arrive at the head of his army. There were cries of "Close the shops, barricade the houses and streets!" It is interesting to speculate what might have happened if Napoleon's generals had been less pessimistic, if Napoleon had not hesitated once again, and once again listened to them—if, with or without his troops, he had gone on to Paris that night to steady his wavering government, rouse the populace, and break off negotiations for surrender. A Parisian royalist who hated Napoleon wrote that had the Emperor appeared, "his presence alone, without any escort, would have suspended all treaties, renewed uncertainties, revived hopes and fears, and changed the entire scene!"

It was within possibility. No capitulation had been signed at the hour Napoleon reached Juvisy, and even after it was signed, nothing prevented his bringing Mortier's troops back to Paris. The capitulation provided only that hostilities could not be resumed until 9 A.M. on the thirty-first. The Allies were still outside the city. They could hardly have bombarded it since they were almost out of ammunition. Had they dared to try to take it by storm, would they have succeeded? Ambushed, strafed by fire from houses and cross streets, they might have failed to win it before Napoleon's forces arrived to encircle them.

On the other hand, Napoleon's venture might have backfired as his generals predicted. He might have been captured, the army might have proven too exhausted to fight effectively, the Parisians too undermined by treachery to support him. It was in Napoleon's character to take the gamble, but in the face of his generals' concerted pessimism, once again he chose a more conservative course and lost the initiative to the Allies.

Napoleon ordered a table, lights, his maps, and his notebooks sent up to a small bedroom of the inn, where he cloistered himself to plan how to win back his crumbling empire. Caulaincourt, once again "with death in his heart," was at Napoleon's side along with Berthier. When they made a move to leave, the Emperor ordered them to stay.

While Napoleon poured over his maps to calculate ways of speeding up his army's arrival, Caulaincourt and Berthier discussed the situation without caring whether the Emperor was listening or not. Napoleon spoke only to ask if news had come yet from Paris, from Dejean, from Girardin, and from Flahaut. From time to time, he sighed deeply, incriminated Joseph, Clarke, and Rovigo—"All they thought of was saving their own skins." Over and over he repeated, "Everything's lost."

Berthier and Caulaincourt offered reassurance. The heart of France was with the army, not in Paris. The essential was to rally the army.

"My army! If only I had it now, but it'll take three days to get here!"

"In three days, Your Majesty can do what you wish to do today."

"Ah, Caulaincourt, you do not know men. Three days, two days—you don't know what can happen in such a short time. You don't know what the intrigues of a few traitors with foreign bayonets behind them can do in a city like Paris."

Caulaincourt suggested sending Berthier to the Allies in Paris because he was on good terms with Prince Schwarzenberg. Berthier demurred. The questions would be diplomatic ones, he said, and he did not know the diplomats. When Berthier left to get some information for the Emperor, Caulaincourt again urged sending him to Paris. Napoleon opposed it.

"Devoted as he is to me, he'd lose his head," Napoleon said. "People would manage to make him believe whatever they wanted. . . . Men are blind, Caulaincourt. My energy irritates them, my constancy tires them, . . . yet I am France's only hope. Without me, you'll fall into revolutions and counterrevolutions. . . . You've all been taken in by the enemy's propositions. If I'd believed their ministers and everyone else, you, first of all, Caulaincourt, we'd have gone down on our knees to beg for a peace that wouldn't have saved us because the enemy is in bad faith. You'd have proof of that soon enough if I decided to give in.

"A few more months of sacrifice and we'll come out of this fight all the greater."

Berthier came back. Napoleon took up his map to review various military questions. He dwelt on the dangerous influence being close to Paris and events there might have on his generals. He decided to make a surprise attack on the enemy. He would arouse the workers and the National Guard, and trap the enemy between Paris in revolt and the imperial army.

"To think of Paris, the capital of civilization, occupied by barbarians!" he said, repeating several times, "Our great city will be their tomb!"

There was a moment's silence.

"What are those generals doing who're separated from their troops in a moment like this? Can I count on them? There are so many intrigues in Paris! Who knows what will happen tomorrow?" A new silence. "My soldiers, my brave officers, won't betray me. There are lots of brave men I can count on. Mortier is a good man, a man of honor. Marmont was brought up in my camp. I've been like a father to him. He may have had weak moments or done foolish things, but he's incapable of treachery. . . ."

Napoleon briefly contemplated the alternate possibility of maneuvering on the Loire, bringing in his armies from the fronts in southern and southeastern France. In either case he would lose nothing by sending Caulaincourt to Paris, he decided. He might gain a day or two and find out whether the Allies were determined to overthrow his government or willing to deal with him. Aside from that, the presence of Napoleon's representative in Paris might stifle some of the intrigue against him, particularly when news spread that he was seeking peace.

In the instructions the Emperor dictated to Berthier for Caulaincourt, he promised "to ratify all Caulaincourt would do for the good of our cause." Caulaincourt was to commend "our faithful subjects" to the Allied sovereigns and the generals commanding their armies. He was invested with full powers for negotiating and concluding peace, and was granted military authority as the city's chief administrator. "All authorities are to recognize him as such and to assist him for the good of our cause and our people."

This time, Caulaincourt did not insist that Napoleon spell out in advance every concession he was willing to make. To argue would have been to overwhelm him, Caulaincourt wrote in his memoirs. Just before Caulaincourt left, the Emperor disclosed what was really on his mind.

"You'll get there too late," he said. "Parisian authorities will be afraid of compromising the inhabitants vis à vis the enemy. They won't want to listen to you, for the enemies have projects other than the ones they've disclosed so far. But you'll find out what we can hope for, and your mission will be useful for that. If you see the only hope lies in our courage, we'll fight and die with glory."

Caulaincourt left the inn between 1 and 2 A.M. Napoleon finished working out the army's orders, which Berthier sent out later from Fontainebleau. Orléans was to become the center Paris had been. All equipment, all depots and reserves were to go to Orléans, along with the government, the ministries, the prisoners of war, and the entire court. The prefect of Orléans was alerted; orders were sent him regarding provisions. Marmont was assigned the command of the advance guard at Corbeil-Essonnes, with Mortier backing him between Essonnes and Fontainebleau. Twenty-four-hour partols were established to keep the enemy from crossing the Seine between Paris and Fontainebleau. The Minister of the Interior was instructed to organize mass levies in Sens and Troyes. When Napoleon had dictated the last details, down to forming new battalions out of the remnants of others, he caught an hour's sleep in his chair after writing Marie-Louise at 3 A.M:

Mon amie,
    I came here to defend Paris but there wasn't time. The city surrendered this evening. I am assembling my army at Fontainebleau. I'm in good health. I suffer for what you must be suffering.
                                                              NAP.

At 4 A.M., Napoleon had to be shaken awake. Caulaincourt had sent a message from the gates of Paris that the capitulation had been signed. Shortly after, Flahaut returned with a discouraging letter from Marmont, advising strongly against any immediate attempt to retake the city.

Napoleon left at once for Fontainebleau, where he arrived at 6 A.M. When the inhabitants saw their Emperor turned back from his capital, they ran alongside his carriage with hands clasped, sobbing. Napoleon's valet Constant, who had gone directly to Fontainebleau from Troyes, found Napoleon paler and more tired than he had ever seen him. For once, the Emperor appeared to make no effort to hide his discouragement. It seemed almost symbolic of his reduced empire that Napoleon installed himself not in the imperial apartment he usually occupied but in a small suite of rooms just off the great horseshoe staircase leading from the main courtyard.

Napoleon closeted himself in his study with Berthier, received a few members of his general staff, and, at last, went to bed. From time to time as the Emperor slept, Constant heard smothered sighs and, occasionally, the name Marmont.

Marmont had fought the battle of Paris with the valor of ten brave men. He had capitulated only after costing the Allies 7000 lives, and only to save his army for another fight, a better chance at victory. In the salon of his private mansion in Paris the night after the battle he proved less steadfast. Napoleon was right to fear the insidious influence of the city.

When Marmont and Orlov came in sight of the marshal's house on the Rue de Paradis, Orlov was surprised to see it lit from top to bottom and crowded with people, who seemed to be awaiting the master. They rushed up to him, broke into separate groups, talked excitedly. When Marmont strode into his green salon on the upper floor, the crowd filling it was hushed for a moment. Marmont was barely recognizable. His overcoat covered a ragged, bullet-ridden uniform, his face was black with gunpowder, and he was splattered with mud and blood from head to boots.

"The armistice has been concluded," he said.

Leaving Colonel Orlov in the care of his adjutant, Marmont went to his study to talk with some of the many people awaiting him.

Everyone left in Paris who was anyone talked to Marmont that night. They gravitated to his house on the Rue de Paradis as if the seat of government had moved there when Napoleon's court and ministers left. Many men of importance had disobeyed King Joseph's instructions to leave. Some were interested in staying to secure a future in the new regime they saw coming. Others were eager to have a hand in bringing it about, and some stayed to protect their property. Among those remaining in Paris were some members of the Municipal Council, seventy-odd senators, and eighty members of the Legislative Corps. The excuses they gave for staying varied. They were ill, they had sick relatives, business to finish, or nowhere to go because their native towns were under enemy occupation. Seventy-five-year-old Archtreasurer Lebrun had made no effort to comply with Joseph's orders, perhaps because he felt too old to bother. Postmaster General de La Valette had stayed. Police chief Pasquier and the prefect of the Department of the Seine had stayed at Joseph's request to maintain public order. And Talleyrand had stayed, despite more than one order to leave.

For the Allies to find half the government in Paris and half outside was to stumble on a situation ready-made for intrigue. When the French took Moscow in 1812, they found no authorities to negotiate with, no one to help arrange for supplies, lodgings, transportation. There was no one to put out fires, keep order, keep the city running. There was no one to subvert. Moscow, empty, quickly proved a hollow victory. In Paris, the Allies were to find a mass of people who thought it their duty to keep business going as usual, ensure adequate provisions for all, and avoid incidents. The prefects, with the enormous services at their disposal, had an imperial mandate to keep order. Their efforts, and the presence in Paris of other imperial officials more or less detached from Napoleon, proved more useful to the Allies than the much-needed stores of ammunition they found in the city.

They were equally useful to Talleyrand. In fact, he was partly responsible for their being at their posts. For days, he and his associates had been persuading waverers to remain to endorse the new regime that would be established. The lady who had helped Talleyrand frighten Rovigo into leaving was one of his most successful advocates in convincing senators to stay. The evening of the thirtieth, he sent her a note to tell her all the senators she had seen were "disposed to act for us," and to urge her to visit a few more who were still vacillating for fear Napoleon might return.

Having arranged to have supporters on hand and placed where he needed them, all Talleyrand would have to do to put his plan into action once the battle was won by the Allies was to win the Allies' support by making himself indispensable to Alexander. He did not anticipate any difficulties there, since he had been cultivating the Tsar for years. But first, the battle had to be won.

The morning of the thirtieth, he had not been certain of the outcome or even that there would be a fight. "*Chère amie,*" he wrote the Duchess of Courlande, "people say the attack this morning was just a reconnaissance and that the enemy is withdrawing. It's positively disgraceful to be as uninformed as we are, and as I am, in such circumstances. Even that all-important question of whether Paris will defend itself is undecided. Some are for it, many others are opposed. There is much agitation, but no action or discussion. I don't believe a mass of men has ever been in such a humiliating situation. I shall come see you early. I am staying on to learn the news. I love you with all my soul, and to know you are anxious, troubled, and perhaps troubled for good reason, distresses me. My angel, I love you, I love you."

As long as the outcome was in the slightest doubt, Talleyrand could not openly disobey the official instructions he received early that afternoon to leave Paris and join the Empress. He went to a great deal of trouble over his excuse, concocting a little ruse recounted in the memoirs of two of the officials he tried to involve in it. He first approached Rovigo. The Minister of Police was riding around Paris, gathering news, when Talleyrand called at his office. Talleyrand soon called again. When he did, he found Rovigo had gotten his own orders to leave and was busy burning compromising papers in his office fireplace in preparation.

As Rovigo describes the scene, Talleyrand explained he was not refusing to leave, but that doing so caused him concern. He blamed others for the disaster, particularly the ignoramuses Napoleon had chosen to listen to. As for himself, though Napoleon's shabby treatment had ended all sympathy he had ever felt for the man, that did not mean he wanted to see the edifice Napoleon had built destroyed. And only by staying in Paris might he have a chance of saving it. Would Rovigo authorize his staying? Surely Rovigo would agree to something so useful to Napoleon and everyone else.

"Not only do I refuse to authorize your staying," Rovigo said, "I urge you to leave and I'll have you watched to make sure you do."

Talleyrand pretended to give in. Rovigo finished burning his papers and left, apparently without setting up any surveillance of Talleyrand, who proceeded to Paris police headquarters to see Pasquier.

Pasquier was doggedly trying to keep order and stay abreast of events. He had not yet heard about the armistice because none of the messengers he had sent to Marshal Marmont and Marshal Moncey on the battlefield had returned. Before he at last got word from Marmont at 7 P.M., Pasquier had a visit he described in his memoirs as "very bizarre." Talleyrand arrived at his office about 6 P.M., accompanied, or rather, led, by Pasquier's cousin, Mme. de Rémusat. It was she who spoke first.

"As you know, Cousin Pasquier," she said, "M. de Talleyrand has orders to leave and join the Empress. Don't you think that's a grave mistake? Are we to have no one left here to deal with the foreigners, no one whose name carries some weight with them? You must be more aware of the inconvenience of that than anyone else since you're about to be facing such heavy responsibilities. M. de Talleyrand is in an awkward position, you see. How can he fail to obey? On the other hand, what a calamity it would be if he really had to leave!"

"I understand perfectly," Pasquier said, "but I don't see what I can do."

"But he has come to ask your advice."

Talleyrand put in a few words, repeating what Mme. de Rémusat had already said, after which she finally proposed in a very roundabout way that Pasquier send some trusted men to the barrier through which Talleyrand would leave. Pasquier's men would arouse people to stop his carriage with the protest that the men who had the most to lose should be forced to stay to protect the city.

"My first duty being to keep public order, I will certainly not risk a move that would stir people up. But you have a simpler way of achieving your end, and without risk," said Pasquier. "M. de Rémusat, having a commission in the National Guard, undoubtedly has jurisdiction over one of the barriers. Let M. de Talleyrand present himself there to leave, and M. de Rémusat can do with his guardsmen what you are asking me to make the populace do."

Pasquier was certain that this idea had occurred to his visitors, but assumed they had hoped to put the responsibility on his shoulders. In any case, Talleyrand did as Pasquier suggested. He made a conspicuous departure from his house. His secretary preceded him on horseback to make sure the passage of his carriage would be noticed. At the Barrier d'Enfer, he was turned away in a noisy scene and came back home to find a group of friends jubilantly awaiting him.

"My dear, I found the barriers closed," he wrote the duchess. "It was impossible for me to continue. . . . I have just written the Archchancellor of all the obstacles that prevented my leaving."

Talleyrand had achieved a major objective. He was still in Paris. His little ruse ensured that if Napoleon retook the city, or if Alexander decided to negotiate with Napoleon, it would appear that he had tried to leave. And in either case, he could make good use of his presence in Paris to regain Napoleon's good graces.

While all seemed to be going well for Talleyrand, Napoleon still held a trump card, the imperial army. As long as Napoleon had a loyal and enthusiastic army, he had strength and the possibility of arousing widespread popular resistance. The battle for Paris was over, but the partisan war the Allies feared was still a threat. If the French army stood firm, anyone trying to overturn Napoleon's government might set off a civil war. It is not surprising, therefore, that Talleyrand was one of Marshal Marmont's visitors the evening of the thirtieth.

Marmont's other visitors were senators, legislators, members of the Municipal Council, the Postmaster General, the Paris police chief, Baron Louis (financier and friend of Talleyrand's), Bourrienne (Napoleon's former school companion turned enemy), bankers, and officers of the National Guard, all mingling with Marmont's staff. The atmosphere was not pro-Napoleon. The handful of senators opposed to Napoleon had doubled in the past few days and a dozen more were at least willing to join in their discussions. The Legislative Corps resented having been dismissed by Napoleon in December for showing too much opposition. The Municipal Council members had gone the furthest, entertaining a proposal favoring the Bourbon Restoration the afternoon of the battle.

The dissenters grew bolder at Marmont's house. Some condemned Napoleon for bringing the armies of all Europe upon them. Others, less vehement, merely condemned Napoleon's government for abandoning them. Few wanted the fight to go on and almost everyone agreed that the capitulation had to be signed. The question was how to save France afterward, and talk was free and open.

"The conversation reflected the opinion of the times faithfully," Marmont wrote later. "In general, everyone seemed to agree that the fall of Napoleon was the only way to save the situation."

A royalist proposed the return of the Bourbons. Marmont pointed out the problems restoration would bring. A prominent banker, cousin to Marmont, answered him: "Eh, *Monsieur le Maréchal,* if we have written guarantees and a constitution to secure our rights, what would we have to fear?" For a member of the upper bourgeoisie to contemplate the return of the monarchy impressed everyone, particularly Marmont.

"When I heard a plain bourgeois banker say this, I thought I heard the voice of the entire city of Paris," Marmont said afterward.

The amiably seditious conversation was interrupted by the unexpected announcement of the arrival of General Alexandre de Girardin, the aide who had been sent ahead by Napoleon from Troyes. The Emperor's name was still magic; the arrival of his messenger evoked his presence. Expressions became serious, officers stiffened, talk dropped to a whisper. De Girardin gave Marmont Napoleon's formal order to continue the defense of Paris and told the marshal Napoleon would follow in person in a few hours. Nothing was signed yet; the battle, he said, could start again the next morning. Capitulating was treason. Loyal men could only be indignant at the thought. The Emperor counted on the population to rise up, to tear up paving stones to throw at the Allies when they entered, capitulation or not.

"That's futile!" Bourrienne said. "The Allies have too many men. It would be breaking the terms of the armistice, and besides, people are already looking forward to a better future. France is tired of tyranny, of the miserable state constant wars have reduced her to, of the ruin of her commerce and industry, the conscription of 300,000 men a year. When people are miserable, all they hope for is change. That's natural enough. Even the Emperor's own brother Joseph gave up trying to save this crumbling empire and left."

"The Allies have run out of ammunition," someone said.

"That's a fairytale," said Bourrienne. "We wouldn't last two hours against them. Who has seen their reserves?"

Everyone seemed relieved when Marmont said he would sign the capitulation as planned and lead the army to meet Napoleon the following day. De La Valette was almost the only one who tried to persuade Marmont to hold out another twelve hours. Marmont was adamant. With less than 28,000 men, it would be useless bloodshed, and he was in any case too committed to change his stand on the capitulation.

As de La Valette left Marmont's house with Pasquier, he saw Talleyrand gliding up the staircase in conversation with Bourrienne.

"They're planning to get Marmont involved in treason," de La Valette said to Pasquier.

"What would you expect?" Pasquier said. "It looks as if it's all over. We have no resources left."

Everyone noticed Talleyrand's silent entrance. Heads turned to watch him limp across the room with his usual calm, dispassionate expression. He stayed rather long in the marshal's study. His pretext, according to Marmont's account, was to find out if communications were still open, or if the Cossacks had already gotten to the left bank of the Seine. He then dwelt at length on the disaster. He praised Marmont's role, his courage, intelligence, and understanding. He hinted that Marmont was the man of the hour, the man on whom salvation depended. What the salvation was, neither said, but from what Marmont wrote in his memoirs, it would seem the marshal was persuaded that Napoleon could no longer save France.

"From then on," he wrote, "I wanted to perform my duties loyally and wait for time and the force of destiny to produce a solution."

When Talleyrand came back into the salon, he paused by a group of men to say a few words everyone rushed over to hear. Orlov was almost alone in a far corner of the room. Talleyrand crossed over to him.

"My Lord, please bear your sovereign the assurance of Prince de Bénévent's most profound respects toward His Majesty."

"Prince," Orlov answered, "I shall deliver this tribute to His Majesty without fail."

Talleyrand turned to leave with an almost imperceptible smile, while Orlov mulled over the sentence he found very significant behind its superficial formality. People standing nearby who had heard Talleyrand but not Orlov said jokingly, "Has Talleyrand gone mad? What is he doing paying homage to the Russian Tsar?"

The night wore on. Dinner was served sometime after 11 P.M. Afterward, men continued to come and go. Servants brought drinks, replaced sputtering candles. Marmont, who had left his study for dinner, was the center of admiring attention.

Orlov sank back in his corner. People arriving and leaving blurred before his eyes. He found it increasingly hard to follow the conversations around him. It had been a long day of fighting, dodging bullets, dashing through the lines on missions, negotiating, struggling. He dozed from time to time, listened from time to time, worried from time to time. He had no powers, no rights; he was merely a hostage. Would the capitulation never come?

At the Hôtel de Ville, Pasquier was asking the same question. With top officers of the Paris National Guard, and other city officials, he had decided to go to the Tsar at Bondy as soon as the capitulation was signed in order to negotiate civil matters, since Marmont's authority was limited to the military.

While the delegation to the Tsar waited in the great hall of the Hôtel de Ville, Pasquier and the Prefect of the Department of the Seine were busy sending orders in anticipation of the problems the morning would bring. They sent orders for bakers to bake more bread, for hospitals to prepare more beds, for more meat, more wine, and more *eau de vie* to be requisitioned for the occupiers. They arranged billets for Allied officers, asylum for refugees coming in from the country, and assigned special patrols to keep order.

The vigil ended about 2 A.M. when word came that the Allies agreed to the terms of the capitulation and would let the army leave freely, reserving only the right to pursue it.

The articles were drawn up in Marmont's salon in front of every-one who happened to be there. Marmont read them to himself, then aloud to the room, and prepared to leave to lead his troops south. Before going, he ordered Colonels Fabvier and Denys de Damrémont to sign the agreement with the Allied representatives, supervise the turning over of the barriers to the enemy in the morning, and then join him on the Essonne river. Fabvier protested. Turning over the barriers was distaste-ful and he had no desire to attach his name to the capitulation.

"It's vital for the Emperor to know the exact strength and compo-sition of the enemy forces occupying Paris," Marmont said. "No one is better qualified than you to gather precise information hastily, at a glance. Besides, the information will be all the more valuable to him because he knows you and has confidence in you. I'm not so much giving you an order as requesting a service on behalf of the Emperor as well as France."

Marmont left to join his troops, who were breaking camp on the Champs-Elysées at 4 A.M. How much he was swayed by the flattery and insinuations of Talleyrand, no one can be certain. Enough, in any case, to answer Napoleon's messenger Flahaut by writing the discouraging letter Napoleon got at Juvisy before leaving for Fontainebleau.

"General Flahaut asked me if I believed the Parisians were disposed to defend themselves," Marmont wrote. "I tell your Majesty the com-plete truth. Not only have they no inclination to defend themselves, they are quite firmly resolved not to. It seems the mood changed completely when the Empress left, and the departure of King Joseph and the entire government at noon brought discontent to a head. . . . No effort could bring the National Guard to fight now. . . . We had a hot and quite glorious battle today, killed a terrific number of the enemy. . . . Unable to continue the fight, we concluded a convention by which we are to have evacuated the city by 7 A.M., and to respect an armistice until nine. My troops will start marching at 5 A.M. . . ." Signing the letter, "Your very humble and very obedient servitor and faithful subject," Marmont left Paris.

As the army departed with Marmont, Talleyrand's friend was making the last call in her night-long round of senators. Senator Count Cornet trembled as he opened the door.

"I've come to rejoice with you over the great event about to take place," she said with a dramatic gesture. "The throne of St. Louis is about to be restored to its ancient splendor."

"God willing!" the count said. "But I'm afraid the devil may interfere."

"We're counting on you, *monsieur le comte*. We pride ourselves you'll be among the first to proclaim Louis XVIII."

"Certainly, certainly, madame, provided the Allies bring him here."

While the Allies camped in an immense semicircle around Paris from Seine to Seine and Marmont's and Mortier's troops continued heading south toward their new positions, the delegation of the city of Paris painfully picked its way north through the dark over the bloody battlefield toward Allied headquarters at Bondy. Alexander and Schwarzenberg slept in the chateau of Bondy for the second night, dreaming of a triumphant entry into Napoleon's capital. Barclay de Tolly slept content with the promotion to field marshal his role in the day's battle had earned him. The King of Prussia had installed himself at Pantin. Marshal Blücher, still half blind, had gotten on a horse at the end of the day, but saw nothing and took no part. He ended in a devastated, pillaged house on the top of Montmartre, while Generals Yorck and Kleist slept, rolled in their coats, on a bale of straw. Far away in Dijon, neither Metternich nor Emperor Francis had any idea Paris had been attacked, much less conquered.

Paris awaited the unknown. The French army awaited another chance. Napoleon awaited his army. And Talleyrand awaited a visitor.

Part Two

TALLEYRAND'S TRIUMPH

"Governments come and go,
but I do not go with them."
—TALLEYRAND

VI

TWO EMPERORS AT THE GATES

March 31

IT HAS BEEN ARGUED that Talleyrand did not direct the events of the following few days, but merely adapted to them. Nothing could be further from the truth. Flexible, pragmatic, and a consummate gambler, Talleyrand awaited each move by the opposition before playing the next card, but by no means did he lack a strategy for winning. Every move he had made thus far was part of a plan worked out long before March 31 dawned, a plan men were acting out like marionettes while he pulled the strings invisibly. Behind his curtain of languorous indifference, king-maker Talleyrand was ready to bring about a change of reign. On March 31, he turned his back on the Emperor of France to welcome the enemy Emperor at the gates.

"I liked Napoleon," Talleyrand wrote afterward, "but beaten, he had to disappear from the scene. That's the fate of conquered usurpers. The duty of good Frenchmen was to consider the fate of France invaded. How much she had against her! What means, what form of government would enable her to meet this calamity? I was neither betraying Napoleon nor conspiring against him. I never conspired in my life except with the majority of Frenchmen and to save France. . . . Napoleon was his own worst enemy."

With the capital about to be occupied, the country thoroughly discredited and on the verge of civil war, Talleyrand believed that in one day of indecision, France might be wiped off the map for all time. He moved quickly to put his plan to save France into action.

On March 31, almost 200 miles away in Dijon, a royalist emissary sent by the Chevaliers de la Foi in Paris was outlining Talleyrand's plan to three important Allied statesmen, Foreign Ministers Prince von Metternich of Austria and Lord Castlereagh of England, and the Prussian Prime Minister, Prince von Hardenberg.

"There are two parties in Paris today," Gain de Montagnac told them, "the royalists and men active in the revolution of the past twenty-five years. Today they are united in wanting the overturn of Bonaparte and the return of Louis XVIII. The majority of the National Guard is with us and half the Senate—Talleyrand will answer for that. The Municipal Council will support us by keeping order in the city if Bonaparte is cut off from Paris. A general in the National Guard will take over the Guard at City Hall. To be sure he can count on his staff, he'll submit a list appointing new officers to replace any he's not sure of. The Municipal Council will approve the list and issue a proclamation to Parisians announcing it is calling on the Senate to safeguard the security of the state. Protected by an élite of the National Guard, the Senate will meet and declare Bonaparte dethroned and Louis XVIII recalled. And then, I boldly predict, messieurs, the spark will set Paris afire and sweep the country."

It mattered little that the Allied diplomats approved the scheme. The letter of approval Metternich wrote Talleyrand that day reached Paris with Gain de Montagnac long after Talleyrand had carried out his plan, more or less as outlined. Napoleon's hesitations at Vitry, St.-Dizier, and Juvisy had kept him from preventing the Allied occupation of Paris that was essential to Talleyrand's success. When the Allies entered on the thirty-first, the initiative passed from Napoleon to Talleyrand.

Emperor Alexander was sleeping at Bondy when Count Orlov returned from Paris about 6 A.M. Passing by the French delegation in the great hall of the chateau, Orlov went directly to Alexander, who received him lying in bed.

"Well, what news do you have for me?"

"I have the capitulation of Paris," Orlov said, handing him the document.

Alexander read it, folded it, and put it under his pillow.

"Embrace me! Congratulations on having attached your name to this great event," he said. He then asked Orlov to tell him all about the evening spent as hostage. He was greatly surprised and amused at Talleyrand's message.

"This is an anecdote now, but it could become history," he said. Sending word that he would receive the Paris delegation at his levee, the Tsar went back to sleep to dream of Paris with the capitulation agreement under his pillow.

The road to Paris looked clear at last. It led directly to Talleyrand's mansion on the Place de la Concorde, physically and figuratively the heart of the city. Every eye turned to Talleyrand to open the door to the future. De Vitrolles pointed to him, Gain de Montagnac in Dijon pointed to him. Louis XVIII's brother, the Count d'Artois, could think of no one else to head an interim government. Foreign diplomats considered him the only authority left in Paris. While Orlov talked to the Tsar in his bedroom, Major General Laborde of the National Guard was telling Count Nesselrode in the great hall below that Talleyrand was the man who knew most about the mood of the people and the government they would accept. The elegant mansion on the Place de la Concorde became the focus of Paris, of France, and of all Europe in the week of Talleyrand's triumph.

When Nesselrode left Bondy for Paris, Talleyrand was in the study of his mansion holding his levee. This was the moment of the day when Talleyrand received his most intimate friends and important visitors, and treated them to a spectacle Grand Judge Molé described in all its curious detail in his memoirs. It is a picture worth preserving, he said, in order to give an idea of customs we will never see again and a manner of treating affairs that will never be reproduced.

When Talleyrand left his bed, usually between 11 and 12 A.M., he went into the study where two or three valets, his doctor, and those of his familiars who had preceded his awakening awaited him. . . . Covered with flannel from head to foot, wrapped in a quilted gray taffeta robe, his head shrouded in several nightcaps, he dragged himself slowly to a mirror to gaze with lackluster eyes at his pale, wan face. All his toilet articles were arranged on a table in front of him. He proceeded to perform a distinctly unappetizing operation. A valet held a huge bowl of water under his chin. Talleyrand plunged a large sponge in it which he ran over his face. Then, putting his nose in the bowl, he discharged into it an incredible quantity of water that cascaded noisily from his mouth. These ablutions and the cascade alternated for a quarter of an hour, during which his study filled with prominent men whose presence he did not seem to notice.

It was not customary to greet him or speak to him first. It was only at the end of half an hour that he gave a sign or said a word in a sepulchral voice, usually with his back turned, to advise each he had been noticed. Sometimes someone had to wait a long time for this sign or word, and it was only when Talleyrand was about to go out the door that an "Adieu, so-and-so," consoled the courtier or solicitor whose patience was running out. Businessmen, bankers, tradesmen, political intriguers, and men in power entered and left throughout.

The preliminary washing was followed by a foot bath while his hair was dressed. He used to exhibit the claws that served him in place of feet to everyone with a cynicism and indifference that always surprised me. While being coiffed, he dried his claws, telling stories and jokes uninterruptedly while signing papers and giving an occasional important order. He then stood up to dress. A sort of promenade that lasted over an hour began, during which he changed shirts and put on his trousers in front of the ladies without bothering to turn his back. The quantity of flannel and number and variety of double waistcoats with which he covered himself was unbelievable. A valet carrying Talleyrand's shirt or waistcoat would follow his uncertain, wavering walk intently, waiting for a favorable moment to slip on his sleeves. The second sleeve was always the most difficult because as soon as Talleyrand had accepted the first, he would start gesticulating to illustrate the story or incident he was telling. These moments were the most active and productive of his day.

On March 31, Talleyrand was busier than usual and up earlier. When Count Nesselrode, the first Allied officer to enter Paris, was announced in Talleyrand's study before 9 A.M., Talleyrand's valet was powdering his hair. Short, elegant, and lively, Count Nesselrode had not seen Talleyrand since their secret collaboration had precipitated Nesselrode's departure from France three years before. Rising joyfully to embrace his friend, Talleyrand covered him from head to foot with powder.

Talleyrand then called in his coterie, the Duke of Dalberg, Baron Louis, Archbishop de Malînes, and his private secretary, Roux de Laborie. With Nesselrode's help, they set about writing a proclamation to Paris which the Tsar would later sign and regard as his own in the belief it had been created under his eyes and supervision. Time being of the essence, Talleyrand thought it best to avoid delay by having the text secretly prepared in advance. He even went so far as to locate a printer, a task that took Roux de Laborie some time since printers, like other tradesmen, were closed on the thirty-first, and using the imperial press was out of the question. Roux de Laborie finally found a young royalist printer named Michaud, and two hours later, the printer submitted the proofs to Talleyrand.

While they were still working on the text, a messenger came to tell Nesselrode one of the Tsar's aides had gotten an anonymous note warning him that explosives had been planted in the Elysées Palace where the Tsar planned to stay. Talleyrand said he disbelieved the story, but offered Tsar Alexander the hospitality of his own house. The unproved rumor fit Talleyrand's plans so nicely that it is impossible not to be suspicious of its origin. Nothing could have helped him more in becoming indispensable to the Tsar than becoming his host. Having the Tsar in his house, Talleyrand could be certain of having the last word with Alexander at all times, an advantage not to be underrated in view of the Tsar's mercurial temperament. Furthermore, no one would be able to talk to Alexander without Talleyrand's knowledge, and some unwelcome visitors might be discreetly prevented from seeing him at all. Visitors like Caulaincourt, for example.

While Talleyrand was working behind the scenes the morning of the thirty-first, Alexander was occupying center stage. A peculiar personality, as one might expect the son of the mad Tsar Paul I to be, Alexander ultimately turned into a bitter, suspicious autocrat. In 1814, however, he was at the zenith of his role as liberator and magnanimous monarch. The praise showered on his fair head brought an inspired light to his intense blue eyes and a glow to his face. Alexander, the handsome, generous, all-powerful victor of the invincible, was the hero of the day. He was the portrait of affability and graciousness. The affability that, Napoleon predicted, would soon tire Parisians charmed them on the thirty-first. The first Parisians Alexander saw and charmed that day were those waiting for an audience at dawn in the great hall of the chateau of Bondy.

Long before leaving for Paris to see Talleyrand, Count Nesselrode had briefed the Paris delegation for its audience with Alexander. When he showed Pasquier the Allied proclamation to Paris that Peyre had brought Joseph on Montmartre, Pasquier tactfully overlooked its implied invitation to restore the Bourbons and remarked simply on the concern expressed for the welfare of Paris. Emperor Alexander's benevolence would only increase if Parisians responded, Nesselrode said. He advised Pasquier to speak frankly to the Tsar.

"Don't feel inhibited in your replies and requests. Bring up everything you feel useful. Just remember he's a little deaf and you'll have to speak loudly to be understood."

Admitted at last to the Tsar's presence, the delegation stood in profound silence while Alexander spoke.

"Gentlemen, you see me at the gates of your capital. By the luck of arms, I am its master and I shall enter it today, but not as the enemy of the French nation.

"I have only one enemy in France, the man who deceived me so unworthily, abused my confidence, betrayed his sworn oaths, and brought an unjust and hideous war upon my country. There can be no reconciliation between us, but, I repeat, in all France I have only this one enemy. Aside from him, I look on all Frenchmen with favor.

"I admire France and the French. I hope they will put me in a position to do them good. I honor the courage and glory of all the brave men I've fought against over the past two years, and I'll always be ready to render them justice.

"Tell the Parisians, then, *Messieurs,* that I do not enter their gates as an enemy. If they so wish, I shall prove their friend."

After repeating this theme in a dozen variations with great vehemence, Alexander allowed the delegates to speak. He was generous in granting their requests. He had every reason to be, his first task being to win the collaboration of city authorities. He promised to preserve the National Guard, the museums, public monuments, and civil institutions. The gesture cost him nothing while giving the French the impression he would allow them to continue running their own affairs. He basked in the glow of the delegates' gratitude.

He asked General Allent if he would vouch for the National Guard. Wounded by Alexander's statements against Napoleon, Allent said, "Yes, if nothing contrary to its oath and honor is demanded of it." Thanks to his bad hearing, Alexander caught only the first word.

Dismissed, the delegation left for Paris post-haste to prepare for the Allies' triumphal march through the city. As they drove through the battlefield littered with bodies of horses and men, Pasquier saw the conquerors forming into columns to martial music beside their smoldering bivouac fires. He noticed they all wore a white scarf or handkerchief tied around one arm. The Russian aide in charge of the Cossack escort explained that the white armband had been adopted after a major battle in which the Allies, in their multinational uniforms and the confusion of the fight, had shot each other instead of the enemy. They had chosen white because it was visible at night, and because every soldier had a handkerchief, shirt, or scrap of lint he could tear up to make an instant armband. That white was the color of the fleur de lys and the symbol of Bourbon restoration had not been considered, but the choice of color turned out to play an influential role.

A short distance from Bondy, the delegates saw Caulaincourt's lanky figure galloping toward them and signaling them to halt. Having left Juvisy with a high sense of mission, Caulaincourt was just beginning to realize he was less a diplomat representing the empire than an impotent observer of its collapse.

He had reached the city hall after the Paris delegation left for Bondy and set off at once on its traces. He talked his way past Allied guards at the city barriers by arguing that since he alone had full powers to negotiate, it was urgent for him to catch up to the delegation without delay. Nothing could be decided without him, he had claimed—and believed. Yet here were the delegates' carriages, not only returning to Paris, but rushing past him.

As he came alongside, Caulaincourt tried to stop them to get news, but he had only the briefest of exchanges while the Cossack guards urged the horses on, encouraged, to Caulaincourt's bitterness, by one of the generals of the National Guard. Pasquier and the department prefect, Chabrol, were embarrassed and icy. The reception, Caulaincourt observed, "gave the measure of the little interest certain people already had in the cause I was charged with defending. . . . The Emperor had foreseen only too clearly what would happen."

His zeal redoubled, Caulaincourt galloped on toward Bondy. Half a mile down the road, he was stopped by Nesselrode, who was on his way to Paris.

"Your mission is useless now," Nesselrode said. "The capitulation has settled everything, and the authorities have assumed responsibility for seeing that the terms are observed. They know our goal is the peace you wouldn't accept, the peace we're bringing to Paris only because you refused it at Châtillon. The Tsar has no time to receive you now. Our columns are already starting to march, as you can see."

Caulaincourt insisted. The delegation the Tsar had just seen had no authority to negotiate peace or even to govern the city. The war was not ended by the Allies' reaching Paris first, but it could be over at once if Alexander would hear his mission of peace. Alexander had won the right to enter Paris, but surely he would prefer to enter peace in hand. It was a greater triumph. Besides, Caulaincourt added, "Our army is intact and growing, ready to fight and only two hours away. Why not spare brave men's blood and avoid risks when the end everyone wants can be achieved in a quarter of an hour?"

After a long argument, Nesselrode consented to turn back to consult Alexander. Reluctant as Alexander was to talk to any representative from Napoleon until he had found out from Talleyrand what the situation was, he agreed to see Caulaincourt briefly. He had known and liked the diplomat as French ambassador to Russia years before, and received him cordially.

"I am always greatly pleased to see the Duke of Vicence again, as a friend," he said. As for Caulaincourt's mission, Alexander was unmovable. It was too late. France and Paris were as tired of Napoleon's government as all Europe and equally convinced peace with him was impossible. Making Caulaincourt promise not to engage in intrigue and to adhere strictly to his role of parliamentary, Alexander agreed to see him again in Paris.

Despondent, aware that intrigue was already gaining ground in Paris, Caulaincourt left, determined to work to the end for Napoleon, and to save the crown for the son if he could not for the father.

As soon as he reached the city, Caulaincourt called on Pasquier. If he hoped the police chief would be more cordial away from Allied eyes, he was disappointed. Nevertheless, Caulaincourt left with the impression that Pasquier was doing his job loyally by ensuring order, keeping track of troublemakers, and making certain no compromising information fell into enemy hands. Caulaincourt appreciated Pasquier's confidence in showing him the declaration to the city he and Chabrol had been preparing. That Pasquier's efforts to keep order were smoothing the way for the Allies does not seem to have struck Caulaincourt. He suggested a few minor changes in the declaration. Pasquier graciously accepted, and the document, commending the honorable capitulation and assuring Parisians of the protection and good will of the Russian Tsar, was ready to be posted. "Remain calm and tranquil through this momentous occasion and exercise the good sense that has always distinguished you," it concluded.

Caulaincourt told Pasquier of Napoleon's arrival at Juvisy the night before, of his hesitations, and his return to Fontainebleau to await the arrival of his army. He showed Pasquier the credentials the Emperor had given him and announced he was to see Tsar Alexander again after the Allied entry into Paris.

"He's undoubtedly bitter," Caulaincourt said of Alexander, "but he's generous and temperate. Perhaps his victory will serve me, if I can make him understand how unwise it would be to risk that glory now. And then, he has the great example of his rival before him."

"I'm afraid you're wrong, but I don't want to shake your confidence," Pasquier said. "You'll need it to succeed."

Tsar Alexander was about to savor his triumph. Choosing, as Napoleon always did, a rather simple uniform to contrast with the peacock splendor of his general staff, Alexander was at the gates of Paris a little past 10 A.M. There he was joined by the King of Prussia with a similar cortège, Commander-in-chief Schwarzenberg, the Tsar's brother, Grand Duke Constantine, and the many princes of many nations.

Inside the gates, Paris had been stirring since daybreak. Not hearing any more firing when they awoke, the citizens had run out to see what had happened. By 8 A.M., everyone knew Paris had capitulated. Everyone knew that, for the first time in four centuries, an enemy army was about to march into the city. No Parisian was going to miss the event. Crowds started gathering as soon as it was light, filling the streets through which the Allies were to pass. People were leaning out windows, hanging over balconies, crouching on rooftops. Many wore their Sunday clothes, which gave them an air of awaiting a fête rather than an enemy occupation. The weather lent itself to the occasion. It was one of those sunny spring days when Paris is at its loveliest, a perfect day for a parade.

There were tens of dozens, perhaps hundreds, of eyewitness accounts. Diarists eagerly filled pages with details of the momentous occasion. There are almost as many versions of the crowd reactions as there are diarists, but everyone agreed the Allied Army was a grand and stirring sight.

The procession of 60,000 was opened with trumpets, followed by the red-uniformed Cossacks of the Tsar's guard, and the Prussian and Russian cavalry on superb horses. The two sovereigns rode abreast with Prince Schwarzenberg, surrounded by 1000 officers, covered with decorations. Grand Duke Constantine, with his Tartar features and near-sighted squint, rode with his own cavalry. Behind came endless columns of infantry, artillery with 40 cannon, and 47 squadrons of Russian cuirassiers with their shining breastplates. The uniforms were resplendent: red, white, blue, green, with plumes and tassels waving, gold helmets gleaming in the sunlight. There were 35,000 cavalrymen alone, hoofs clattering over the cobblestones while the crowds pressed so close the riders barely had room to pass.

They came from all over Europe; from Sweden, Silesia, Prussia, Bavaria, Austria, Russia, and parts of Asia. The Cossacks attracted particular interest and were found quite handsome, not at all like the monsters pictured in French posters. Bushy-bearded, dressed in sheepskins, wide pantaloons, and cylindrical bonnets a foot high, they rode lively little light-footed horses and carried more arms than the other cavalrymen: a lance, a saber, two big pistols hanging from a wide leather belt, the little whip called a knout around their necks, and sometimes a rifle as well. The Kalmucks and other Tartar tribes were there, distinguished by their flat noses, small eyes, and dark-red complexions. The Bashkirs and Tunguses from Siberia were armed with bows and arrows. Circassian chiefs from the Caucasus were covered from head to foot in brilliant sheets of mail with long pointed helmets on their heads like those worn in the early Middle Ages, and in the midst of the troops rolled Russian carriages driven by long-bearded coachmen wearing dark robes and flat, small-rimmed hats.

At the barrier, the crowds were still. The silence was sullen as the Allies passed through the gates into the workers' quarters before faces saddened and concerned. Only when they neared the heart of Paris was there any favorable response, yet there, too, the majority was silent.

To stir a reaction when the Allies appeared, a small group of young noblemen associated with the Chevaliers de la Foi created a royalist demonstration in the central part of the city. There were the usual twenty or thirty activists, all on horseback, led by the Duke of Fitz-James, Sosthène de Larochefoucauld, Chateaubriand's nephew, and the Marquess of Maubreuil, who tied his Legion of Honor to the tail of his mount. Not daring to venture more than a few blocks from the Place de la Concorde, they repeated the same round five times to give the illusion of growing numbers. Carrying white handkerchiefs aloft on the ends of canes, they shouted, "Long live the kings! Long live the Bourbons! Down with the tyrant!" One of the spectators said the young men inspired neither anger nor hatred, but also failed to evoke any enthusiasm on the part of the onlookers.

The most avid anti-Bonapartists seem to agree that the crowds were fairly neutral, though curious, up to this point. A few regarded the young men with pity. No one tried to stop them. A handful of ladies in balconies along the Boulevard des Italiens threw down white cockades and waved white handkerchiefs, but people seemed more astonished than anything else until the imposing spectacle of the Allies approaching caught their attention.

All eyes centered on Alexander, erect, six feet tall, young, handsome, riding a white horse. His fair hair shone above his green uniform with gold epaulets, eclipsing the splendor of the King of Prussia in blue with silver epaulets and a hat with a trailing cock feather. In contrast to the stiff, serious-faced Prussian monarch, Alexander was smiling, bowing, and waving.

How many cried, "Long live Emperor Alexander! Long live the sovereigns! Long live the Bourbons!" no one can say. In a crowd of 20,000, a hundred voices can make a great deal of noise. The young noblemen pressed around Alexander, shouting and cheering. There was an echo in the crowd. Some of the Parisian ladies mounted behind the Cossacks' saddles for a better view. From the Madeleine to the Champs-Elysées, where the Allied sovereigns halted to review troops for two or three hours, the crowd was noisy. The fake demonstration helped, the magnificence of the spectacle helped, and the white armband the Allies wore restrained some who might have protested the cheers had they not assumed the armband meant the Bourbon restoration was already agreed upon.

The cheers were partly an expression of relief, too. To Parisians who had been dreading pillage, massacre, and revenge, who had expected to be inundated by savage hordes from the Don, the sight of this handsomely uniformed, orderly army marching to military bands that played French tunes while Alexander waved affably to the crowds was a surprise. Without thinking beyond the moment, without considering what foreign occupation meant, the relief the onlookers felt exploded in a burst of gratitude that led to the shameful spectacle of a crowd enjoying the enemy's parade. The enemy sovereigns and soldiers cried "Peace! Peace!" so gaily. Even the Cossacks did not look so dreadful, the ladies exclaimed, with cries of, "Oh, here come some more. Look how handsome they are!" Sadly, Caulaincourt wrote Napoleon that night: "Many saw this painful and humiliating day as just one more spectacle."

To a few, the spectacle brought a discovery and a change of heart. Young Charles de Rémusat, a second cousin to Pasquier, was one of those surprised by his own reactions.

"I admit that the attitude of Alexander throughout the procession struck me in an unexpected way," he wrote. "While I hesitate to give too precise an account in retrospect of what was then a succession of fairly confused impressions, there is no doubt that when I saw this warring army, come from so far, steel and fire in hand, marching peacefully through a city that appeared neither saddened nor bitter; when I saw the naturally gentle and affable expression of Emperor Alexander, and the pacific character of the entire ceremony, in which any triumphant insolence was studiously avoided, I realized there was such a thing as civilization. It was civilization that was the real victor that day. The contrast between the haughty, solemn allure of force, as Napoleon taught us to know it, and the moderation—affected if you will—on the part of a conqueror who seemed to be paying homage to the glory of a vanquished people crossed my mind. I began to see the painful event taking place before my eyes in a new light."

While the Duke of Dalberg and the Archbishop of Malînes ran out into the streets at the sight of ladies distributing bits of white handkerchiefs to the crowds in the Place de la Concorde, Talleyrand watched from his windows. He was there, looking down with interest, when Caulaincourt was announced. Talleyrand seemed surprised to see him.

"The Emperor lost everything by not letting you make peace at Châtillon," were Talleyrand's first words.

"Can he count on you now our luck is down?"

"Up to two days ago, I'd hoped to save him by keeping the Empress and her son here," Talleyrand said, "but the Emperor persists in giving secret orders and distrusting everyone. His letter to his brother ruined everything. Everyone was paralyzed by the fear of displeasing him, of disobeying, and now he's lost and France is lost with him. It's not up to us to save him today. Why did he let things go so far? Why did he prefer to listen to flatterers?"

"This isn't the moment to go into his faults," Caulaincourt said. "He sent me to Emperor Alexander to plead his cause and sign the peace everyone wants. Will you support me? Are you abandoning him now his luck has failed? Will you sacrifice the Empress, the King of Rome, and the true interests of France?"

"I did everything I could to save them at the last council meeting. I tried to keep them from leaving. However unjust the Emperor has been to me, I fought for him and for them almost alone, and all for nothing, thanks to the Emperor's secret orders. His interference was fatal. You'll find out for yourself that I did everything I should have."

Just then, Count Tolstoy, Grand Marshal of the Russian court, arrived to announce that the Tsar had accepted the invitation to stay at Talleyrand's house. Count Nesselrode entered the room right behind Count Tolstoy, who left while Nesselrode and Talleyrand ignored Caulaincourt to engage in a long conversation in a corner of the room. The little Caulaincourt overheard made it clear he could hope for no support from Talleyrand. It was equally clear he was in the way. As he left, he passed through a series of antechambers already filling with people eager to learn which direction matters were taking in order to side with the winner. Caulaincourt pretended not to notice them as he hurried back to his sister's house. As a mere parliamentary, he could not return to his official residence in the foreign ministry on Rue du Bac.

"I left with death in my heart," Caulaincourt wrote Napoleon. "I don't know what your plenipotentiary can hope for. For the moment I see nothing but cause for worry."

Caulaincourt's reasons for worry multiplied. While awaiting his promised interview with the Tsar, he dispatched messengers to everyone he thought might be able to give him details on the departure of Napoleon's court, the arrangements made for delegating authority in its absence, and the events of the thirtieth. He was totally unsuccessful. As he put it, "Everyone who might have known something either had left Paris or was not at home. Some had gone out because of curiosity or anxiety, and the rest pretended to be out because no one wanted to receive anyone in those first uncertain moments."

Talleyrand was the first Frenchman to greet Emperor Alexander when the Tsar finished the interminable review of troops on the Champs-Elysées. He arrived at Talleyrand's mansion modestly on foot, surrounded by an admiring crowd of young royalists. At the bottom of his monumental staircase, Talleyrand made a gracious speech about the honor he felt at being the great Tsar's host. Alexander entered in an exalted mood.

A conference was held at once in Talleyrand's *salon de l'aigle*, a long, elegant room overlooking the Rue de Mondovi. The enormous chandelier and glittering sconces, the delicate Pompeian-style tracery on the wood panels, the row of narrow windows with their deep embrasures and gold and white boiseries gave the room a pompous air. It was a suitable setting for deciding the fate of an empire.

The King of Prussia arrived shortly after the Russian Tsar, followed by Prince Schwarzenberg. Count Nesselrode and the Prince of Liechtenstein had spent the day with Talleyrand. Also present were the Tsar's right-hand man and aide, Corsican Pozzo di Borgo, a bitter enemy of Napoleon, and Talleyrand's closest consultant, Dalberg.

Alexander paced the room in great agitation.

"*Eh bien,* here we are in the famous city of Paris! And it's you who brought us here, M. de Talleyrand," he said. "We now have four possible choices, to negotiate with the Emperor Napoleon, to establish a regency, to make Bernadotte head of state, or to recall the Bourbons."

"Emperor Alexander is under a slight misapprehension," said Talleyrand. "There are not four choices, there is only one, the last His Majesty mentioned." He proceeded to eliminate the first three. "Napoleon if you could, but you can't—there are no adequate guarantees," he said. "The regency if Napoleon were dead, but what would you do with the little Emperor's father? Napoleon would always be listening behind the door. His recapturing power would be only a matter of time. As for Bernadotte—a soldier again? We don't want one anymore, and if we did, we'd keep the one we have. He's the first in the world.

"No, not even you, who have conquered France, can impose a king on the French nation. All-powerful though you are, you're not powerful enough to choose for France. If you did, the country would rise up en masse against the invasion, and Your Imperial Majesty is well aware of the terrible power of a nation aroused.

"To achieve something lasting, one must act on a principle. With a principle, we are strong, we meet no resistance, and any objections will be effaced in little time. There is only one principle. Louix XVIII is a principle. He is the legitimate king of France."

Alexander raised objections, just as he had in talking to Baron de Vitrolles. In the months the Allies had spent in France, the only sentiments they had encountered were indifference, resentment, and hostility. No voice was ever raised against Napoleon, and as for the Bourbons, the first voices they had heard in favor of the restoration were the acclamations of the past hour, hardly the voice of the country.

Talleyrand took up the arguments de Vitrolles had used with

Alexander. If people had not expressed themselves in the Allies' presence. it was because they resented the miseries of the invasion, not because they were attached to the government that had brought those miseries upon them. Besides, who would dare declare himself against Napoleon as long as the Allies were ready to negotiate with him? That would be suicidal. Bordeaux had come out in favor of the Bourbons only after foreign occupation made it safe to do so. It would be the same in Paris.

Alexander hesitated. He prided himself on being a product of eighteenth-century enlightenment. The Bourbons were passé, absolutist, inflexible, and vengeful. Alexander agreed with Napoleon that in twenty-five years of well-deserved misfortune they had learned nothing and forgotten nothing. France would never accept them.

The Bourbons would become liberal monarchs out of necessity, Talleyrand said. They would have to accept a constitution to win the throne. A constitution guaranteeing the truly sound principles of the revolution would satisfy the Jacobins, or old revolutionaries. It would satisfy the constitutional monarchists, and the ultraroyalists would be glad to see the Bourbons back one way or another. Everyone would accept Louis XVIII, and only Louis XVIII would be accepted by everyone.

"What would have to be done to attain your end? I don't want to impose anything," Emperor Alexander said. "I can only cede to the wishes expressed by the country."

"Of course, Sire," Talleyrand said. "All we have to do is put people in a position to make themselves heard. The constituted authorities will call for the Bourbons themselves in a deliberation in the Senate, which I'll take the responsibility of holding, and whose results Your Majesty will see immediately."

"Are you sure of it?"

"I guarantee it, Sire, and I guarantee the Senate's example will be followed by Paris and all of France."

Alexander still hesitated. The combat of Fère-Champenoise was constantly on his mind. He kept seeing the thousands of young recruits choosing certain death over surrender and falling, row by row, before his eyes. Their cries of *Vive l'Empereur!* as they fell rang in his ears. That raw recruits were ready to die futilely for Napoleon's cause was undeniable evidence that a part of the population had no desire to abandon him.

Talleyrand suggested that Tsar Alexander listen to the opinions of responsible Frenchmen and judge for himself. If Dalberg had not had a

German accent, Talleyrand might have asked him to express the will of the French people. He had his star witnesses ready, however. His collaborators Baron Louis and the Archbishop of Malînes, both upper-class Parisians, openly anti-Bonaparte, and devoid of any contact with the country at large, were solemnly introduced into the salon. Alexander lent himself willingly, perhaps even knowingly, to the farce. Possibly all the Tsar wanted was a workable solution he could accept under the guise, however thin, of its having been presented to him by Frenchmen as the will of the people.

As the Archbishop of Malînes recalled the scene in his memoirs, the King of Prussia was on the far right. Schwarzenberg was closest to the heavily ornamented table in the center of the room. Dalberg stood on Schwarzenberg's right, with Nesselrode, Pozzo di Borgo, and the Prince of Liechtenstein lined up next to him, while Talleyrand stood to the left of the King of Prussia.

Facing the assembly, Alexander made his usual speech with emphatic tones and gestures. It was not he who had started the war. He had not come to Paris for conquest or vengeance, nor was he making war on France. He and his allies, he said, turning to get the agreement of the King of Prussia and Prince Schwarzenberg, had only two enemies in France—Napoleon and any foe of French liberty. The French had a completely free choice, he went on, turning back to the archbishop and Baron Louis. All they had to do was tell him what the nation felt, and the Allied forces would support its wishes. He then questioned each separately.

De Malînes burst into an impassioned speech. We are all royalists, he said. All France is royalist. If she hasn't shown it yet, only the drawn-out negotiations of Châtillon are to blame. As soon as the public can declare itself in complete security, it will do so, and the example of Paris will be followed everywhere. Baron Louis repeated the same view in his brusque, staccato voice. The Tsar turned again to the King of Prussia and Prince Schwarzenberg, who said they fully agreed with the opinions expressed.

"Very well," the Tsar said. "I hereby declare I will no longer deal with Emperor Napoleon." When it was pointed out that he was excluding only Napoleon and not his family, the Emperor added, "nor with any member of his family."

The debate that determined the future of France was over. From then on, all followed as if the script had been rehearsed. Had Talleyrand written every word of it, he could not have been more satisfied. After the archbishop and Baron Louis left, Count Nesselrode and Dalberg were asked to withdraw to draft a declaration of Tsar Alexander's intentions. Since the document had already been written and even set up in proof, the two men produced a draft after a token delay of half an hour. Happily, as Talleyrand had expected, Alexander found that it expressed his ideas perfectly.

He changed little. To the Allied promise to respect the integrity of French borders, "under France's legitimate kings," he added a hint that the Allies might be more generous. "They may do more, since their principle has always been that, for the good of all Europe, France must be great and strong." The rest of the document he left unaltered: the announcement that the Allies would not negotiate with Napoleon or any member of his family, the invitation to the Senate to appoint a provisional government to administer the country and prepare a suitable constitution, and the promise to recognize and uphold the constitution France chose.

Talleyrand's secretary rushed from the room with the declaration in hand. The printer was waiting discreetly in an adjoining room, ready to run off the approved text. Thanks to Talleyrand's advance preparations, the document that most influenced the opinion of Parisians was posted within the hour. It cut short much extraneous intrigue and convinced many Frenchmen that France would get better conditions from the Allies under a new government than under Napoleon. It soothed French pride by implying that the government, not the country, had been defeated. That the Russian Emperor was, in effect, calling the French Senate into session was generally overlooked.

Everything was going marvelously, but neither Talleyrand nor anyone else had forgotten that Napoleon was only a few leagues from Paris with his army. After producing the archbishop and Baron Louis as the representatives of France, Talleyrand set them to work to win the support of Napoleon's most influential generals while preventing or counteracting efforts by spokesmen for Napoleon in Paris.

"If we could not keep them from coming," wrote the archbishop, "we at least managed to shorten their stay and diminish their effect."

Napoleon's main spokesman, Caulaincourt, was making no headway.

"Emperor Alexander received me this afternoon for only a moment, had no time to listen to my claims, and put me off till tomorrow," he wrote Napoleon. "I am rejected everywhere.... I am afraid the sovereign's declaration, posted this afternoon, proves treason has already made great strides.... Sire! Take counsel only from your courage.... No doubt much will become clear between today and tomorrow, but everyone is avoiding me.... I haven't seen a friendly face.... This reserve, if it is only that, will give Your Majesty the measure of opinion and the character of the men remaining here. I stimulate the good ones, I encourage the weak. I find very few Frenchmen, I must say with pain to Your Majesty. Many intriguers are anxious for me to leave. I've already been asked to. My presence is embarrassing, though I am only here in a private capacity. If, as I fear, I am unable to put myself in a position of leadership, I'll probably be sent back tomorrow.... I won't give up until I'm put out the door."

If persistence is a virtue, Caulaincourt was a saint. He repeated his round of calls that night. A few people, taken by surprise, let him in. They sighed and said it was time to think of France, sacrificed for so long to one man's ambition. Caulaincourt found everyone he knew "decidedly against the Emperor." He was stunned and contemptuous, called them wretched, ungrateful cowards.

"The old senators are bewitched," he wrote, "their heads completely turned by Talleyrand's maneuvers and Emperor Alexander's speeches. Far from being afraid of dishonoring and compromising themselves, they rush ahead excitedly as if their only fear were not doing enough ... not appearing supple enough, eager enough.... They are ready to subscribe to everything Talleyrand proposes."

Talleyrand and his supporters had preceded Caulaincourt everywhere. They dazzled senators and legislators with the prospect of playing a role in great events, of forming a peerage, writing a constitution to be imposed on the Bourbons. And they reminded the politicians that they would guarantee their own positions and privileges in the process. Those opposed were absent or silent, but all would come around in a surprisingly short time. While Caulaincourt hung on doggedly, Talleyrand grew stronger by the hour. The myths and illusions he had fabricated were becoming reality. The cause of a small band of royalists was taking on the semblance of a popular movement through his clever manipulation.

For months, growing discontent, subtly encouraged by Talleyrand, had unwittingly aided the royalist cause. The ground in which royalism took root was prepared by every defeatist, by everyone who repeated alarming news from the battlefields or called for peace at any price. It was helped to grow by everyone who spread the belief that Napoleon was the sole obstacle to peace. When the Allies entered Paris, the seedling idea, still unrecognizable to the layman, was ready to burst into flower in a few days.

Talleyrand had planned it that way. The man who believed a diplomat should show talent even in his choice of leisure activities never made a purely casual gesture. His contemporaries called him lazy, but they simply failed to understand his peculiar methods of working. It could be said that he was working all the time, though he was careful not to let it show. When he limped into Minister Rovigo's office to shake his head sadly at the news from the French army, when he sympathized with Pasquier over the desperate straits of Paris and the overwhelming superiority of the Allied forces, when he warned of the possibility of a popular revolt, he was preparing men to accept the solution he would propose when the time was right.

Most officials remaining in Paris were quickly persuaded to cooperate with the Allies, whether from a desire to keep their jobs and salaries, a belief that public order was in the best interests of Parisians, or from the premature conclusion that the empire was finished anyway. The few who refused to cooperate, like de La Valette, were replaced. After raising almost the only voice in Napoleon's defense at Marmont's the night of the thirtieth, de La Valette resigned as head of the postal services the following day. He was replaced at once by Napoleon's bitter enemy Bourrienne, who got the vital postal system working by the next dawn so that news of the changes in Paris could reach the provinces and start the revolution there.

Men of de La Valette's integrity were few. Few were as honest as Pasquier, who broke openly with Napoleon before the new regime was secure. But by accepting the illusion that Napoleon was already dethroned, both helped Talleyrand overthrow him. It was by spreading and strengthening that illusion that Talleyrand made it a reality. He promoted it by every means at his disposal: newspaper propaganda, street propaganda, and the word of mouth that has always been a peculiarly effective force in Paris. He manipulated the Allies, the Senate, the administrators. He acted as head of the new government before it came into being. Besieged all day in his mansion by old and new royalists, he sent them out to spread word of the hope for and near certainty of the Bourbon restoration. To men with lingering attachments to the empire, he spoke in practical terms. They had already compromised themselves with Napoleon by remaining in the capital. The Allies were in Paris and had the power. What was one to do? Why, make the best of it and get the best for France.

Though most of the population was opposed to the overthrow of the empire, it remained silent and leaderless. Had anyone stepped forward to lead a rebellion in Paris, the Allies might have been ousted. No leader appeared. Men had stopped making an effort to win on the grounds that Napoleon's cause was already lost.

"It's too late," Talleyrand said to Caulaincourt. "You come too late," Alexander told him. Waverers and weaker men gave in to what appeared inevitable. Every underling remaining at his post bent to the wind as soon as he saw clearly which way it was blowing. Sooner or later, almost every official or politician who stayed in Paris was compromised.

Even those who, like Pasquier, welcomed the return of a monarchy found themselves in the equivocal position of betraying the man who had given them wealth, honors, position, and trust. Some ultraroyalists felt humiliated by the occupation and ashamed by the ease with which Paris accepted it. Only the émigrés greeted the events of the day with a clear conscience. For men who had left France years before to fight in enemy armies, the occupation resolved an unhappy dilemma. Count Langeron, who had commanded the Allied assault on Montmartre, later wrote, "By the unexpected and welcome restoration of Louis XVIII to the throne of his fathers, I found myself in the position of having fought for my native land."

The Allies were not as easily convinced that the change of government was a *fait accompli*. They had invaded France with great apprehension and continuous worry. Astonished and more than a little anxious at finding themselves in Paris, they were not to be blinded by a handful of royalists to the power Napoleon still had. They feared him even with his remnants of an army. Emperor Alexander later said he had attacked Paris against the opposition of all his generals. The attack could have been a disaster for the Allies. Many Russian officers, once safely in Paris, admitted they had only sixteen hours of ammunition left. General Yorck said he had none at all. General Langeron replied to one of the young men who congratulated him on the ease and speed with which the capital had been taken, "It's easy to see you did not fight the campaign, Monsieur. I, who fought, and find myself in Paris, am still astonished at being here."

While royalists rejoiced prematurely and Talleyrand maneuvered, the Allies started sending troops south to cover the roads to Fontaine-bleau and Orléans in case of an attack. They built up a line of defense on the southeast and made plans to attack Melun to take the bridges over the Seine. Allied Staff Headquarters was moved south to the chateau de Petit-Bourg at Chevilly, just across the Essonne River from the French on the road to Fontainebleau. Allied soldiers were kept on the alert, ready to fight at a moment's notice.

Napoleon's army of 60,000 men was assembling with incredible speed, but most of it was still far away in eastern France. Forced marches went on through the night. Officers' horses could barely stand. Soldiers were hungry and exhausted. Despite superhuman efforts, the Imperial Guard was over sixty miles away, Ney slightly farther, and Macdonald and Oudinot almost 100 miles from Fontainebleau on the thirty-first.

At hand, Napoleon had only his guard, the garrisons of Melun and Fontainebleau, and the men who had just fought for Paris. Marmont commanded the strongest arm, the 12,000-man advance guard at Cor-beil-Essonnes, at the juncture of the Essonne and Seine Rivers, while Mortier, five miles farther south, had fewer than 6000 men. To the northeast, the prefect of the Seine-et-Marne, the Count of Plancy, was staunchly determined to defend the garrison town of Melun and its vital bridges, but he lacked the means to hold out for long.

Except that not one of Napoleon's strongholds, from Paris to the Rhine, had surrendered, the war was going very badly for the French. The Austrians had taken France's second city, Lyons. The English were approaching Toulouse. Men around Napoleon were glum. Many urged him to retreat to the Loire to join the imperial government and regroup all available forces before attacking the Allies. He seriously reconsidered doing so. The evening of the thirty-first, he sent orders to Macdonald and other generals to halt in place, but by 9 A.M. the following morning, he sent new orders to continue the march to Fontainebleau post-haste. This time, Napoleon decided against his generals. He preferred to stay close to Paris in the hopes his nearness would discourage intrigue and force the Allies to keep their forces concentrated. At Fontainebleau, he had a favorable strategic position. The Essonne River constituted a barrier between Fontainebleau and Paris; the Seine and the Yonne offered protection to the right and rear. He awaited the arrival of his army with mounting impatience.

The majestic palace of Fontainebleau, in the center of an immense forest, had been Napoleon's favorite country residence in his days of glory. How different it was for him now, in the suite known as *les petits appartements*. Napoleon had stamped this part of Fontainebleau as firmly with his taste as the *grands appartements* he stayed in when there with the court. Reminders of his glory were all around him. He had slept in the iron camp bed, hung with green-velvet curtains, after his victory at Austerlitz. The caryatids recalled his Egyptian campaign. Everywhere there were his favorite greens, olive, jade, and hunting green—curtains, upholstery, and rugs, embroidered in the imperial emblems, the eagle with its spread wings, the golden bees, and the simple *N* with which he sometimes signed his letters to Marie-Louise.

With a fire burning in the grate behind him, Napoleon looked out two long narrow windows at the garden around the statue of Diana with a stag. Large mirrors on the gold-decorated, pale-gray walls reflected the short, plump figure of the man who was still Emperor of France, but was almost alone at Fontainebleau. His capital was occupied; his government, his army, his son, his wife, were all far away. In the uncertainties, his thoughts turned often to Marie-Louise.

"Take courage, take care of your health," he wrote her. "Give the little King a hug from me, and love me always."

VII

TALLEYRAND'S TRIUMPH

April 1

MOST OF THE PALACE of Fontainebleau was dark and deserted. In Paris, lights burned day and night in the Hôtel Talleyrand. Count Nesselrode occupied the second floor with his secretaries, Tsar Alexander occupied the first with his aides-de-camp, while Talleyrand reserved the six rooms on the entresol for himself.

There was continuous hubbub everywhere. Every room was filled with people, activity, coming and going, excited talk. The only difference between day and night was that at night, the Tsar's Cossack guards curled up on their bales of straw in the broad entrance courtyard to sleep.

The center of activity was Talleyrand's headquarters on the entresol, one flight up the marble staircase flanked by Alexander's statuesque Imperial Guard. The three rooms on the court were given over to the public. In the first, there was a group of lowly intriguers—"the sort who appear the minute you tolerate them," wrote Count Beugnot, who shortly became minister of the interior, "the ones who inevitably emerge to form the cortège of the new power." Past this antechamber was a second room for more important intriguers. In the third, Roux de Laborie, who became assistant secretary to the provisional government, gave private audiences when he could fight his way through the crowd of applicants and favor-seekers who besieged him as he passed.

The disorder was duplicated in the three so-called private rooms overlooking the Rue de Rivoli and the Tuileries gardens. There was Talleyrand's bedroom, which became the headquarters of the provi-

191

sional government; a salon filled with secretaries, ministers, and men awaiting orders or making reports; and a library where, in the words of an observer, "M. de Talleyrand listened privately to those lucky or clever enough to get him there, which was anything but easy." When Talleyrand crossed from his bedroom to the library to give a private audience, he was waylaid by one person after another as he tried to get through the salon. Talleyrand listened to everyone, rejected no one, promised nothing.

The hub of all this activity was Talleyrand's bedroom. On the morning of April 1, he was holding his levee there at the unusually early hour of 6 A.M., after spending the night aligning as many senators as possible for the vote he had promised Alexander. Napoleon had given the Senate constitutional powers of sorts to smooth the transition from republic to empire. Talleyrand planned to use those powers to depose Napoleon and change the empire to a constitutional monarchy.

That afternoon, he would get the Senate to approve a provisional administration, which he would head. Once the senators had been induced to vote for a rival administration in Paris, they would be sufficiently compromised to take the next step and declare Napoleon's government defunct. Next, encouraged by promises of a glorious role in the new regime, the senators would go along with the restoration; or at least enough of them would for the rest to follow.

The senators clearly had no right to meet and no right to vote out of existence the government that gave them their authority, but Talleyrand dismissed that as parliamentary gibberish. What mattered was that the illegal vote of a rump senate would not only be accepted by Tsar Alexander as the voice of the government and the people, it would set in motion waves of acceptance that would end by engulfing Napoleon's most loyal supporters.

Some of the senators Talleyrand or his emissaries talked to sighed, lamented, or feigned indignation, but their desire to continue being senators kept them from closing the door to the man of the hour. There would be a constitution, Talleyrand promised the Jacobins and constitutional monarchists. To those who argued that the Bourbons were unknown, unpopular, and long isolated from French affairs, Talleyrand answered, as he had to Alexander, that this was precisely what made them such a good choice. Their obscurity and unpopularity would oblige them to listen to the will of the people and support the constitution that would be presented them. When ultraroyalists objected to having a constitution at all, Talleyrand said it was impossible to bring back the Bourbons without it. To men loyal to Napoleon, he said the empire was finished and it was now every patriotic Frenchman's painful duty to save the country from partition and pillage by setting up a new authority without delay. To the senators, he sent an invitation as novel as it was illegal:

> The Prince of Bénévent has been invited by His Majesty Emperor Alexander to present to the Senate the propositions of the Allied powers. He will be at the palace of the Senate at 3:30 P.M. precisely. Your presence is requested.

Presiding over the session required giving a speech. Talleyrand disliked speechmaking and never wrote a speech himself if he could get someone else to do it. He does not seem to have given this address much importance since he turned the writing over to the Archbishop of Malînes, whom he considered totally incompetent. The archbishop composed the text under Talleyrand's desultory supervision while Talleyrand dressed at 6 A.M. on April 1.

Talleyrand's second concern was completing his slate for the provisional government. The principle members, Talleyrand's collaborators, he had chosen weeks earlier. Having manipulated most crises from the card table, Talleyrand not unnaturally selected his whist partners to see him through this one. His cabinet was soon known throughout Paris as *La Table de Whist de M. de Talleyrand.*

With Talleyrand as president, there were four other members in the cabinet. Arnail de Jaucourt and Emerich de Dalberg were intimates of long standing. General Pierre de Beurnonville, a respected man who knew how to get on well enough to start his career as an abbé and end it as a marshal, was, like Jaucourt, a senator, and thus certain to help get senate support for the slate. The fifth member, Abbé Francois-Xavier de Montesquiou-Fézensac was chosen to please the royalists. Nicknamed *le petit serpent* during the revolution, he had amused himself by conspiring for the Bourbons throughout the empire, but never in brutal conspiracies using explosives. His were the well-mannered plots of good society, "spun in salons and never reaching farther than the antechambers." To balance his reputation as an extreme royalist, the day the government was installed, Talleyrand took one of the survivors of the old Constituent Assembly, Dupont de Nemours, as secretary general. The latter's work was really done by the indefatigable assistant secretary, Roux de Laborie, who ran day and night from one interview to another, never saying more than two or three sentences before rushing on to the next.

The new government ministers were called commissars. Police Chief Pasquier and departmental prefect Chabrol, who suited Talleyrand perfectly, kept their jobs. Bourrienne kept the post office. Talleyrand's close friend, Baron Joseph-Dominique Louis, became commissar of finance, Jules Anglès, the police official who used to supply Talleyrand with foreign newspapers, became minister of police. General Pierre Antoine Dupont took over the army; Pierre-Victor Malouet, the navy; Count Jacques-Claude Beugnot, the prefect at Lille, the interior; Count Antoine de Laforêt, foreign affairs; and Pierre-Paul-Nicolas Henrion de Pansey, justice. General Jean Dessole became commander of the Paris National Guard, replacing Marshal Moncey, who had joined Napoleon at Fontainebleau. Most members of the new government were respected men, but most remained figureheads while Talleyrand ran the government from his bed.

"I'm the shadow of a minister," Count Laforêt complained, "like the man in the fable of hell, a shadow of a man shoveling air with a shadow of a shovel."

The comings and goings of messengers, constant interruptions by visitors from the Allied staff and the city administration, and hordes of petitioners and office-seekers, made it impossible to carry on serious business. One could hope to catch Talleyrand for a private interview only between midnight and 2 A.M.

Talleyrand enjoyed himself hugely. He disliked routine. He was at home in the midst of this human comedy. He was getting everything he wanted done in a setting that offered him endless opportunity for amusement. His favorite entertainment was sending eager royalists out to cry, *Vive le Roi!* and distribute white cockades. They were sometimes beaten up, but the mission pleased them and kept them occupied.

After finishing Talleyrand's speech in midmorning, the Archbishop of Malînes was restless. He felt hurt at being left out of the provisional government. What was he to do? he asked Talleyrand. He could not be shunted aside in such a moment.

"Eh! No one wants to shunt you aside," the prince answered. "In fact, you can render a vital service right now. Do you have a white handkerchief?"

"Yes."

"Really very white?"

"Definitely."

"Let me see it."

The archbishop pulled his handkerchief from his pocket. Taking it, Talleyrand waved it in the air in all directions like a flag while crying, "*Vive le Roi!*"

"You see what I just did. Now go down, take the Boulevard de la Madeleine up to the Faubourg St.-Antoine, waving your handkerchief and crying *Vive le Roi!* all the way."

"But, Prince, you can't be serious. Think how I'm dressed. I'm in clerical clothes, wearing my cross, my Legion of Honor."

"Precisely. If you weren't dressed as a clergyman, you'd have to go change first. Your bishop's cross and tonsure will all help create a scandal, and it's scandal we need."

The archbishop left to play the masquerade. He followed the boulevards, gathered a large train of curious and idlers, but at the Boulevard Poissonière, he was charged by a group of Bonapartists who forced him back. He arrived at Talleyrand's breathless, covered with mud to his neck, and boasting about his success and daring. He had won over a large part of the population. If he had hesitated to go beyond the Boulevard Poissonière, it was only because he had taken on a mission no one else would have dared to try without a few cavalry squadrons as escort.

Talleyrand merely said, "Didn't I tell you you'd make a prodigious effect dressed like that?"

While events moved forward in a turmoil inside Talleyrand's house, a reassuring normalcy was cultivated in Paris by the government and welcomed by most of the inhabitants. The workers' quarters remained sullen, but the center of Paris came back to life. Shops opened. The Allied military were welcome customers. Allied officers rushed eagerly to the boulevards and the Palais Royal, then a center of gambling and prostitution for the upper class. Gold flowed, prices rose, cafés and restaurants filled, lines formed outside theaters.

Parisians continued to be dominated by shameless curiosity. They visited Allied cavalry bivouacs along the Champs-Elysées, infantry bivouacs on the quays. They flocked around Allied officers and pelted them with questions which were often answered, to their delighted astonishment, in intelligible French. "A warrior who speaks our tongue alarms us less," one Parisian commented.

The foreign officers made every effort to be liked. They were polite. They were kind to children. They threw money to the poor and to groups crying, *Vive Alexandre!* Rumors of a few days before that the Russian Tsar called the conquered French provinces *Russian France* were dissipated, along with fears that the Allies would burn down the capital, carry off the treasures, and turn the Cossacks loose on the inhabitants.

The Cossack bivouacs on the Champs-Elysées attracted the largest crowds. The Champs-Elysées then ran through an area half woods, half market gardens, stretching from the fashionable mansions of the Faubourg St.-Honoré to the Seine. In April 1814, it was an exotic sight. Inside their low-pitched tents, Cossacks were mending bizarre, semi-oriental clothes, boots, harnesses, and bridles, or looking over their plunder. Some sold shawls and watches to eager French bargain hunters, who never stopped to think they were encouraging the pillage of their own countrymen. Elegant French ladies picked up the Cossack's hand-iwork for a closer look and peered into pots of food cooking over campfires. They smiled at the sturdy little Cossack horses, tied three or four to a tree and busily eating all the bark off under the branches hung with tremendously long lances, arrows, quivers, bows, sabers, and out-size pistols. There were always Cossacks sprawled next to their animals. They had to stay near their horses, one Parisian observed, because they never walked anywhere. He saw one Cossack mount his horse to go thirty feet for water, get off, fill his dipper, and mount his horse again to ride back to his tent. The picturesque disorder was further enlivened by an occasional exotic song that stopped in midair without a final cadence.

"Everything, even the rhythm of their drums, was novel," wrote an enchanted royalist lady, adding, "Ah! We felt conquered and liberated all at once."

French papers carried glowing accounts of the Allies' entry into Paris. Emperor Alexander's nobly worded proclamation of the thirty-first was posted on the walls of Paris. The Prefects of the Seine and of the Police announced that all people and property were under the protection of Emperor Alexander. No one could be persecuted or molested for expressing a political opinion or wearing a political emblem.

Alexander's magnanimity was lavishly praised, and he sought every occasion to display it. He had never been in Paris before. He rode all over the city, visited, complimented. Everywhere he was accompanied by what was a small escort for an emperor, especially in an occupied city, just two or three generals and a few servants. His ally, the King of Prussia, sometimes rode by his side but was overshadowed by Alexander.

"The Prussian King," wrote Pasquier, "always had a rather timid air and passed almost unnoticed in public."

"It was touching to see the two great monarchs surrounded by crowds that showered them with praise and blessings," a royalist wrote in his diary. "They stopped every moment to speak to the people nearest them, to repeat they had entered France only to rescue France and Europe from a yoke of misery. The French had nothing to fear from their army, they said. No retributions would be demanded, even though Bonaparte had collected them in other countries."

Emperor Alexander invited peasants to camps outside Paris to reclaim horses, cows, and sheep commandeered by Allied soldiers. Hearing from Pasquier that the Cossacks' horses were destroying trees on the Champs-Elysées, the Tsar went to see for himself and gave orders for damages to be made good. He was a model of tact at all times. When someone said, "Your Majesty's arrival at Paris has been long awaited and desired," he replied, "I should have been here sooner. You must attribute my delay to French valor." On finding empty pedestals at the Louvre because the director had hidden some of the best objects, Alexander took offense. He had promised to respect public property, he said, and ordered everything put back in place. Asked to provide special protection for the Bank of France, Alexander replied that none was needed because all Paris was under his guarantee.

He offered something for everyone. The royalists saw him as the restorer of legitimacy; the constitutionalists as the champion of constitutional monarchy. Democrats marveled at a monarch who proclaimed the people's right to choose their own government. Philosophers praised his magnanimous maxims, tolerance, and moderation. That Russia had no territorial claims on France made his protests of personal disinterest convincing. He became a sort of demigod. He was compared to Marcus Aurelius, to Trajan. His previous ambitions and the schemes he had hatched with Napoleon were forgotten. Even Napoleon said Alexander was precisely the sort of emperor the French should have, since they put form above content. "With manners like Alexander's, one could ruin France and still be adored," Napoleon told Caulaincourt.

Pasquier proved to be one of Alexander's best lieutenants in those first few days. As indefatigable as he was indispensable, Pasquier kept the occupation running smoothly, suppressing any manifestation that might arouse Allied resentment, any incident that might lead to violence. For three days, he slept only an hour or two a night. Keeping order was not easy. Bands of imperial soldiers and officers threatened uprisings. The workers, who had not forgotten the Revolution, were angered by the occupation and the royalist manifestations that hailed it. They tried to provoke quarrels with Allied soldiers. Allied soldiers committed brutalities in villages around Paris. The Cossacks, while respecting property within the city, made regular forays outside to come back loaded with booty which they put on sale at a market they set up on the Pont Neuf. Sometimes the owners of stolen cows or pots or blankets ran after them to recover their goods, and the fray that followed, in which bystanders took sides, was potentially explosive. Food was lacking for many people, and finding forage for the horses was even more crucial. Cossacks would starve for two days before they would tolerate a three-hour delay in feeding their animals, Pasquier was warned, but there was little grain stored in Paris and the farmers in the surrounding area, assuming the city gates were closed, were not making the usual deliveries.

To solve these difficulties, Pasquier went to Emperor Alexander early the morning of April 1. Alexander wisely gave Pasquier his confidence, and urged the police chief to communicate with him directly when problems arose.

"I guarantee you a reply to any question in half an hour if I'm unable to see you personally," he said. Thanks to the easy and rapid cooperation thus established, problems were settled promptly.

Announcements were posted declaring barriers open and circulation normal. Public coaches began leaving on schedule, farmers started bringing in supplies. In another proclamation, Pasquier informed French soldiers and officers in Paris that they were free to leave or stay and had no need to hide. Alexander contributed his usual touch by adding an invitation to the military "to assist in deciding the great question at hand for the happiness of France and the entire world." The Allied governor, General Sacken, disciplined unruly Allied soldiers in and outside Paris severely. When fish failed to arrive at the Paris market for the fifth straight day, he had some Cossacks who had stolen herring hanged as an example.

The thorniest problems were posed by the army and the gendarmerie, who remained staunchly loyal to Napoleon. Pasquier convinced the Allies not to dismiss the gendarmes. They were needed to help the National Guard keep order, he said, particularly since they had the only mounted French troops in Paris. Pasquier found the task of convincing the gendarmerie to cooperate difficult.

The company was drawn up at arms to receive him, but when he told them the city of Paris counted on their zeal and devotion to maintain order he was interrupted by cries of "To the Emperor! We want to join the Emperor!" A dozen rushed at Pasquier in fury. The officers closed around him in protection and calm was somewhat reestablished. The city would keep no one by force, Pasquier said. Those who wished to give up the advantages of their service were free to do so. He ordered the captain to draw up a list of those resigning, to take back the arms belonging to the city, and to send the names to the prefecture so that he could issue passports at once with the proviso that the men leave the city gates before 6 P.M. Only four or five chose to resign. From then on, there was no sign of insubordination.

The ultraroyalists were as hard to control as the Bonapartists. Uncontained, they would have destroyed their own cause. They were too fanatical, too intolerant of the feelings of people whose support they needed. Convinced that they were the true representatives of the new power, they tried to take the government into their own hands. They wanted the Count d'Artois to come take over Paris without delay. The mere mention of a constitution drove them to fury, and they failed to see the point of playing charades with the Senate. De Vitrolles, back in Paris on April 2 after escaping his captors and traveling across France in various disguises, was indignant to find the Senate being given a role. Dalberg had to warn him to watch his words.

"Matters of state aren't accomplished with the heart," he told the impatient baron.

Talleyrand and his colleagues saw to it that ultraroyalists were shunted aside as much as possible and kept out of Alexander's sight. Government decrees seized the initiative from a group of young noblemen who were tearing down imperial emblems, trying to overturn Napoleon's statue in the Place Vendôme, opening prison doors, and papering walls with abusive proclamations that defamed Napoleon and his army. The provisional government took over these activities itself, but in an orderly manner and after issuing sanctioning decrees.

"Poor devils of legitimists," Chateaubriand complained, "we were shut out everywhere, we counted for nothing."

The extremists could not be completely suppressed. They were delirious to find the dreams they had dreamed alone echoed everywhere. They were intoxicated by their own voices, their own posters on the walls.

"We felt we were in an enchanted palace," one royalist wrote, "that what we saw was a mirage. Reading all these posters only increased our feeling of unreality. Time alone could convince us it was true."

Propaganda that bewitched the royalists was less enchanting to men of other persuasions. Louis XVIII's proclamation from Hartwell, issued February first and posted all over Paris by royalists after the Allies entered, belittled decorations won under Napoleon. In an effort to win over the Emperor's officers and soldiers, Louis offered them "rewards more real, distinctions more honorable than those they had received from a usurper." To avoid alienating the army, the provisional government was forced to deny the authenticity of the proclamation though it was completely genuine.

Chateaubriand's vituperative pamphlet *De Buonaparte et les Bourbons* was even more harmful. It was acclaimed with joy by royalists, who thought it a great asset to their cause. According to Pasquier, "It almost caused an explosion among the military we were trying to bring around, and whose support the foreigners regarded as the only possible foundation for a solid agreement."

Royalist posters accused Bonaparte of cowardice, of abandoning the throne he had been too incompetent to defend. The Allied declaration refusing to negotiate with him reduced him to the status of robber chief, they said, and pursued as he was by all the powers of Europe, even that role would not be his for long. They called him a Corsican tiger, a monster, disowned even by Corsica. One royalist newspaper carried matters so far as to speak of "the enemy army at Fontainebleau."

Fourteen of the sixty-four members of the Municipal Council assembled to publish one of the most violent attacks signed by any official body. After renouncing Napoleon and pledging loyalty to Louis XVIII, the council's poster excoriated Napoleon as the most oppressive tyrant the human race had known. Talleyrand did not object to diatribes against the Emperor in principle; it was a matter of timing. With such insults bandied about, how could he hope to win over waverers who were holding back out of loyalty to Napoleon? Talleyrand had the Municipal Council's posters taken down and refused to print the text in the *Moniteur* (though he failed to stop its appearance in the ultraroyalist *Journal des Débats*). Such violent language was premature on April 1, though the course of public opinion was changing fast, and that of its leaders even faster.

Calculated self-interest played a large part in that rapid change, but it was not the only factor. To understand what happened, one has to picture the upheavals and chaos of twenty-five years of revolution, crises, and almost continuous war. The empire had been hailed as a way out of the morass. When it collapsed and the imperial army that had seemed invincible was decimated, everyone was profoundly shaken. Illusions were shattered along with the empire. Even regicides, revolutionaries, and democrats began to suspect they might have been wrong. Many hurried to join the new order in self-protection, but others were groping for a new vision. In the chaos of April 1814, the idea of a reign that had lasted eight centuries was appealing. New illusions replaced old ones. The Bourbon rule was remembered as a time of peace and prosperity, while the revolution and empire became synonymous with terror and war.

The restoration was still an abstraction. People did not picture Louis XVIII on the throne. He was unknown. Instead, they thought of Henri IV, popularized in legend and song under the fetching nickname of *bon Henri*. They dreamed of rescue by a knight in shining armor, riding his white horse through the land, uniting it in peace and prosperity forever after. They were to be as astonished by the real Louis XVIII as Baron de Vitrolles had been on learning that far from being ready to ride through his kingdom, Louis was often so crippled by gout that he could neither walk nor mount a horse. For the moment, however, daydreams about *bon Henri* were irresistibly appealing after the disasters of the past two years.

"The feebleness, ambition, cowardice, and shortsightedness of men!" Caulaincourt exclaimed, but he did not give up. By turns deceived, outraged, indignant, and sad, on April 1 he continued his rounds despite the cold reaction he had met everywhere.

His first call was on Prince Schwarzenberg. Perhaps being in Paris had changed the prince's mind. Perhaps the Emperor of Austria or Metternich might be arriving with new orders, new views. The wait in the antechamber was long; the prince cold, dry, and above all embarrassed. He seemed astonished to find Caulaincourt still in Paris and suggested he prepare to leave. When the conversation was interrupted by a dispatch bearer, it was obvious, even to Caulaincourt, that Schwarzenberg was relieved.

Alexander admitted Caulaincourt more promptly, but warned him there was great pressure to send him on his way. The diplomat's presence was keeping some men from declaring themselves against the empire because they took it to be a sign the Allies might yet negotiate with Napoleon.

That, Caulaincourt said, was his hope. Once more, he marshaled every argument in favor of negotiations with Napoleon. The unshaken loyalty of the French army never failed to impress Alexander, and the onus of bringing on a civil war alarmed him. The Tsar was laying the grounds for revolution in France, not peace, Caulaincourt told him. The opinions he accepted as representing France were merely the views of Talleyrand's cohorts.

"Though I officially represent Napoleon," Caulaincourt concluded, "my views are those of every good Frenchman, of every man concerned with the welfare of France and Europe."

Alexander claimed that his mind was still open. The Allies were not going to be duped by intrigue or led by passions, he said, but they had learned Napoleon could not be trusted. If Napoleon remained on the throne, they would have to reduce his empire to a size that would limit his ambitions, and that would mean humiliating France and laying the grounds for new wars. Therefore no peace was possible with Napoleon; even Austria agreed.

Caulaincourt walked down one flight to Talleyrand's bedroom, where Talleyrand received him briefly and evasively. Leaving the bedroom by the salon, Caulaincourt found Pasquier, Dalberg, Jaucourt, the Archbishop of Malînes, and some fifteen other followers of Talleyrand. Caulaincourt wheeled on Pasquier and drew him to a window embrasure. He was insulted by Pasquier's having deceived him the morning before, he said. After their talk, he had counted Pasquier among Napoleon's supporters, and now he saw that Pasquier was on the enemy's side.

"I can explain, but this isn't the time or place," Pasquier began when he was interrupted by the archbishop, crossing the room with head high to challenge Caulaincourt.

"*Monsieur le duc,* go tell your master the stocks that dropped to 45 francs on the twenty-ninth have risen to 63."

"I will," said Caulaincourt, "and I'll also tell him that the man who was always the first to flatter him is the first to insult him today. At least there's some consistency in always being first."

Caulaincourt rushed at the archbishop with the intention, as he later confessed, of throwing the clergyman out the door or window, whichever came handiest, but others came between them.

Discouraged, but not without hope, Caulaincourt returned to his sister's house. Clinging to the few words the Tsar had said that indicated everything was not completely settled, Caulaincourt renewed his visits to key men in Paris, senators, legislators, and administrators.

"*Hélas!* I knocked at every door in vain. Even men who had held posts in the Emperor's household seemed to feel released from all obligation as his subjects. Fortune had abandoned the Emperor. Saddened, but all the more determined at finding myself alone in the lists, I redoubled my efforts. . . ."

Once again Caulaincourt returned to his sister's house. Pasquier came to explain that he had decided to join the Bourbon cause only after seeing the Allies and reassuring himself of their intentions toward France. By now, Caulaincourt could understand that only too well. What had swayed Pasquier had won over other prominent men less frank and honest. Every hour brought the loss of key men who might support a regency, if not Napoleon himself. Once men openly declared themselves against him, they rejected the regency as well for fear Napoleon might regain influence and punish them for their disloyalty. In twenty-four hours, Napoleon's cause would be lost in the capital, and the provinces would follow suit. Napoleon had foreseen it all clearly when he told Caulaincourt, "You don't know what can happen in such a short time, what the intrigues of a few traitors with foreign bayonets at hand can do in a city like Paris."

At 3:30 P.M., Talleyrand was at the Senate session to read the speech the Archbishop of Malînes had written. He read it badly, with a kind of indifference. He was a poor orator anyway. No one seemed to think the speech a good one, nor did it matter. Any senator likely to raise objections at that first session had been omitted from the list of invitations.

It was a peculiar session, more like a party than a senate meeting. The thirty senators present out of the seventy or more in Paris wore their usual official costume, but instead of sitting, they stood divided into small groups or gathered around the podium, talking among each other.

The Bourbon name, uppermost in everyone's mind, was not mentioned. After Talleyrand's nonchalant reading of appeals to their staunch and enlightened patriotism, the senators voted without discussion or opposition for the five-member provisional government headed by Talleyrand. Throughout the meeting, Talleyrand's emissaries scurried about Paris rounding up additional Senate votes. Editing the *procès-verbal* was postponed until 9 P.M., by which time 64 senators had been convinced to sign. Among them was de Pastoret, Secretary of the Senate, who had found it improper to attend the irregular afternoon session, but yielded to his colleagues' pressure to endorse the measure passed. Sixty-four votes was a minority of a senate of 140 members, but then, the entire procedure was illegal anyway. To cover abstentions, the announcement Talleyrand put in the *Moniteur* stated blandly that "senators unable to attend because of illness sent in their adhesions."

Talleyrand was president. It had taken him less than forty-eight hours to become officially as well as actually the most powerful man in France.

As he had expected, the Allies accepted the vote as the voice of the nation, or at least they said they did. That it was unanimous greatly impressed Emperor Alexander. It impressed others too, and the thin semblance of legality brought an ever-increasing flow of adherents. Some had doubts. Several senators who lingered over their doubts got together privately the night of April 1 and the following morning. While they found Senators Beurnonville and Jaucourt acceptable as members of the provisional government, they balked at de Montesquiou, a known Bourbon agent, and Dalberg, a German who had collaborated with the enemy. Nevertheless, the doubters voted with the rest. The moment they found themselves at the illegal Senate session, they felt there was no turning back. Step by step, the enthusiasts and the reluctant were drawn ahead, and what began as a hollow charade took on flesh and substance.

The unexpected calm of the city contributed greatly to Talleyrand's success by encouraging the conspirators and the Allies to move ahead quickly. Men who disagreed with Talleyrand's course grew more and more reluctant to compromise their futures by offending the party that was gaining ground every hour. Astonished at the influence accorded the invaders, confused by the rapidity of events, and terrified by the cataclysmic alternatives hanging over them, Napoleon's would-be supporters failed to act.

"They moaned softly in my presence," Caulaincourt wrote, "but made it clear I could hope for nothing from them. I found myself fighting alone for the Emperor and his dynasty."

Treason stalked the land with soft footfalls, masquerading as peace, as duty, and even as courage. Peace was a magic word. "Anyone who used it appeared divine," Caulaincourt wrote. "The population and the army were so tired of war that peace at any price became the real power of the day, and this power aligned itself entirely against Emperor Napoleon, who was still said to be the obstacle to peace.

"Intrigue knocked at the doors of the valiant in the name of the interests they valued most. The citizen was shaken, the general disarmed, the former aide-de-camp deceived. Men became ungrateful, then false, and finally traitors, perhaps in spite of themselves."

Only a battle won at the gates of Paris could save Napoleon, Caulaincourt concluded.

"The mass of Parisians were for him. His cannon would have won back plenty of friends, and those who had come out openly against him were still few. . . . As for the foreigners, the Emperor still represented such a formidable force in their eyes that it took the cowardice and treason of the entire administration and every prominent man, plus all the passion of a few like Talleyrand and Pozzo di Borgo to reassure the Allied sovereigns they would succeed. In those early days, the sovereigns felt they were sitting on a volcano."

Despite this conclusion, Caulaincourt was a diplomat first and warrior second. Besides, he was on a mission of negotiation. He decided to make one final effort before returning to Fontainebleau. Mounting Allied fears gave him hope. He knew the Allies must realize the outward calm of Paris was only a stupor, a momentary astonishment that would pass. He knew Alexander was capable of reversing his opinion if persuaded his interest lay elsewhere. He was aware that the arrival of Napoleon's army at Fontainebleau, unit by unit, hour by hour, was adding to Allied alarm. Everything indicated that Napoleon was preparing an attack. If the Allies had to leave Paris to fight him or to avoid a battle in the city itself, their future would become uncertain at best. The prospect of being caught between Napoleon's army and a city aroused against them chilled the staunchest Allied generals. Besides, the Allies did not want to continue the war, they wanted to spare their armies in case they had to fight each other afterward. Why risk everything? was the unspoken thought of many. Why not negotiate with Napoleon? Who cares who governs France so long as we make sure Napoleon's hands are tied?

Caulaincourt sensed these unspoken thoughts. While Talleyrand was out reading his indifferent speech to the Senate, Caulaincourt returned once again to Talleyrand's mansion to plead with Emperor Alexander. This time, Alexander was at his most affable. He spoke of Napoleon without personal resentment, expressed interest in his welfare, discussed everything without hesitation. Touched by Caulaincourt's loyalty, he took the diplomat's hands affectionately several times and urged him to calm himself.

If the Allies refused to tolerate Napoleon on the throne of France, they should support a regency rather than the restoration, Caulaincourt argued, provided Napoleon and the army would accept it. The regency would have a popular following, while the Bourbons had no supporters outside a handful of intriguers. By taking the intriguers' side, Alexander risked losing the glory he had won.

"Alexander seemed greatly shaken, even disposed in my favor," Caulaincourt wrote. "He told me, 'Don't despair, nothing is decided yet,' and a moment later, he added, 'Tomorrow I'll see you to give you a reply to take to Fontainebleau. Don't hope for too much, particularly for our agreeing to negotiate with the Emperor, for that could happen only if we demanded guarantees, fortresses in France, and other great sacrifices we believe it would be unwise to demand.'"

Caulaincourt paid attention only to the words that encouraged him: *Nothing was decided yet.*

Napoleon was as aware as Caulaincourt that his support diminished every hour. He also knew he had to fight or disappear. His thoughts were fixed on preparing his attack. Day and night he planned, issued orders, consolidated decimated units, called up local gendarmeries, and made new levies. He sent supplies and reinforcements to Melun and Essonnes, where the bridges he held over the Seine would cut off an Allied escape eastward. No detail was too small: the distribution of flour, *eau de vie*, hay; the baking of bread; the repair of saddles, boots, harnesses.

Statistics poured in on the status of regiments, battalions, infantry, cavalry, artillery, munitions. Army notebooks were brought up to date. Incoming dispatches confirmed the continued advance of the eastern garrisons and the spread of uprisings in Champagne, Burgundy, and Lorraine. As soon as the last of his troops arrived from the east, Napoleon would be ready to attack with at least 60,000 men. After trapping the

Allies between his forces and Paris, he would block their escape eastward at the Seine until the partisans and garrisons could join him to annihilate them. The Allies' immobility encouraged him to believe he could push them back to the wall quickly. It was a good plan, a feasible plan, one he longed to put into action. As troops arrived, he reviewed them with an inspired, thoughtful expression in the huge entrance courtyard at Fontainebleau Palace and sent them on north at once to their new positions.

On April 1, when Marmont came from advance headquarters to Fontainebleau for supper with Napoleon sometime between 2 and 3 A.M., Napoleon heard the full details of the battle for Paris for the first time. He praised Marmont heartily and lamented the lack of energy the government and Parisians had shown in defending the capital. At three, o'clock that afternoon, Napoleon returned the visit, reviewing Marmont's Sixth Corps at Essonnes. The review was splendid, the troops ardent. As always, their enthusiasm aroused Napoleon's optimism. The commanding general at Allied headquarters just across the Essonne River, on hearing drums, cavalry mounting, and loud cries of *Vive l'Empereur!*, thought he was about to be attacked.

There was bad news for Napoleon, however. Colonels Fabvier and Denys de Damrémont rode in from Paris with the requested reports on Allied forces and the news of Alexander's declaration that he would not deal with Napoleon or his family. Fabvier also brought a depressing tale of the welcome Paris had given the Allied occupiers. The cheers for the enemy and the white flags had been bad enough, but Fabvier had witnessed worse scenes, such as a crowd tearing the uniform off a French soldier in the heart of Paris. When Fabvier poured out his indignation to one of Napoleon's aides, the aide urged him to tell his story to the Emperor.

"I won't hold anything back if he asks," Fabvier replied. Five minutes later, an orderly came to bring him to Napoleon, who was on horseback, ready to leave for Fontainebleau. Fabvier rode beside him through Essonnes.

He was struck by the Emperor's serenity and consideration. Napoleon smiled reassuringly at Fabvier and urged him to simply tell what had happened minute by minute. The Emperor insisted on hearing every detail, every insult. He was so preoccupied that he often let his horse stop in front of a furrow or slight obstacle; then, instead of urging the animal on, he would reach over absent-mindedly to calm Fabvier's horse with his hand. His comments were mild.

"They are unhappy and the unhappy are unjust," he said of the

Parisians. He questioned Fabvier about the Bourbon movement, adding, "You're too young to know what a popular movement is." When Fabvier told him it was not the rabble, but young Parisians of society who had cried *Vive le Roi!* and distributed white cockades, Napoleon said, "They are émigrés who arrived with the enemy."

Fabvier answered that he had recognized several he had seen in Paris.

"Name them," the Emperor said, but Fabvier was reluctant. Napoleon did not insist except to say, "Sosthène de Larochefoucauld?"

"I didn't see him," Fabvier answered.

Napoleon changed the subject to the battle of Paris.

By the time he had asked a few questions and praised the troops, they had reached the road to Fontainebleau. Amiably he turned to Fabvier.

"Here is our road and there is yours. Adieu. Tell them you're not to be forgotten in the rewards accorded your army corps."

Fabvier never saw him again.

At Fontainebleau, Napoleon shut himself up with his maps and notebooks and reports once again. He sent couriers to Orléans to keep in touch with his government. He sent scouts to gather information on Allied movements. He dictated a series of orders for the review and dispatch of French troops scheduled to reach Fontainebleau on April 2. It was already clear that his army would not be completely assembled by that date. He issued new orders urging speed, had more guns, bread, and reinforcements sent to Essonnes, and wrote a reassuring bulletin to be carried to every part of the empire his couriers could reach:

> The occupation of the capital by the enemy is a misfortune His Majesty feels deeply, but it should be no cause for alarm. The presence of the Emperor at the gates of Paris with his army will prevent the enemy from indulging in his usual excesses in a city so large and so difficult for him to keep without rendering his position extremely dangerous.

As worsening news arrived from Paris, Napoleon was somber but determined. The Allies had good cause to worry.

VIII

THE TRUMPS ARE PLAYED
April 2, 3

To NAPOLEON, racing against time at Fontainebleau, the hours seemed too short. To Caulaincourt, awaiting his promised interview with Alexander in Paris, they dragged.

"How long the hours seemed! How could I hope for success when everyone was against me, French and foe alike! ... Words can't tell how much this thought added to my anguish and darkened my feeble hopes."

Caulaincourt's hopes were quickly dashed when the hour came. "Emperor Alexander's reception froze me ... my heart sank before he spoke.... No government would negotiate with Napoleon ... only his abdication could put an end to the war and the misfortunes of France ... my continued stay in Paris would no longer be tolerated, and in any case, there was nothing more for me to do.... Emperor Alexander could not receive me again until I was authorized to negotiate on the basis of Napoleon's abdication."

Negotiate for what? Alexander committed himself to nothing. No government would be imposed on France, he repeated, and once Napoleon was excluded, anything suited the Allies. First, Napoleon must be removed from any possibility of exercising influence on France or Europe. What of a regency? There, too, Caulaincourt could not get Alexander to commit himself. Let Napoleon abdicate unconditionally, then we'll see, was his stand. All he promised was that Napoleon would have a "suitable establishment."

"The Allies," Caulaincourt wrote, "felt sure enough of the course of events and the support of traitors to offer our Emperor an asylum, a handful of earth in some remote corner of the world, as if it were a favor. I rejected the Emperor's abdication as an insult to our honor."

He rejected it, perhaps, but he also discussed it at length with the Tsar. "Our situation was already so critical that I tried to clarify what Alexander meant by a suitable establishment," he explains. Austria was a possibility, Russia also.

"If he comes to Russia," said Alexander, "I will treat him as a sovereign." The island of Elba was mentioned for the first time. When he dismissed Caulaincourt, Alexander said, "Trust me and urge him to accept my offers. I'm a better friend of his than he thinks, and I'm your friend too. I like men who are faithful to duty."

Playing unwittingly into Talleyrand's hands, faithful Caulaincourt left for Fontainebleau, once more "with death in his heart." Talleyrand was glad to be rid of him. His presence in Paris froze everyone, and if he persuaded Napoleon to give up the throne voluntarily and unconditionally, the difficulties still facing Talleyrand would be more than half solved.

The Allies were worried. They saw their military position as untenable unless they could consolidate their political position. Deposing Napoleon and his family was a perilous course, one that required winning the support of Napoleon's government in Paris, of the people, and of the army. The first was easy. The Senate docilely voted Napoleon's deposition the evening of April 2. It was inevitable, since they had already excluded Napoleon's government by implication when they voted in the provisional government the day before. Late as it was, the Senate act of deposition was rushed to the newspapers. A few senators walked out on the session, but the vote was unanimous again. Alexander was impressed.

Getting the support of the people was proving more difficult. The explosion of popular sentiment against Napoleon and in favor of the Bourbons that the Allies had expected was simply not happening. To the contrary, the longer the Allies stayed, the less popular support they saw. The Parisians' initial relief at not being sacked had passed. They could now safely indulge in resentment at the incidents an idle occupation force was bound to provoke. Violent royalist propaganda was ruffling popular feelings. Anyone wearing a white cockade outside the center of Paris was insulted and roughed up, and the Allies had to prudently retract their request that the National Guard abandon the tricolor for the cockade. Some men were saying that Paris would not be in its current state if everyone had behaved like the commander of the chateau of

Vincennes, still holding out with his garrison of 400 men in the fortress just outside the city.

There were rumors that Napoleon was about to return with 300,000 men. More and more people blamed the Allies for delaying peace by refusing to deal with Napoleon. He was still Emperor for most, while Talleyrand's whist table goverment was a caricature. Popular cartoons were circulated of Talleyrand as *Prince Bien au vent* and *du Bonvent*, puns on his Napoleonic title Prince of Bénevent.*

Talleyrand had to keep reinforcing the Tsar's vacillating enthusiasm. He fêted him at dinner and went with him to the opera, where Alexander and the King of Prussia were acclaimed. On April 1, Talleyrand arranged for the Tsar to receive and congratulate the Senate immediately following the session at the Luxembourg Palace. A few senators balked at being presented to the enemy emperor, but Talleyrand ensured a large, imposing, and amiable audience by filling in the ranks of the absent with actors. Wearing the official senatorial dress, a gold-embroidered suit and coat lined in yellow silk, a lace cravat, white silk sash, white trousers, and a black, turned-up felt hat with gold cord and white feathers, the false senators were indistinguishable from the rest.

Tsar Alexander paraphrased his now familiar speech of being the friend of the French people and enchanted to find himself among them. His sole aim was to protect their decisions. As a generous afterthought, he announced that, following the resolutions the Senate had just taken, he had decided to grant the Senate what the provisional government had already requested of him, the return of all French prisoners in Russia. This was quite meaningless, being a normal consequence of peace, but the gesture filled the Senate with gratitude.

Talleyrand's chef Carême then gratified their appetites with a magnificent supper, at which Alexander rose, champagne in hand, to toast Louis XVIII. The senators drank under the impression it had somehow been settled with everyone else in advance that Louis XVIII would be king. Only afterward did they ask themselves and each other what had happened. Not that it mattered. As soon as the Senate was officially asked to confirm Louis XVIII as king, it did so without a murmur.

Napoleon's army remained the greatest danger to Talleyrand and

---

*The puns play on the words *vent* (wind) and *bene, bien,* and *bon* (well or good). Thus *Bien au vent* and *du Bonvent* meant *going with the prevailing wind.*

the Allies. Napoleon's officers were proving far less vulnerable than his officials.

"Until you have the army on your side, gentlemen, you have nothing," Alexander said. "In the end, the army will always overthrow everything set up against its will or even without its consent."

For two days, articles in Paris newspapers had appealed to the army to abandon a pointless war. A proclamation to the army, signed by all five members of the provisional government, appeared in the evening papers April 2 alongside the Senate act ending the empire. The proclamation was so vituperative that one wonders to whom Talleyrand left the wording of this one.

> You have never fought for the motherland. You can't go on fighting against her under the flag of the man who ravaged the country and delivered it, unarmed and defenseless, to the enemy . . . a man who isn't even French. . . . You are no longer Napoleon's soldiers. The Senate and all France release you from your orders.

Talleyrand's emissaries brought newspapers and copies of proclamations to officers of Napoleon's army at their posts south of Paris. Since Napoleon was legally deposed, loyalty to him was rebellion, they said. The only way for Napoleon's officers to win peace and preserve their ranks, pensions, and dignity, was to join their country's new government. The alternative was to be surrounded by 400,000 enemies and cut off to a man.

All military men who cooperated with the provisional government were given prominent billing. The appointment of General Dupont as minister of war was not of much help. His surrender to the Spanish at Bailén six years earlier had clouded an otherwise brilliant career. Senator General Beurnonville had been out of the active army too long to wield influence. General Dessole's appointment as head of the National Guard was more effective. His intermittent disfavor with Napoleon had made him willing to accept the appointment, while his unblemished and powerful reputation gave his acceptance great impact. General Ricard, who had fought valiantly with Marmont during the battle for Paris, joined Dessole as second in command.

The day the appointments were announced, General de Nansouty, who had commanded the Imperial Guard cavalry during the campaign and was in Paris recovering from battle wounds, announced his adherence to the new government and his support for the Bourbons.

All these officers were in Paris, however. It was Napoleon's army outside Paris that had to be undermined, and not by a meaningless trickle of isolated defections. Fabricated rumors of overtures made to the Paris government by Napoleon's marshals were useful only in Paris. What was needed was the real thing, the defection of a man highly placed, brave, famous, and known for long, loyal association with Napoleon. Someone prominent in his current military plans. A man whose defection would bring an army corps with it.

Talleyrand had chosen Napoleon's Brutus. Cynical as Napoleon was about human behavior, accurately as he had predicted what Caulaincourt would encounter in Paris, this blow would fall where Napoleon expected it least.

Napoleon spent most of April 2 closeted in his study at Fontainebleau, avoiding what Baron Fain called his "military family." The advice of his marshals and generals was unwelcome; their attitude discouraging. He emerged from isolation only to review arriving troops from the top of the horseshoe staircase leading into the massive front courtyard of the palace. His eyes lighted only at the *vivas* of his faithful soldiers.

Napoleon sent units out as quickly as they arrived. Most went to reinforce Marmont. General Souham's division, reviewed between 9 and 10 A.M., went to Essonnes. General Piré's light cavalry brigade, returning from the eastern border of France, was reviewed between ten and eleven and sent to Montceaux, a few miles south of Essonnes. Faithful General Sébastiani, who had been at Napoleon's side in every campaign, paraded his cavalry for Napoleon at the same hour before continuing to Pringy, four miles south of Montceaux, where he shortly received a horse regiment of gendarmes. Two other regiments, one infantry, one cavalry, went to St.-Germain-sur-Ecole on the road to Orléans.

The soldiers and the line officers commanding them were as lusty and loyal as ever, but inside the palace, the marshals' opposition to an attack on Paris continued to grow. Some saw it as a form of vengeance for the city's failure to hold out. They were ready to fight, they said, but on the Loire. The government was already there, the population was loyal, and the armies fighting on other fronts in France could join them quickly. A move to the Loire would draw the enemy farther inside France and make it more difficult for him to keep Paris.

Only to each other did they admit that they were afraid for their families in Paris. Only to themselves did they admit that they were tired and wanted at least a pause to regroup if this war must go on. And not even to each other did they admit they were afraid. Ney was called "the bravest of the brave." His marble calm under fire was the admiration of all. Oudinot was intoxicated by war and envied men who died in battle. They were all brave, vigorous men, reveling in feats of glory, but however fearless they were in battle, they were afraid of the bleak, dishonored, useless end they foresaw if they attacked Paris and lost.

While the news coming from Paris was bad for the empire, it proffered hope for immediate peace. Perhaps it was possible to avoid the catastrophe about to fall on them. Dissatisfaction was open, but it was not yet treason.

"The fall of the empire had become the object of every wish," Marshal Oudinot's wife wrote, "but each kept his reserve."

When Napoleon remarked at dinner with his staff on April 2 that he would abdicate if necessary to save France from civil war, his words fell on attentive ears. When Caulaincourt arrived in late evening with a similar theme and more bad news, his listeners began to speak out among themselves.

What Caulaincourt told Napoleon did not surprise him. "He listened impassively," Caulaincourt said, "as if these events, betrayals, and threats pertained to someone else. He looked and acted in disaster exactly as he had at the peak of his glory."

Napoleon talked at length, calling Caulaincourt back twice during the night for long, rambling conversations that touched on the Bourbons, the Allies, Paris intrigues, and the army. Napoleon repeated he would rather give up the throne than sign a humiliating peace.

"Talleyrand is right," he said. "Only the Bourbons can bow to a peace dictated by Cossacks. They can endorse the nation's humiliation because they have nothing to lose. They would find France just as they left it. They suit Alexander perfectly."

Napoleon still hoped Emperor Francis might step in to salvage matters. He refused to believe the Austrian Emperor would be duped into removing his daughter from the French throne and allowing Russia the upper hand. Austria had always been afraid of Russia's dominating Europe. Napoleon wrote Marie-Louise to make another appeal to Papa François. Time might be gained, if nothing else.

As for his government in Paris, Napoleon criticized both those who had left and those who had stayed. That Talleyrand should be leading the party against him, he found quite natural.

"It's legitimate vengeance," he said. "I treated him badly and I was wrong not to put him in prison before I left, after abusing him as I did . . . but if he manages to restore the Bourbons, it's they who'll avenge me at his expense one day."

Who else was in the plot with Talleyrand? Ah, Alexander, of course. How ungrateful! "If I'd freed Poland and the serfs, Alexander wouldn't be in Paris today!" The other sovereigns were ingrates too, trying to overthrow him when he had left them on their thrones. "I could have deposed the King of Prussia. . . . I could have deposed my father-in-law. I could have freed Hungary. . . ."

As for his marshals, Napoleon believed their fears and fatigue would vanish the moment they faced the enemy. They would fight as well as ever, for honor and glory. The problem was only to have that battle soon.

"No one abandons the fight on the eve of the battle," Napoleon said, "but there's no time to lose. Forty-eight hours from now, I might be unable to keep things going."

Had he had all his troops, he would have attacked at once, but Macdonald would not be in position until the following afternoon, the third of April, at the earliest. That put the attack off until at least the fourth. He would address the troops and his Guard again at noon on the third, Napoleon told Caulaincourt. When he roused his "old mustaches," everyone would recover his spirits.

Caulaincourt, as usual, saw his duty in the pursuit of the negative. According to his own account, he made every effort to be as discouraging as possible. Schwarzenberg's cold reception had convinced him there was nothing to hope for from the Austrian Emperor. He harped on what Napoleon already knew without offering a solution. Contact with Paris was contaminating the army, he said; there was no time to lose.

"Napoleon was still lulling himself with hopes and spinning illusions which only my rigorous sense of duty brought me to destroy in that cruel moment," Caulaincourt wrote in his memoirs. "I did my duty as I had to, and I noticed he began to view more seriously than before not only the difficulties of his situation, but all the consequences it might have. . . . What concerned him most was the humiliation of France, the country he had wanted to make so great, so powerful. That, and the army. His own fate hardly entered the picture. When I forced him to speak of himself, he said, 'Six feet are enough for a man.' "

April 3

Napoleon was not buried yet. At 3 A.M. on April 3, he was dictating. Still hoping to have enough units in position to be able to attack on the fourth, he announced that General Headquarters would move that night to the chateau of Tilly, at Ponthierry, twenty-eight miles south of Paris. Only Oudinot's and Macdonald's troops had yet to arrive at Fontainebleau. Impatiently, Napoleon sent Macdonald orders to quicken his march and to warn him, "We may be fighting."

The Allies were on the move too. April 2 and 3, Allied units camping north of Paris marched through the city from morning till late afternoon, hurrying south. The cavalry of all the Allied nations clattered and rumbled across Paris for hours on the third, each regiment with formidable artillery, a large number of reserve horses, and vehicles of all sorts. When the Parisians saw the foreigners on the march, they came out of their houses with serious faces. Concern replaced the curiosity they had shown at Allied parades.

Schwarzenberg left only his guards and reserves in Paris. His orders of April 3 anticipated a surprise attack at any of three points: on the road to Fontainebleau; west of that, on the road to Orléans; or east of it, if the French crossed the Seine to the right bank. All bridges were guarded. Everyone was on the alert.

"Focus all your attention and use every means to ensure being informed the moment the enemy moves," Schwarzenberg's orders read.

Tension was high. There was one alarm. Napoleon was sighted on horseback a few leagues from Paris, but he was only reviewing his advance troops behind the Essonne River.

Paris had become unpleasantly aware that the war was still on and the victor undecided. The Allies were still fighting in the north, east, south, and southwest of France, and in Italy.

"Our affairs are highly promising in France," Foreign Minister Lord Castlereagh wrote on April 3, "but whilst Buonaparte can call himself Emperor and has half the fortresses of Europe in his hands, we can in wisdom risk no relaxation or diminution of strength in any quarter."

The Allies were so afraid of a battle for Paris that they were planning a withdrawal to Meaux. Orders to withdraw were ready to be sent, though they were kept secret to avoid alarming the provisional government and its supporters. The secrecy was so successful that even long after, police chief Pasquier not only did not know that orders had been prepared, but insisted it was impossible. He knew, however, how terrified the Allies were of fighting Napoleon over Paris, and he assumed the Allies would lose. He had voiced his fears to Dalberg at Talleyrand's house the morning of the second.

"When generals in their position, with their numerical superiority, are so obviously afraid of the army they're about to fight, how can one help anticipating a resounding defeat?"

"You're right," Dalberg said. "That's why we're seeking other guarantees of security."

"And where do you expect to find them?"

"Measures have already been taken. We're going to try to eliminate the risk of losing the battle."

"He then explained to me," Pasquier wrote afterward, "that a certain number of determined individuals, led, as he put it, by an energetic bastard, would put on uniforms of *chasseurs de la garde* taken from stores in the Ecole Militaire, and either before or during the action, get close to Napoleon and free France of him. My indignant expression kept him from giving me any more information despite my efforts.... All he would say when I asked him where men capable of such a deed were to be found, was, 'That's easy enough. We have them in every color. Chouans, Jacobins, etc. ...' "

Pasquier went home, dismayed. He had barely sat down at his desk when he received a note from de La Valette, obviously written in great haste.

> I know how incapable you are of being involved in the infamous plot afoot to kill the Emperor. Perhaps you're not even aware of it. That's why I'm warning you, certain you'll do everything in your power to foil it.

For de La Valette to have found out about it, the plot must be well advanced, Pasquier thought. Another warning arrived almost simultaneously from a police inspector in whom Pasquier had great confidence. Again, no details.

"It was one of the most painful positions I've ever been in," Pasquier wrote, "I was entrusted with the secret, but had few details and no names. How was I to prevent this horrible coup? There were traps everywhere. The most faithful risked being accused of treason."

Pasquier was still anxious and undecided at midnight when a French soldier arrived from Fontainebleau in disguise with a note hidden in a knife handle. Pasquier recognized the writing of Secretary of State Maret. The short message was from Napoleon: "Can I count on you?"

Pasquier decided to show it to Talleyrand and get his approval of the reply. Dalberg was present when Pasquier consulted Talleyrand the morning of the third and, oddly enough, also approved his warning Napoleon. Pasquier gave Napoleon the latest news, including the deposition by the Senate, the pending deposition by the legislature that noon, the release of the French army from its oath, and General Nansouty's declaration of support for the provisional government. He described the "remarkable animation" of the National Guard under its new commander. He warned Napoleon that there were various plots against him, and prominent bankers were offering twelve million for his head.

"Don't count on me for anything more," he concluded. "What I shall do should be clear from what I have done."

At Fontainebleau, Maret grimaced on reading the reply in the presence of the Count of Plancy, the loyal Prefect of the Department of Seine-et-Marne, who had just come to consult on the defense of Melun. A town of 7000 on the Seine southeast of Paris and near Marmont's advance headquarters, Melun was vital to the impending attack. Before leaving, Plancy had left orders for the bridges over the Seine in the middle of town to be destroyed if the enemy approached in his absence. Melun would be cut in half, but the enemy could be blocked from continuing south toward Fontainebleau.

When Plancy arrived at the palace, Napoleon was having lunch with Marshal Berthier. The Emperor was holding a leg of lamb in the air in his right hand while cutting off the entire skin around it with his left. Plancy was astonished to find the Emperor eating so heartily when he had "reason to be troubled and anxious at the least," but what surprised him most was the subject of the conversation. Hat under his arm, sword at his side, Plancy stood respectfully in front of the Emperor, ready to listen with the greatest attention to the grave matters he assumed were being discussed. Instead, Napoleon and Berthier spent lunch talking of an old love affair of Prince Eugène de Beauharnais with La Bigottini, a pretty dancer at the opera, whom all the officers had known. The officer serving the Emperor supplied some details for Napoleon, who joined jovially in the conversation.

As the Emperor left the table for his study, he gave Plancy a friendly slap on the cheek, a sign of high spirits and approval.

"You're in favor, Plancy!" the officer on duty said laughing.

"It's a little late," Plancy answered, and asked to be given an audience with the Emperor as soon as possible. He was told he would be received as soon as Marshal Lefebvre, then in conference with Napoleon, had left.

Plancy wanted to present a plan to win back the empire. If all France had responded like the Department of Seine-et-Marne, the enemy would never have gotten a foothold, he believed, and the Allies could still be driven out with the Seine-et-Marne as a base.

Plancy wanted Napoleon to march on Paris at once with the forces at hand after announcing rewards for every man taking part, bonuses for every soldier, a rise in grade for every officer, and promotion to vice-marshal for the first twelve superior officers to establish and maintain themselves in Paris. Simultaneously, all prefects would order mass levies in their departments, towns would be transformed into strongholds, roads would be barricaded, and bridges cut. The tocsin would ring day and night to call all France to arms.

The plan was far less ridiculous than it might sound, Plancy believed: it was far less desperate, for example, than the Russians' successful tactic of burning down Moscow.

"I could have transformed my entire territory into an immense, unassailable stronghold in one gallop," Plancy wrote afterward. "The 50,000 well-organized national guardsmen of my department would have launched the movement.... We were in a devil of a fix if three million men who took over the roads and turned their houses into fortresses couldn't drive 200,000 foreign soldiers out of France."

Marshal Lefebvre left. Plancy first gave the Emperor news from Paris he had received by letter. He then made the mistake of asking Napoleon if he was sure of all the marshals and generals around him. Questioned, Plancy elaborated. He had heard one of Napoleon's marshals make light of serious matters in the course of a dinner in a way that seemed to find an echo among the many superior officers present. He had also heard one of the bravest officers in the army, a general, speak ironically and sarcastically about the war.

"I am afraid, Sire, that men may be weary and tired of war," Plancy concluded.

Napoleon frowned. He demanded names. Plancy demurred. The facts were not grave enough to justify his compromising anyone. He did not know the men well enough to judge their true intentions from casual remarks. Napoleon insisted, striding vigorously around the room. "Speak!" he ordered at last, stopping in front of Plancy, who blurted the name of a high-ranking general.

"Bah!" the Emperor said. "He's a troublemaker, a grumbler who always says anything that goes through his head, but he's one of the best and bravest officers in the army."

There was a moment's silence. Abruptly, Napoleon left his study. Plancy waited, eager to present his plan, but he had lost his chance. Napoleon had gone—gone, he later learned, to order the general's arrest. Events moved too quickly for the man to be found, and too quickly for Plancy to propose his plan. The drums were already beating for Napoleon's noon review of the Guard.

Plancy left the study to join the generals surrounding the Emperor on the stone balcony overlooking the courtyard. The courtyard was filled with waiting troops, the Old Guard on one side, the Young Guard on the other. Drums rolled, arms were presented. The men around the Emperor, Caulaincourt in particular, had long faces. While his staff stayed on the balcony, Napoleon, followed only by Berthier and three other officers, walked down the horseshoe staircase and passed among the troops to review them unit by unit. Napoleon looked a little agitated, one of his officers said. He stopped often, addressed the soldiers, read all the requests they presented, and granted medals to most of those who asked for them. At last, realizing the number was too great to pass in such detail, he began referring them to two of his generals. He often asked the soldiers their age and seemed to be assuring himself of their strength and good will. At the end of the review, the Emperor placed himself in the middle of the courtyard and called the officers and subordinates of the second regiment around him.

"We formed a circle around His Majesty," wrote General Pelet, commander of a brigade of the Old Guard. "He was rather flushed, his eyes a little enlarged, his hat a bit askew, his head raised and turned slightly to the right. He spoke in a loud, animated voice, more or less in these words:

" 'Officers, subordinates, and soldiers of the Old Guard! The enemy has stolen three marches on us. He is in Paris. I sent Emperor Alexander an offer of peace at great sacrifice on our part. France would be reduced to its old borders. We would renounce all our conquests, lose all we've won since the Revolution. He not only refused, he went beyond that. Through treacherous suggestions to émigrés whose lives I spared and whom I've covered with benefits, he authorized the wearing of the white cockade. He'll soon try to substitute it for our national colors. In a few days, I shall go attack him in Paris. I count on you'—There was silence. 'Am I right?'—A thunder of cries burst. '*Vive l'Empereur! Vive l'Empereur! To Paris! To Paris!*' "

The men had been silent at first because they thought it superfluous to answer, Pelet explained in his record of the event. Napoleon continued.

"We'll show them the French nation is master of its fate. If we've been master of others for so long, we shall always be master of ourselves. We can defend our colors, our independence, and the integrity of our territory!"

Swearing to conquer or die, the officers moved off to repeat Napoleon's words to the troops. The *Marseillaise* played, the troops shouted deliriously. Napoleon turned back to the palace with a glowing face.

The sight of his staff on the balcony sobered him at once. All animation in his face died as he entered the palace. He would have it out with them, he decided, inviting his staff into his study. They were discouraged and disillusioned, but not disobedient. Just half a year earlier, before the battle of Leipzig, his generals had dared to hold a secret council and send Berthier and another officer to tell him the battle should not be fought because the enemy's forces were too great and the French troops too demoralized. Napoleon's response then had been withering. This time he would seize the initiative.

As his generals stood before him in timid, if resentful, respect, Napoleon spoke of the danger of being duped by the Allies. The Allies had won by deceit what they had been unable to get by fighting, but they could be defeated in battle. That was the only way to save France, Napoleon assured them. He would gladly give up the throne if that would serve the country, but his abdicating in favor of his son would not work. The Allies had no intention of allowing a regency in France. They dangled the idea before the French only to lure them into a trap.

Quickly, Napoleon moved on to the subject of intrigues on behalf of a Bourbon restoration, a subject on which the marshals were all vehemently united. Ney was particularly emotional. Only the empire could guarantee his future, his children's future, and that of any man who had been through the Revolution, he said. "The Bourbons and their courtiers would lose no time in letting my children know their father was nothing but a peasant." There the discussion ended for the moment.

"My marshals and many of my generals have lost their heads," Napoleon said to Caulaincourt afterward. "They can't see there's no army without me, and without an army, no security for them. . . . They're throwing themselves into the lion's mouth. They didn't say anything, but I could see they favor my abdicating. They think they'll just be exchanging one man for another. The imbeciles don't see that France's future and theirs lies with me. . . . My son can't guarantee them a thing. . . ."

He could pull his generals back under his control, Napoleon thought. Men were pawns, their doubts and hesitations weaknesses he had always turned to his advantage. In any case, as soon as they started fighting, they would stop thinking.

"I'm going to fight," he told Caulaincourt. "The Parisians are sure to back me. . . . What's happening now is just the work of fifty traitors. The Senate deposition won't mean a thing if I push the enemy back fifty leagues."

Unfortunately, no battle was possible before all the army arrived, and the marshals and generals were fast slipping away from Napoleon's sway. If Napoleon is wrong, who is right? they began to ask themselves. As they agonized over that question, they became ready to play into Talleyrand's hands, just as the Senate had.

On April 3, the rump Senate dutifully completed the revolution it believed it was leading. Convened at noon, by 4 P.M. it had approved a virulent list of accusations against Napoleon, to be published as a preamble justifying the act of deposition. Napoleon was accused of abrogating the people's rights, making war illegally, depriving his ministers of responsibility, depriving the press of liberty, refusing honorable peace terms, and abandoning Paris. He was held responsible for the ruin of cities, depopulation of the country, and spread of contagious diseases and famine. That same day, the Legislative Corps, with fewer than 80 of its 380 members present, voted for the deposition and imitated the Senate in proceeding to pay homage to Emperor Alexander and the King of Prussia. Napoleon's government had destroyed Napoleon's government.

That night, the decree of the provisional government declaring Napoleon dethroned was read in all public places. There were cries of

"Down with the tyrant!" and *"Vive* Louis XVIII!" The texts of decrees and propaganda of all sorts covered the walls. Allied placards told their soldiers, "From this moment, the French are our friends. Let your arms destroy the few unfortunates still clinging to ambitious Napoleon, but treat the farmer and peaceful inhabitant of the towns with consideration and friendship." French placards praised the Allied monarchs for having answered the wishes of the French nation by embarking on "a holy crusade against the monster Napoleon."

While evening crowds pressed around the proclamations posted in the streets, twenty-five French political figures crowded into one of the small rooms on Talleyrand's entresol to hear the draft of the new French constitution. In Talleyrand's plan, the constitutional draft would prepare the senators to accept the King it was designed for without actually mentioning him. The overall concept was astute. In the details, which probably bored him, Talleyrand was less clever. He had left the drafting of the constitution to old Archtreasurer Lebrun. It was a logical choice. Lebrun had the prestige of his position, a long respectable record of government work, and a good reputation as a writer. Among those gathered to hear Lebrun's draft were Pozzo di Borgo for the Allies, the five members of the provisional government, the Paris National Guard commander, General Dessole, a number of senators, and Pasquier. Pasquier described the scene in detail.

When everyone was seated as well as possible in the tiny room, Talleyrand took the floor. Lebrun had graciously accepted taking on this preparatory work, he said, and, coming from a man so enlightened and profoundly versed in these difficult matters, his work would no doubt shorten the task and light the way for ensuing discussion.

Pulling a handsome volume bound in red leather out of his pocket with great difficulty, Lebrun said in his bantering, surly voice, "Messieurs, as you will see, my task didn't cost me much effort. I found it already done. I didn't have to reflect long to be convinced I wouldn't do better by working hard, and probably not as well. Believe me, it's never too late to go back to an indisputably good thing." With those words, he laid the handsome red volume on the table. It turned out to be the constitution of 1791.

His audience exchanged glances of mute stupefaction. The most discomfited was Talleyrand, but he quickly and tactfully let Lebrun know how mistaken he was. After praising the merits of parts of the 1791 constitution, Talleyrand showed how inapplicable it was to present circumstances.

Seizing on the point on which he was most certain of being understood, he said, "For example, there is but one legislative body, one house in this constitution. We need two. We have a Senate we cannot get along without. . . . What we need," he concluded, "is a declaration of principles, a solid framework to which details can be added later." Everyone applauded this way of bringing the question back into proper perspective.

Cleverly, Talleyrand gave the impression of considering the Bourbon restoration so inevitable that he only mentioned Louis XVIII at the end of his speech, as if taking advantage of a natural occasion to praise the King about to be crowned.

"We must bear in mind, Messieurs, that the constitution you will be making will be judged by a man of superior intelligence. The prince who must accept it and give it life, the prince it must support, will be its best critic. . . . He will be in a position to discuss everything that should enter into a wisely moderate constitution article by article, and perhaps better than any of us. We would do poorly to offer such a prince a weakly conceived work that would satisfy neither his strong mind nor his lofty views. Consequently, we must do it well and above all avoid losing ourselves in details."

Talleyrand could not have presented the new King more persuasively. Every quality that would enhance his image was mentioned. He was strong, enlightened, skilled in constitutional matters, had high principles and good judgment. Furthermore, Talleyrand conveyed the message that it was best to avoid details and get a constitution written. No time was wasted. The draft was in final form the following day, complete with Article Two, which read, "the people of France call Louis-Stanislas-Xavier to the throne of France." The draft was adopted unanimously by the Senate two days later.

So much for the constitution. And yet, like Napoleon, Talleyrand knew that all this was meaningless if the Allies were pushed back fifty leagues.

Talleyrand advanced his trump card that night as Napoleon advanced his loyal guard. Their destinations were the same: Essonnes. The fate of France, and of the two men struggling to control its future, was about to be decided.

As Napoleon suspected, Talleyrand was trying to establish contact at imperial advance headquarters at Essonnes. His emissary, disguised as a Cossack and bearing a proposal from Schwarzenberg, crossed the lines the afternoon of April 3. How amusing it had been to fix him up, complete with baggy trousers and knout! "I'll always remember how extraordinary he looked in that disguise," Pasquier recalled.

The emissary was Charles de Montessuis, aide-de-camp to Marmont for six years, turned civilian, financier, and royalist. He brought Marmont letters from Bourrienne, Pasquier, General Dessole, and Prince Schwarzenberg, along with copies of current newspapers and the latest decrees, including the act of deposition and the release of the army from its oath. Last but not least, he brought strong arguments from his briefing by Talleyrand and Nesselrode the night before.

Only the provisional government could rescue France from occupation and prevent civil war, de Montessuis told Marmont. The leaders of the provisional government urged Marmont, as a well-known patriot and famous warrior, to set the army a courageous example by rallying to their cause and leading his corps to their side. Marmont had been chosen, de Montessuis explained, because he, of all the marshals, was the only one politically sophisticated enough to understand the situation. In agreeing, Marmont would merely be obeying the Senate, which had released him from his oath of loyalty to Napoleon. He and his troops would be sent to Normandy, a province untouched by war, where he could preserve his Sixth Corps intact for France. He would soon have more than a corps under his command, however. His troops would be the nucleus that others would join. Under his leadership, a new army would form that would give the new government the strength to negotiate with the Allies to France's best advantage.

If Marmont refused, de Montessuis's argument continued, no one could predict the magnitude of the disaster that would follow. France would be ruined, and her soldiers would have fought and died in vain. The path of true patriotism lay in bringing a rapid end to the crisis. The power to do so lay in Marmont's hands. If he used it, he would earn the nation's eternal gratitude.

The afternoon of April 3, Marmont's aide Colonel Fabvier saw his chief talking to a bald-headed civilian in the garden of the chateau in which the marshal had established his headquarters. The civilian was, of course, de Montessuis, who had shed his Cossack disguise after crossing Allied lines. After his visitor left, Marmont told Fabvier of the proposal and asked how he should respond. By hanging the man, Fabvier answered.

For Fabvier, the matter ended there, but Marmont continued to think about what de Montessuis had said. Talleyrand had chosen his target well. As commander of the Sixth Corps at Napoleon's advance headquarters, Marmont's position was vital. If the Sixth Corps defected, Napoleon was unlikely to be able to continue the war. The Emperor's confidence in Marmont and Marmont's isolation from Fontainebleau made it easy to approach him without arousing suspicion, while Marmont's character and his recent difficulties with Napoleon made him susceptible to an approach.

Marmont was still bitter over Napoleon's tongue lashing for his errors at Laon. He was sensitive about having had to assume the unpopular duty of arranging the capitulation of Paris. He was always getting the worst assignments, always being sacrificed. He and Napoleon had been junior officers together. If Napoleon was emperor, it was just luck, not his superiority. Luck and Marmont's stepping aside. It was time he had a greater part on the world stage for himself, Marmont thought. His vanity and ambition were not satisfied by his present role, and defeat followed by exile or partisan warfare was hardly a tempting future. All one had to do to win Marmont was to woo him with the prospect of becoming a national leader, and this is what Talleyrand and Nesselrode had briefed Charles de Montessuis to do.

Marmont was flattered to be the first approached by the provisional government to reconcile the army with the people. He was swayed by the letters de Montessuis brought from old friends he liked and respected, impressed by the views he read in the newspapers. He was moved by the appeal to his courage to make this sacrifice for the good of his country. The vision of himself as savior of France and commander of the new army was irresistible. He had already been influenced by Talleyrand, by the sentiments Parisians expressed at his house on the thirtieth, and by Fabvier's accounts of the Allies' reception in Paris. It was a time in which an honest man could have one opinion at Fontainebleau and another at Paris. Marmont was halfway in between.

IX

BETRAYAL

April 4

MARMONT AGONIZED through the night. "It is hard to express the crowd of emotions this news brought me," he wrote in his memoirs. "Attached to Napoleon for so long, I felt my old affection for him aroused by his misfortunes, the affection that once dominated all other feelings. Yet, being devoted to my country and finding myself in a position to influence its destiny, I felt I had to save it from ruin. . . . Happy are those who live under a stable government or have an obscure position in which they never face such a cruel dilemma. They can't judge that situation without having lived it. It is easy for a man of honor to do his duty when it is clearly marked, but how cruel to live in a time when one can and must ask oneself where duty lies.

"On the one hand, I foresaw the fall of Napoleon, a friend, a benefactor. His fall was certain no matter what happened because we had no means of defense left and no hope of support with public opinion in Paris and a large part of France against us. He might win a brief delay, but he would soon fall and bring the country down with him. Hadn't he boasted he would bury the world beneath his ruin? But if France separated herself from Napoleon and took the sovereigns at their word, couldn't she force them to respect her? Couldn't one look upon the changes in public opinion and the Senate's decrees as the lifeline that could save the country from complete shipwreck?"

And what of Napoleon, Emperor, commander, companion of his youth? What was happening was Napoleon's fault.

"He alone dug the abyss that was swallowing us. What efforts we had made, I, more than any man, to keep him from falling into it!"

227

What of his debt to Napoleon? His dukedom, wealth, marshal's baton? The Emperor had not given him much compared to others, he reasoned.

"When he finally made me a marshal, wasn't he simply giving me my due? I don't have to feel any great gratitude, and as for the chance to enjoy the pleasures of court life, I have only to say that during the ten years of the empire, I spent all of six weeks in Paris in visits of two weeks each."

There remained the tie of friendship.

"Napoleon was probably the person I loved most in my life, but when I saw this great genius fading . . . indifferent to France's interest or his soldiers' lives, my heart, which had already cooled, was turned to ice."

The duty of an officer to his commander?

"Hadn't I more than fulfilled my duties toward him? Shouldn't the country have its turn and hadn't the moment for it come? Aren't there circumstances in which a man of pure and honest character ought to rise above all common considerations to embrace new obligations? . . . In my inner struggle, I leaned toward the revolution in Paris."

Later, Marmont recalled a prophetic conversation he had had with Napoleon in the early-morning hours before the battle at Leipzig in the fall of 1813. One of the many subjects touched on in the four-hour conversation was the distinction Napoleon drew between what he called a man of honor and a man of conscience. Napoleon preferred the former. One could count on him to keep his word and his engagements, while the man of conscience would consult his own judgment.

"Take you, for example," Napoleon had said. "If the enemy had invaded France and was on the heights of Montmartre, and you believed, even correctly, that the salvation of the country dictated your abandoning me, and you did so, you would be a good Frenchman, a good man, a man of conscience, and not a man of honor."

Sometime during the night of April 3, Marmont decided to lead his corps to the side of the provisional government. He wrote two letters explaining his motives. One, never sent, was to Napoleon:

"I devote myself to France in taking an action my heart condemns, but the future of my country demands. I must leave your ranks on the day the nation rejects you, but after saving the motherland, I am ready to bring you my head if you ask for it!"

The second letter, sent the fourth of April, was Marmont's reply to Schwarzenberg's proposal:

"The people and the army having been released from the oath of loyalty to Emperor Napoleon by the Senate decree, I am ready to agree to a rapprochement between the army and the people to prevent civil war and put an end to bloodshed. Consequently, I am ready to leave with my troops. . . ."

His only condition was a promise that the troops be allowed to go to Normandy freely, fully armed and equipped, and that if, in the hazards of war, Napoleon should fall into Allied hands, his life and liberty would be guaranteed in a place to be chosen by the Allies and the French government.

The morning of the fourth, Marmont worked out the details of the defection and secured the cooperation of a few select members of his staff, including his senior officer, General Souham.

While Marmont was struggling with his conscience through the night of April 3 and wondering where the path of duty lay, Napoleon's loyal guardsmen were marching on the path of duty they never questioned, toward Essonnes and almost certain death. They were tired, but their fatigue, unlike the marshals', was purely physical. A good meal, an hour's sleep, and they were ready for anything again. Even if they had heard talk that Napoleon was to blame for the war, they would never abandon him. Abandon Napoleon? Napoleon, who would ride through the ranks under fire calling, "Unfurl those colors! The moment is here at last!"? Napoleon, who led the charge that reversed the rout at Arcis? Napoleon, who was always in the thick of the fight during the day and who rode through their camp each night to see for himself that his men had what they needed? The rank and file, the subordinate officers, the officers leading the ranks were as loyal as ever.

Napoleon's Guard, the most fiercely devoted of all, marched by moonlight in a silent column through the imperial forest of gigantic oaks. All was still, except for the muffled sound of cannon rolling, the regular tramp of footsteps, the rattling of sabers and bayonets. The soldiers were grave, somber-faced, thinking of the oath they had sworn to fight or die, determined to end their military careers beside the walls of Paris or under its ruins. They marched with sublime devotion, a devotion the despair of their leaders was to render useless.

April 4 was the last day of the campaign of France, but it was Talleyrand's words, not Napoleon's bullets, that ended the struggle. The Allies' all-night alert against an attack was lifted the morning of the fourth after Schwarzenberg completed arrangements for Marmont to lead his troops to Versailles that night. Orders readied for the evacuation of Paris were canceled, just as they were about to be sent. The provisional government and the Senate were twittering with joy.

Talleyrand seemed to have won. Before another twenty-four hours passed, his adversary would find himself deprived of his advance guard and 12,000 of his best soldiers. The defection was certain to undermine army morale and bring a new wave of adherents to the provisional government. Alexander's fear of the French army vanished along with his growing doubts about the degree of popular support his French advisers and their program enjoyed. If the army was half won, the battle was over. It was time to send for the Count d'Artois.

Baron de Vitrolles was once again Talleyrand's messenger, but this time the baron saw Talleyrand in person. When de Vitrolles called at 10 A.M. on April 4, Talleyrand was still in bed. It was not unusual for men as important as Talleyrand to receive in bed. Beds were warm, rooms cold. One of the privileges of the privileged was remaining in bed while lesser men attended, shivering, in the barely heated chamber.

Details were quickly settled for the Count d' Artois's arrival and reception in Paris as lieutenant general of France pending the coronation of his brother as Louis XVIII. De Vitrolles wrote everything down beside Talleyrand's bedside, making two copies, one to take and one to leave with Talleyrand. There was no disagreement, at least in de Vitrolles's mind, that the so-called constitution the foolish senators were to approve would not be allowed to limit the new King's powers.

Like many others, de Vitrolles was so distracted by the confusion in which Talleyrand operated that he failed to see that Talleyrand and his provisional government were doing anything at all. "It was difficult," de Vitrolles later wrote, "to get an idea of what the provisional government was. The entire thing was contained in Talleyrand's bedroom on the entresol of his mansion. A few clerks, assembled under the direction of Dupont de Nemours, the last and best of economists, formed the office, with Roux de Laborie as assistant secretary. M. de Talleyrand's bedroom was open to everyone he knew, men and women, and the conversations of the crowds entering and leaving constituted the deliberations on affairs of state.

"Some more or less witty articles for the newspapers were the main bit of work, under the heading of forming public opinion. Aside from that, if an idea that happened to please Prince de Talleyrand crossed the mind of one of those coming and going, he made it into a decree which the other government members signed in blind faith when they took their turn in paying a visit to their president."

When the baron rose with the intention of leaving at once for Nancy, Talleyrand announced he wished to give him a personal letter for the count that would not be ready until midafternoon.

"Ask *M. le Comte d'Artois* if he remembers our rendezvous at Marly," Talleyrand said, and with a show of indifference, he told of that last meeting. The story, which de Vitrolles later verified, completely cleared Talleyrand of any guilt vis-à-vis the Bourbons during the Revolution.

The date was June 16, 1789, two days after the fall of the Bastille. Louis XVI was still on his throne, but the country was heading for full-scale revolution. With two companions, Talleyrand made a secret midnight trip to the royal chateau at Marly to see the King. Louis XVI refused to receive them, but authorized his brother, the Count d'Artois, to act for him. For two hours, Talleyrand and his colleagues pleaded for the King to use force to repress the rebellion before it exploded. They had a plan and were willing to accept all responsibility and risks. It was no use.

"As for me," the count said, "I have made my decision. I leave France tomorrow morning."

"In that case, Monseigneur," said Talleyrand, "since the King and the princes are abandoning their interests and those of the monarchy, we have no choice but to look out for our own."

"That is what I advise you to do," said d'Artois. "Whatever happens, I shall not blame you, and you can always count on my friendship."

While waiting for Talleyrand's letter, Baron de Vitrolles made the rounds of everyone he thought might give him a message of support for the Count d'Artois. Though constantly confronted by evidence that his unlimited enthusiasm for the Bourbons was not shared by all, the baron was sublimely blind. He was particularly eager to get a letter from Tsar Alexander for the count, but accepted it as fact when Talleyrand told him the Tsar regretted being too busy to receive him. (De Vitrolles was the sort of arrant royalist Talleyrand kept away from Alexander.)

Though he was frustrated, even baffled, by the turn his visit to General Dessole took, it did not shake his faith. He merely found it bizarre. Baron de Vitrolles found the general busy organizing his new command in an improvised headquarters, with only a few tables and a few clerks. The baron had no one to announce him, had trouble getting to Dessole, and found that Dessole had never heard of him or his mission.

"The only way I could get a private word with him was to push him into a corner of the room," the baron recalled. Hastily, de Vitrolles explained he would probably be the first to reach the Count d'Artois with news of recent events and of the important services the general had rendered. It was only fitting that he should bring the count some concrete testimony of such touching and deserving devotion.

Neither the count nor his brother Louis owed him gratitude, Dessole said. He did not know them and was doing nothing for them. Called upon to serve his country under difficult circumstances, his only thought had been to accept the call and whatever risks it implied. If the Bourbons turned out to play a role in the future, as seemed likely, he would have nothing against serving them, but until then, they played no part in his decisions.

By 3 P.M., de Vitrolles had finished his rounds. The post horses were harnessed to his carriage, but Talleyrand's letter was not ready. De Vitrolles's departure was deferred till evening.

For Talleyrand, the Allies, and the provisional government, the day had been one of successful progress. New adherents were pouring in. Those already cooperating with the new order were rushing to publicize their support to make sure they would get full credit from the man about to be crowned.

Influential men like Pasquier and Prefect Chabrol printed circulars listing their reasons for backing the provisional government. "Happy to see an end to my country's troubles," Pasquier wrote, "I have accepted the new way of serving it."

New acts were passed April 4 to undermine the vestiges of imperial power. The Senate issued decrees disbanding mass levies and giving draftees and newly levied units liberty to return home. The veterans might fight on, but Napoleon would be unable to continue for long without reserves of manpower.

The restoration was still a delicate subject (talk of a royal guard was instantly squelched), but there were no holds barred in propaganda against Napoleon. As soon as he was voted off the throne, the provisional government had become as vicious in its attacks as the royalists. A government manifesto posted on the walls of Paris April third called

Napoleon "just an adventurer seeking fame," and accused him of having laid the nation to waste in a few years. "He could at least have become French in return. . . ."

Talleyrand, the Allies, and their supporters had every apparent reason to feel confident. They were not, however. Something, they felt, still might happen. Napoleon had fought too hard to build his empire to give it up without further struggle. The calm of Paris in the midst of the overthrow of its government and occupation by foreigners was un-natural. Things were going too well. "I confess I do not like the excessive tranquillity, even indifference, that seems to exist," wrote the English diplomat Sir Charles Stewart.

In fact, something was happening, something quite unexpected.

Everything seemed tranquil and in order at Fontainebleau the morning of April 4. The battle was delayed once again. Napoleon had not yet left for his new headquarters, but his forced wait was almost at an end. Most of Oudinot's and Macdonald's men would reach Fontaine-bleau during the day, and by the fifth, the army would be in position for the attack.

Napoleon spent the morning of the fourth issuing final orders in preparation for the coming battle. He modified the disposition of his troops in reaction to incoming reports of an Allied advance on the road to Orléans, and the news, denied and then confirmed, that the Allies had taken Etampes, directly west of Fontainebleau. He sent orders to prevent the enemy from repairing the bridge the French had destroyed at Melun to block the road south. At 11 A.M., he again announced that he would move his headquarters to the chateau of Tilly that evening. Reviewing troops at noon in the courtyard prior to his departure, he found his soldiers and line officers eager for battle. "To Paris! To Paris!" they shouted.

Ignoring the stony-faced marshals and generals on the horseshoe staircase, Napoleon headed for his suite.

"Only an abdication can get us out of this," Ney said after Napoleon brushed past.

He may not have intended to say it. Ney was a man given to sudden impulses and equally sudden regrets, but the shocking statement found an immediate echo. There was an explosion of fears and resentment. The marshals had been shaken that morning by news from Paris of the Senate deposition. They already felt that fighting to retake Paris was fighting

Paris itself. Now that Napoleon was deposed, were they to follow him to war against their own Senate? Against some of their colleagues? Their families? The Emperor had no right to plunge the country into civil war. He had no right to drag everything and everyone down with him out of pride. If he would step out of the way, the Allies would accept his son, and country and empire would be saved.

Red-headed, hot-tempered Ney led the way down the long, mirrored gallery leading to the Emperor's suite. As Napoleon entered his private salon, he noticed Marshals Ney, Lefebvre, and Moncey striding rapidly behind him. Dragging the others with him, Ney burst into the room.

"Sire, it's time to put an end to this! Your situation is desperate, you must abdicate for the King of Rome!"

Out of surprise or restraint, Napoleon merely answered that they could still fight and regain their lost fortunes.

"No," Ney said. "The army won't follow any more, it has lost confidence."

"The army will obey well enough to punish you for insubordination," said Napoleon.

"Ah, if you still had that power, would I be standing here now?"

Ney's voice rose, his gestures became wild. Witnesses say he was on the verge of attacking Napoleon physically. There was a painful silence. Napoleon's mute surprise struck Ney into self-awareness. The moment passed, but the blow had been struck.

Napoleon dismissed the officers, had a hasty lunch in silence in the adjoining room, retired briefly to his study to write, and called in the same men.

He had little choice. He could yield. He could arrest the rebel officers and promote a new general staff from the ranks of eager and loyal junior men. Whether or not Napoleon considered that, it was not the course he chose.

The marshals stood in a circle, immobile, attentive. Neither the fire nor the rose-violet upholstery and wall coverings warmed the stiff, pompously furnished room. Reflected over and over in the mirrors on all four walls, Napoleon stood near the fireplace, drumming his heels on the black hearth. The men waited in silence to the ticking of the Sèvres porcelain clock on the mantelpiece. At last, raising his head abruptly, Napoleon looked over those present. Avoiding Ney's eyes, he paused in front of modest old Marshal Moncey, one of the few who had never shown personal ambition.

With a glance at Caulaincourt, Napoleon said, with effort, *"Eh bien, oui.* Since they'll no longer deal with me, since my resistance would be the cause of civil war, I will sacrifice myself to the happiness of France. I will abdicate!"

Moncey ran forward at these words, seized Napoleon's hand, and kissed it.

"Ah! Sire, you are saving France! Please accept my admiration and gratitude."

Napoleon looked at him in surprise.

"Don't be mistaken, Sire, that's how I feel, but order me where you will, I am no less ready to follow you!"

Napoleon called in Baron Fain, took the draft of abdication from his hand, and gave it to Caulaincourt. Caulaincourt read it. It was not enough, he said in a sad, firm voice. The Allies would reject it. He cited the conditions without which there would be no point in presenting it to Emperor Alexander. Napoleon objected, refused. Ney broke his silence, eyes blazing. Time pressed, there wasn't a moment to lose, he said.

Napoleon sat at the gueridon in the middle of the room, modified the act with his own hand, and gave it back to Fain to copy. Once again it failed to satisfy. Napoleon retired to his study to produce a third version. "There it is, this time as it will remain," he said as he handed it to Caulaincourt. "I won't change anything more." Caulaincourt read the act.

> The Allied powers having proclaimed that Emperor Napoleon is the sole obstacle to the restoration of peace in Europe, Emperor Napoleon, faithful to his oath, declares he is ready to give up the throne, France, and even life itself for the good of the country, inseparable from the rights of his son, the regency of the Empress, and the maintenance of the laws of the empire.
>
> Written in our palace of Fontainebleau, April 4, 1814.

As he finished reading, two new arrivals were announced. Marshals Oudinot and Macdonald had at last gotten to Fontainebleau with their troops, or what was left of them. In one month, they had lost close to three fourths of their men. The survivors were weary, hungry, and demoralized by the news of the fall of Paris. When Macdonald learned the Allies had taken the capital, he wrote a fellow general, "We are stunned. I've no news from headquarters, I don't know what we're supposed to do. What will happen to our unfortunate country now?"

Many soldiers deserted en route to Fontainebleau. Their officers were dispirited. One of Macdonald's generals refused to charge the Cossacks harassing the rear guard. "Damn it, let us have peace!" he cried in the hearing of his troops.

When Macdonald got Napoleon's dispatch ordering him to hurry to Fontainebleau and warning him, "We may be fighting," the marshal wrote back that his troops were unfit for combat. His officers asked him to ride ahead in person to persuade Napoleon to make peace and save what was left of France and the army. Some urged him to ask Napoleon to abdicate in favor of his son if necessary.

Fearing that Napoleon might think his coming part of a plot if he left his troops without orders, Macdonald continued to Fontainebleau with the remnants of his Eleventh Corps, reduced from over 10,000 to under 3000 men. As soon as he reached Fontainebleau, officers crowded his quarters to beg him to tell Napoleon what the army felt. Macdonald had trouble getting rid of them long enough to change his mud-spattered clothes.

While he was dressing, one of Marmont's aides-de-camp arrived with a letter de Montessuis had brought to Essonnes on April 3. An officer read the letter aloud while Macdonald finished dressing. The account of recent events in Paris by his intimate friend, General Beurnonville, astonished Macdonald. It was hard to believe so much had happened in three days. The Allies had refused to negotiate with Napoleon. The Senate had dethroned him and was about to recall the Bourbons under a constitution modelled on England's. The war was over in Paris, the city peaceful under the harmonious rule of the magnanimous Allies and the provisional government, of which General Beurnonville was a member.

Macdonald passed the letter among his staff, who became all the more eager for him to speak to Napoleon. Accompanied by Marshal Oudinot, he headed for the palace. Though he tried to get rid of them, a crowd of excited officers followed him across the cobblestoned courtyard. At the foot of the outside staircase, he turned to order them to let him continue alone because their presence might give Napoleon the impression of an officer revolt. They refused to abandon him for fear Napoleon might punish him on the spot.

"Times have changed," said Macdonald. "He wouldn't dare, particularly when we have the army behind us." The men agreed to wait in the gallery.

Macdonald and Oudinot strode into Napoleon's private salon.

Napoleon had not seen Macdonald since the marshal tried in vain to persuade him to head east toward his strongholds from Vitry.

"Good day and how goes it, Duke of Tarentum?" Napoleon said.

"Badly, Sire," said Macdonald. "So many unhappy events. A surrender without honor! Without our being there to help save Paris! We are all overwhelmed and humiliated."

"It is indeed a great misfortune. What are your troops saying?"

"They say you've summoned us to march against the capital. They're as disheartened as we are, and I've come to tell you they refuse to expose Paris to the fate of Moscow. My men are dropping of hunger. . . . If they advance, they'll find themselves exposed on an open plain. The cavalry is weak and exhausted, the horses can barely stand. We don't have enough ammunition for a skirmish and no way of getting more. If we fail, as we probably will, what's left of us will be destroyed. All France will be at the enemy's mercy. We are determined to have no more to do with it. For my own part, I declare to you that my sword shall never be drawn against Frenchmen nor dyed with French blood. Happen what may, we've had enough of this ill-fated campaign without kindling a civil war."

"No one intends to march *against* Paris," Napoleon said.

"But, Sire, do you know what's going on there?"

"They say the Allies refuse to deal with me."

"Is that all you've heard?"

"Yes."

"Read this." Macdonald handed the Emperor Beurnonville's letter, adding that since it was written by one of the members of the provisional government, it would give Napoleon an accurate picture of what was happening. Napoleon read it without a change of expression.

"May I have it read aloud?" he asked.

"Certainly. It has already been made public in my room. As you'll see from the address, it wasn't sent to me alone. The Duke of Raguse [Marshal Marmont] forwarded it to me by an aide-de-camp, opened."

After the Secretary of State read it aloud, Napoleon returned the letter to Macdonald with thanks for his mark of confidence.

"You should never have had any doubt of it."

"Quite true. I was wrong. You're a good and honorable man."

"The important thing is to make up your mind, Sire. Opinion is hardening. There's no time to lose."

"I've tried to bring France happiness," Napoleon said. "I haven't succeeded. Events have worked against me. I am abdicating and retiring."

"Ah! Sire, what a catastrophe!" exclaimed Macdonald, thinking this sudden decision had sprung from his words alone.

Napoleon glanced around the room.

"Yes, I am abdicating. But as for you, do you all agree to recognize my son as my successor and the Empress as regent?" Each was asked in turn; each agreed, Macdonald effusively.

After announcing that he had chosen Caulaincourt, Marmont, and Ney as his envoys, Napoleon said, "Gentlemen, you may withdraw. I shall prepare my envoys' instructions." As they were leaving, he threw himself on a sofa, striking his thigh with his hand. "Nonsense, gentlemen! Let's forget it all and march tomorrow. We'll beat them!"

Macdonald again said his army was in no condition to fight. The others insisted that they, too, had had enough. They added that every hour diminished the chances of the envoys' success. Napoleon did not insist.

"Be ready to start at four o'clock," he told his envoys as he dismissed everyone.

The generals had barely reached the gallery when Napoleon, touched by Macdonald's effusion, called him back.

"I've changed my mind about Marshal Marmont. Since he commands the advance guard, I may need him at Essonnes. I want you to take his place as envoy. Will you accept?"

Macdonald promised to do his best. Before leaving, he returned with Ney and Caulaincourt for the Emperor's instructions. They were to negotiate a peace treaty between France and the Allies in the name of the regency. "As soon as the principle articles of the treaty are agreed, and before signing them, they will inform us so we can make our abdication known either by message to the Senate or proclamation to the French people. They will then receive the powers of the regency to sign the treaty."

As Napoleon's instructions and the wording of his so-called abdication make clear, he was not abdicating. He was only offering to abdicate if certain conditions were guaranteed, and the conditions were ones he was sure the Allies would not meet. In effect, faced with his marshals' ultimatum, Napoleon had chosen to let the Allies turn them down. He was sure the regency would never be accepted, but he knew the marshals would not believe it until they saw for themselves. Let them try. Their mission would gain a day or two's rest for the army, satisfy the marshals, and no doubt win back their support, since they would be left with the alternative of the return of the Bourbons, to whom they were unanimously opposed. In his own mind, all Napoleon had done was tender a futile offer to abdicate in order to settle his current dilemma and put things back where they were before the marshals confronted him.

What Napoleon failed to foresee was that his marshals, his soldiers, and the public at large would not distinguish between an abdication and a conditional abdication. For the soldiers and the public, the distinction was too delicate. For the marshals, it was unwelcome. Napoleon's voluntary withdrawal relieved them of having to choose between abandoning him and negotiating peace. They trembled at their own boldness and were dazzled by its success. Napoleon's old companions at arms were his old rivals for power. This time, they had gotten the upper hand.

Among themselves, from that moment, they no longer regarded Napoleon as emperor or commander. Had he not abdicated? Had he not given them a mandate to make peace? They decided to make sure he could not change his mind in their absence and throw everything aside to proceed with the war. From now on, we alone represent the army, Napoleon's envoys told Marshal Berthier. To keep Napoleon from compromising our effort by starting hostilities in our absence, you must obey orders only from us. Berthier agreed.

Napoleon took his own precautions. Confiding the act of conditional abdication to Caulaincourt, he warned him to keep an eye on Ney.

"He's well disposed now, but he'll find the ground in Paris too slippery. Nothing guarantees me what he'll do an hour from now because he has no head. He's as weak as he is brave, and his excessive ambition makes him vulnerable."

It was not Ney's vanity that should have concerned Napoleon most, but the vanity of his favorite, the man of whom he had just said to Caulaincourt, "No one inspires me with more confidence. I can count on him. He was brought up in my camp, he has principles of honor, and there isn't an officer for whom I've done as much as I have for him. I'm lucky it's his corps that is at Essonnes."

Marmont was more displeased than surprised to see the envoys' two carriages draw up outside his headquarters about 5 P.M. The aide-de-camp who had carried Beurnonville's letter to Macdonald at Fontainebleau had returned to Essonnes with news of the abdication two hours before. When the three envoys arrived, Marmont was surrounded by his top-ranking generals. "All acted more embarrassed than astonished to see us," Caulaincourt commented. While the envoys told Marmont what had happened, they noticed everyone around them whispering and exchanging looks.

They got a partial explanation of this peculiar behavior while awaiting their permit to pass Allied advance posts. In a roundabout way, Marmont admitted he had had overtures from the Allies inviting him to separate himself and his corps from the Emperor's cause. He had sent counterproposals and was afraid word might come any moment that they had been accepted. Now that there was a chance for a regency, he regretted his response, since the regency would solve the dilemma in a better way. Never would he have acted on his own except that the army was so dispersed that there had been no way of consulting his colleagues. Why hadn't he been invited to the meeting at Fontainebleau?

Ney, Caulaincourt, and Macdonald were stunned. To urge Napoleon to abdicate to save the empire, as they had, was one thing. To abandon advance headquarters, defect the entire Sixth Corps, and leave Napoleon and the army exposed to an enemy surprise attack was treason. How could Marmont have gone so far as to discuss such a thing with the enemy? They repeated Napoleon's praise of Marmont and confidence in him as advance commander. They pointed out how imprudent he had been, and how terrible the consequences could be for France and the army.

Marmont tried to justify himself. He had thought the Emperor and France lost, had hoped to save them both by helping to bring about a prompt peace. He had feared the Emperor would sacrifice the last Frenchman to his stubborn pride. He complained of the Emperor's silence. Now that Napoleon was willing to sign a peace treaty, all was changed; the terrible onus of abandoning him could be avoided. He would join his colleagues, Marmont declared, never to separate himself from them and the cause of the army. He cut short his colleagues' reproaches. "First get me out of this, then lecture me."

There were two ways of getting out, Napoleon's envoys told Marmont. The first was to go to Fontainebleau and explain everything. Marmont was afraid Napoleon might have gotten word of his private dealings. If so, he would be arrested and shot.

"Then come to Paris with us, since you say nothing is fixed with the enemy," said Macdonald.

Privately, the envoys thought they would prevent any possibility of a defection at Essonnes by removing the commander. Besides, by taking Marmont with them, they could keep an eye on him. Marmont agreed to go, perhaps with a view to being farther from Fontainebleau in case one of the generals he had consulted should leak something to Napoleon about his plan to defect.

Before leaving, he turned his command over to fifty-four-year-old General Souham, senior officer at his base. Souham, who resented not having won a marshal's baton after twenty years as general, was one of those Marmont had confided in. After explaining the reason for his departure, Marmont instructed Souham not to make a move until his return, and gave orders for the troops to be assembled and informed of the Emperor's abdication.

As soon as permission to pass Allied outposts arrived, the envoys set off in two carriages, Ney and Caulaincourt in one, Macdonald and Marmont in the other.

Marmont was startled to see Macdonald's carriage turn up the avenue to the castle of Petit-Bourg at Chevilly.

"What's wrong?" Macdonald asked.

"But this is Allied advance headquarters."

"Well, what of it?"

"What if Prince Schwarzenberg insists on my carrying out my bargain?"

"Stay in the carriage, then. I'll tell the other two envoys when we stop."

The three concealed Marmont under their cloaks before going into the castle, where Schwarzenberg and the Crown Prince of Wurtemberg met them. The Crown Prince, who had once served in Napoleon's army under Ney, received them very badly, but after delivering a bitter harangue blaming the French for all the misfortunes of Europe, he left the room in a temper and went to bed.

While waiting for Tsar Alexander's permission to continue to Paris, the envoys talked with Schwarzenberg of their mission. Ney and Macdonald were surprised to find the prince strongly against the regency, which they assumed Austria would support. Nothing could convince them that the Austrian Emperor would abandon his daughter, and they were encouraged to learn that Metternich and Emperor Francis were expected in Paris soon.

There was clearly nothing to hope for from Schwarzenberg, however. The more adamant he was, the more indigant the marshals became. The exchange was growing heated when Schwarzenberg was rescued, sometime between 10 and 11 P.M., by his servants' announcing supper. Having eaten at Marmont's headquarters, the envoys joined the prince at the table without taking part. Supper was silent, melancholy, with everyone keeping his eyes on his plate. Before leaving, Macdonald visited Prince Wurtemberg in his bedroom. The prince told him Marmont had agreed to lead his corps over to the Allies.

"That was merely under discussion," said Macdonald.

"To the contrary," said the prince. "Everything Marmont asked was granted and the agreement was completed."

Determined to get the truth from Marmont, Macdonald rushed back to the carriage. Marmont was gone! Startled, Macdonald hurried back to the salon, where he found Ney and Caulaincourt alone, Prince Schwarzenberg having been called out of the room.

Shortly, Marmont himself walked in, to his colleagues' surprise. He was smiling and relaxed, as if just relieved of a great weight. He had gone into the chateau, he said, and sent for Schwarzenberg to tell him he no longer entertained any thought of the arrangement discussed between them since he was now acting in concert with Napoleon's envoys in the name of the entire army.

There was more to it than Marmont was saying, his companions thought. Yet, after such positive assurances, how could they doubt a man who had always been honorable? In any case, offending him by expressing new doubts would have alienated him.

Toward midnight, they all rode on together after getting their safe conduct and taking leave of Schwarzenberg. The twenty-mile ride to Paris over encumbered roads bristling with checkpoints was an uneasy one.

X

CRISIS AND ABDICATION
April 5

WORD OF THE ENVOYS' mission reached Paris about 8 P.M. The provisional government was meeting at Talleyrand's as usual at that hour, with all thoughts centered on Marmont's defection. De Vitrolles, about to leave on his much delayed journey, was in private conversation with Talleyrand. The latter had his letter to the Count d' Artois in his hand when he learned that Caulaincourt and the marshals were at Petit-Bourg awaiting permission to continue to Paris to see Tsar Alexander. Talleyrand put the letter back in his pocket.

"This is just an incident," he said, "but we must wait to see how it turns out. You can't leave now. Emperor Alexander is capable of the unexpected. One is not the son of Paul I for nothing."

By the time the meeting of the provisional government broke up between 10 and 11 P.M., Talleyrand and the Tsar had gotten details of Napoleon's envoys' mission from Schwarzenberg. The Tsar decided to receive the marshals as soon as they arrived, and to consult the provisional government immediately after. Messengers ran to call the members back.

They assembled in alarm—"terror" was the word the Abbé de Montesquiou used—in the salon of Alexander's suite on the first floor of Talleyrand's mansion. There they could look out the long, balconied windows onto the Place de la Concorde, where the blood of the Bourbons they were about to recall had splattered the cobblestones to the cheers of Parisians. They shuddered and waited.

The marshals arrived well after midnight. Talleyrand, escorting them to see Alexander, said only, "Messieurs, what are you trying to do?

If you succeed, you'll compromise everyone who has entered this room since the first of April, and there are many of them."

The Tsar seemed startled to see Marmont, but said nothing. After the marshals stated their objective, Alexander asked them to listen. He expressed warm admiration for the French army. Once again, he recalled the indelible impression made on him at Fère-Champenoise when he saw "a mere detachment, almost all raw recruits in blouses and round hats, immortalize itself by its courageous resistance." He declared he was no longer Napoleon's enemy, now that Napoleon's luck was down. He respected the French army and its marshals for being devoted to duty "instead of doing as many others have done, throwing themselves into our arms and doing their best to overturn Emperor and empire." The Allies refused to deal with Napoleon because no peace made with him would last, but they did not want to take part in the government of France or infringe on her traditional territory.

Macdonald saw through this, but did not interrupt. When the marshals' turn to speak came, Ney made an impassioned speech about how eager Napoleon's generals were to get rid of Napoleon and have done with the sufferings of war. To the growing horror of his companions, he dwelt bitterly on Napoleon's blind ambition and abuse of the army's devotion and sacrifice. Caulaincourt and Macdonald tried in vain to stop him from weakening their cause by picturing the army as divided and no longer devoted to its commander.

"Let me speak, you'll have your turn," Ney said angrily.

When Ney at last finished, Caulaincourt and Macdonald praised the Allies' generosity, Emperor Alexander's magnanimity, and returned his compliments with praise of Russian troops. The Tsar seemed touched. Caulaincourt and Macdonald took advantage of his favorable disposition to ask his support for the cause of the regency. Napoleon's abdication and the recognition of his son as successor and the Empress as regent should satisfy the Allies, they said.

"Has Napoleon abdicated?" Alexander asked.

"On behalf of his son," was the reply.

That still wouldn't ensure peace, Alexander said, because Napoleon would be bound to exercise influence over his wife. Besides, he added, it was too late.

"Public opinion has gone too far. We haven't checked it and it is growing every moment. Why didn't you come to an understanding with the Senate?"

The envoys' anger burst. The people were afraid of giving the Bourbons, émigrés, and royalists the power to revenge themselves. That miserable Senate did not represent public opinion. It had no right to act. As a mere tool of the empire, once the empire was overturned it had no right to exist.

"Will Your Majesty let us speak plainly to this miserable Senate? Every institution, everything we have today, would be threatened by the restoration. . . . There would be a terrible civil war. The nation has paid too high a price for the little liberty she has gotten not to defend it, and the army won't let its glory be trampled on. Reduced to sad straits by the fault of its commander, it will spring from the ashes, stronger and more dedicated than ever."

Emperor Alexander was struck by these arguments. He did not want to make a lifetime enemy of Napoleon's army by rejecting the envoys' plea. The marshals switched to an appeal to Alexander's vanity.

"You have declared you made war on one man alone," they said. "He is beaten. Your Majesty has a chance to show he is a generous victor. Be our mediator on a fresh field of glory, one worthy of Your Majesty's noble soul. Earn the gratitude of the great national majority as you have earned ours by your generous moderation."

Alexander seemed moved. "I have no objection to your seeing the Senate," he said, "and I'm not partial to the Bourbons. I do not know them, but I'm afraid the regency is out of the question. Austria is very much opposed to it. If I were alone, I would be glad to agree, but I must act in concert with my Allies. If the Bourbons won't do, choose a foreign prince or one of your marshals—there are plenty of illustrious men in France.

"In closing, gentlemen, to prove my sincere esteem and deep regard for you, I will make your proposals known to my Allies and will support them. I am most anxious to have the matter settled. Resistance in the Lorraine and the Vosges is growing all the time. One of my columns lost 3000 men crossing those regions without seeing a single French soldier. I don't hesitate to tell you these things because your frankness has encouraged mine. Come back at nine tomorrow morning, we'll finish then."

When they withdrew after this long conference, the envoys crossed the great drawing room, where they saw the members of the provisional government, along with Pozzo di Borgo, Nesselrode, and some Russian officers. The French looked anxious and fearful, Macdonald noticed with disgust, and were all in disgraceful undress, whereas the Tsar had been in full military uniform.

Some of the French officials flaunted an air of authority. An argument erupted. The marshals called the officials a set of factious, ambitious men who had broken their oaths. Macdonald rejected Beurnonville's hand, and told him he had wiped out thirty years of friendship. He turned on his former colleague, Dupont, the new Minister of War. Napoleon might have been severe, even unjust, toward Dupont over the Bailèn affair, but that didn't justify his behavior.

"Since when does a man seek vengeance for personal wrongs at the expense of his country!"

Caulaincourt interrupted the heated exchanges. "Gentlemen, you're forgetting you're under the roof of the Emperor of Russia here."

Talleyrand, who had just left the Tsar, added, "If you want to continue arguing and discussing, come down to my quarters."

"That would be pointless," said Macdonald. "My colleagues and I do not recognize the provisional government."

On that note, Caulaincourt and the three marshals left for Marshal Ney's house to await their audience with the Tsar the following morning.

As soon as the envoys had gone, French officials went into huddles, asking what had happened. They were soon told by the Tsar himself.

When they were ushered into the Tsar's study, he was standing. The French officials formed a semicircle in front of him. Alexander summarized the marshals' proposals and arguments with warmth. The regency would settle everything. It would assure France of a government that would respect old customs and new interests. The government would remain in the capable hands of the experienced men who had guided it through the past years. Austria's lively interest would be a guarantee against pressure from other powers. Most important of all, the regency had the support of the army, and that resolved the last remaining difficulty facing them.

The French officials carefully avoided reminding Alexander that he had solemnly promised not to negotiate with Napoleon or any member of his family. They did, however, point out that the Senate had gone along with the plans for the restoration, that Bordeaux had already declared for the Bourbons, and that several towns in the provinces were ready to follow suit. Could one regard all that as not having happened?

Talleyrand's argument that the regency offered no guarantee against

Napoleon's seizing power and his fortuitous summing up in the phrase, "He would always be listening behind the door," was probably the most telling single blow against the regency. The argument the French at first hesitated to use also proved effective. It was General Dessole, a simple, forthright soul, who at last blurted out what everyone was thinking and no one was saying. In a pathetic speech, he said he had always been opposed to Napoleon, but had decided to follow the banners of the provisional government only after Alexander's formal assurance that the Allies would not negotiate with Napoleon or any of his family. If the Allies recognized the regency, now all he could do was seek asylum in Russia. He hoped the Tsar would at least give all his French backers passports to go there.

Alexander reassured everyone that whatever he decided, he would never abandon to Napoleon's revenge men who had compromised themselves to support the Allies.

When the French officials left in the early hours of the morning, the Tsar was visibly shaken. He would discuss the issue with the King of Prussia, he said, and give his decision the following day at 9 A.M.

The officials were terrified. They talked of exile. Talleyrand had trouble keeping them from dissolving the provisional government on the spot. Anglès, the new minister of police, later told Rovigo he was so sure it was all over that night that he loaded his traveling carriage to be ready to leave. Count Rochechouart, the French émigré who had been appointed commander of the city by the Allies, dismissed the royalist delegation awaiting him that night.

"I find I have neither the time nor the desire to busy myself with the restoration," he said. "For all we know, we'll have to evacuate Paris tonight."

There were anxious faces in the Faubourg St.-Germain. The old royalists got ready to emigrate again. Their new supporters panicked.

"When we reached Marshal Ney's," wrote Macdonald, "we learned more than 2000 white cockades had fallen off people's hats during the night."

It seemed almost certain that the treaty would be signed the next day. Napoleon's army was still feared. His envoys sent him a hopeful account of their interview, saying they anticipated concluding negotiations the following morning.

No one slept that night in the Talleyrand mansion. Talleyrand was busy until dawn acting as intermediary for royalists, senators, and officials coming to plead with the Tsar and the King of Prussia. He spent most of the night with the Tsar, who vacillated over his decision while Talleyrand frightened him with his picture of Napoleon listening behind the door. Alexander had been impressed by the envoys. Napoleon's resources, the rights of Napoleon's son, the cause of the army, and Alexander's own promise to support French views, all weighed in their favor. Besides, he liked the Bourbons no better now than he had before. Unimpressed by the response to the Bourbon cause in Paris, he did not consider the example of Bordeaux significant. The Bordelais would have acclaimed anyone who opened their harbors to ship out five years' accumulation of wine.

Alexander agreed with Caulaincourt that restoring the Bourbons was not going to be as easy a task as Talleyrand would have had him believe five days earlier. The new powers were fighting over the succession to the empire before it was dead. Quarrels over the constitutional draft that morning had pointed up the difficulties of relying on ex-republicans to support a royalist cause. The Abbé de Montesquiou had exposed the gap and shocked most of the senators by objecting to their imposing conditions on "the natural rights of royalty." What right did the senators have to make a constitution without the participation of either the nation or the King? he asked. All Talleyrand's tact had been required to conciliate the contenders.

As usual, Talleyrand listened to everyone without a word, letting his rapt attention convince each of his approval. When he spoke, he used the language he had mastered that made people his dupes without his committing himself at all. He persuaded the royalists to tone down their demands in order to achieve their aims; the details could come later, he implied. He consoled the republicans with visions of Louis XVIII's wisdom, liberalism, and the influence upon him of long years in England, haven of constitutional monarchy.

Alexander sensed that the reconciliation Talleyrand managed to achieve could not last. The schism was bound to grow as exterior dangers diminished. Royalists made little effort to hide the fact that the only use they had for the Senate and provisional government was to help put Louis XVIII back on the throne. "Afterward I hope we'll get rid of these monsters. They should almost all be hanged," wrote Chateaubriand's sister.

Alexander was aware that while the privileged part of France was conniving to keep its position, the bulk of the nation was watching the spectacle with increasing coldness. The provisional government reigned only in Paris and Allied-occupied territory. Most of France was loyal to Napoleon; much of it had as yet no word of the changes in Paris. If the Bourbons suppressed the veterans, republicans, and bourgeois when they got into power, if they sought vengeance or insisted on their old privileges, there might be a civil war in which the country would call on Napoleon to rescue it.

France was by no means exhausted. There was a large reserve of men able to fight, and many of them were disgusted with the turn of events in Paris. There were plenty of Frenchmen like the innkeeper outside Paris who had told de Vitrolles it was those 800,000 Parisian rats who had caused all the trouble during the Revolution and ever since.

With the Senate and royalists in disagreement, the population unenthusiastic, and Napoleon's army gathering just the other side of the Essonne River, Alexander was anxious to have done with it all. He respected Macdonald and Ney. He liked Caulaincourt. He had once genuinely admired Napoleon, and had never completely forgotten the spell Napoleon had woven at their first meeting seven years earlier, when the two Emperors had exchanged cravats, handkerchiefs, decorations, and high-flown words of friendship. He was tempted to be generous to his fallen enemy. And he wanted to avoid appearing to go back on his promise to respect the will of the French people.

Talleyrand repeated all his old arguments. Napoleon's family had no legitimate claim to the throne and could only keep it by force. A regency with a three-year-old king would be weak and constantly threatened. If Napoleon did not take back his crown, others would try for it. Napoleon's generals perhaps, why not? The only stable government was a legitimate one, and the only legitimate ruler was Louis XVIII. Any other solution invited civil war and threatened European peace. Talleyrand's past aid to the Tsar in foiling Napoleon's designs assured him of a hearing. Vacillate Alexander might, but he listened. Talleyrand was determined, Alexander indecisive. The scales hung in the balance once again, when once again, something happened that no one had foreseen.

Napoleon grew restless at Fontainebleau after Caulaincourt and the marshals left. He wrote Marie-Louise to ask her father to intervene in the negotiations begun with Alexander. Then his thoughts turned again to the postponed attack in which he expected to win back his throne or add to the splendor of his fall. It had never occurred to Napoleon that he would fall any way other than in battle. His impatience grew as he waited, closeted in his study.

Outside the walls of his study, the rumor of his abdication spread. The troops at Fontainebleau were charged with emotion. Some officers refused to believe the rumor. The oath they had sworn the day before and their orders to prepare for an attack seemed to rule it out. At dinner that night, however, Napoleon confirmed it. He had written a conditional abdication in favor of his son because the marshals wanted it, he said, but he expected nothing to come of it. The Allies feared him too much to let his son rule so long as he lived.

News that Napoleon had abdicated radiated confusion everywhere. At Essonnes, rumors spread on the return of Marmont's aide from Fontainebleau. Men and officers were equally bewildered. Napoleon defeated, perhaps; Napoleon killed in battle, yes, but Napoleon abdicating? General Lucotte at Essonnes found himself unable to comply with Marmont's order to announce to his men that Napoleon had abdicated.

"The Emperor will do whatever is necessary to save the country," he told his assembled troops, "and he counts on you to follow him." Follow him where? Lucotte himself no longer know. "Sire! I no longer know where to turn," he wrote Napoleon that evening after Marmont had gone. "Heads here are confused. I beg you to point the way."

Shortly thereafter, the generals at Essonnes who had been party to Marmont's plans to defect the Sixth Corps were alarmed by the arrival of a dispatch from the Emperor summoning Marmont to Fontainebleau at 10 P.M. Napoleon was merely convoking a meeting, for which he sent similar orders to eighteen of his key generals at other posts. Not knowing this, the conspirators, in their guilt, feared Napoleon was summoning Marmont because he had discovered the marshals's secret agreement with the enemy. How were they to explain Marmont's absence? What were they to do?

Following the dispatch, one of Napoleon's orderlies, Colonel Gourgaud, arrived at Essonnes in person and demanded Marmont in his gruff, peremptory manner. Marmont's aide, Fabvier, was lying on a couch in headquarters, unaware of what was going on, when Gourgaud stormed in angrily about 10 P.M.

"Where's the marshal?" he said.

"In Paris with the other gentlemen," said Fabvier.

"What? He left his corps without orders to do so? The others had a mission. He doesn't."

"What do you expect?" said Fabvier. "You can see everything's crumbling. The machine is falling apart. The Emperor is abdicating. Lots of people are leaving. Everyone's thinking of himself. But don't be angry," he added. "The marshal's gone, but General Souham is in command. Any order you have for the corps, you can give to him. He's just twenty minutes from here on a height. Have some ham and a glass of wine while I get an orderly to take you."

Fifteen minutes later, Gourgaud left. Fabvier returned to his couch.

Souham and other members of Marmont's staff who had agreed to the marshal's plan to defect the Sixth Corps were panic-stricken when Gourgaud presented Napoleon's second message. Forgetting that the Emperor's orders were often sent in duplicate, Souham saw Gourgaud's visit as proof that Napoleon knew everything.

"The bastard will have me shot!" he said, assembling his colleagues to decide what to do.

About midnight, one of Marmont's servants came to Fabvier to ask for orders. There was talk of leaving, he said. Fabvier replied he had heard nothing about it, and he'd have received orders to leave if there were any. He opened the window to look out at the advance posts. Nothing unusual there, no sound. He decided to stay where he was so he could be found if needed.

Between 1:30 and 2 A.M., while Fabvier was lying, sword buckled, on the couch in the orderlies' room, General Digeon came in. The general seemed surprised. Wasn't Fabvier leaving with the army? Leaving where? asked Fabvier, leaping to his feet.

"It's all agreed," Digeon said evasively.

Fabvier ordered his best horse saddled and hurried to the lines. To his astonishment, he saw the troops massed. He pushed through them to find the generals gathered around a big fire.

Not being in on the coup, Fabvier did not understand what was happening, but he knew the troops were not supposed to leave Essonnes. Planting himself in front of General Souham, Fabvier demanded an explanation.

"It's all agreed," said Souham.

Fabvier insisted. Marmont had told him the army would not move until his return from Paris.

"I'm not in the habit of accounting to inferiors," said Souham. Then he added, "The marshal has put himself in safety in Paris. I'm taller than he, I don't have any desire to be cut down."

"If you think he went to Paris for safety, follow him, but leave the army here."

Fabvier argued in vain. Even General Compans, who had just fought so many desperate battles to fend off the Allies, turned against him. It was dangerous to leave troops under Napoleon's command now the Emperor had abdicated, he said.

Glancing at a unit about to march, Fabvier thought briefly of rushing over to tell the men where they were being led. Then he considered the danger to the troops of an armed clash among them so close to the enemy. His own habit of obedience was strong. Souham was a senior general. Fabvier pleaded for at least a few hours' delay. He would kill his horse to get to Marmont in Paris and bring back a counter order.

"That's all well and good," said Souham, "but the wine is poured, it must be drunk."

As Fabvier galloped north to Paris to tell Marmont, Baron de Bourgoing, the aide to Marshal Mortier who had been present at the bombardment of the chateau of Soudé St.-Croix on the twenty-fifth, was galloping south to Fontainebleau with the same news for Mortier.

Mortier had left de Bourgoing at Marmont's headquarters, with orders to bring him instant word of any movement among the enemy troops just across the river. Toward two in the morning, the baron was awakened by noise. He was told the French troops were about to march. When he asked to see Marshal Marmont, he was told the marshal had left. The baron questioned one general after the other. As aide-de-camp to Marshal Mortier, he had the right to be informed, he insisted, but the generals were reluctant to explain. When their evasive replies left the baron no doubt of their intentions, he abruptly rode off to Mortier's headquarters at Mennecy before they could stop him. When he arrived, Mortier was just getting out of his carriage after a late supper meeting with the Emperor at Fontainebleau, the meeting to which Napoleon had summoned Marmont.

"Go tell the Emperor at once," Mortier said. "Assure him of my unshakable loyalty and the absolute devotion of the Young Guard. We are his for life and death."

Changing horses, Baron de Bourgoing dug in his spurs again.

When Marmont had worked out the details of the defection of his corps, he had planned to deceive his men into thinking they were marching into position for an attack on Paris. Though his soldiers respected him and were trained to obey blindly, he knew they would mutiny if they suspected they were being led over to the enemy. He counted on the habit of discipline to make them continue in silence even when the generals in on the plot led the columns west off the road to Paris in the direction of Versailles.

Such staunch supporters of Napoleon as Fabvier and General Lucotte had been left out of the plot. To the others, first sworn to secrecy, Marmont had presented the restoration as a *fait accompli*. They would all be rebels if they continued to fight against France's chosen new government, he said. Most of his staff was shocked at first, but quickly persuaded. Several, like Souham (who thought he should be a marshal), bore grudges against Napoleon.

To keep his line officers from discovering the deception, Marmont had prepared orders for them to march to their posts alongside their men so that they would be isolated from each other and unable to communicate any suspicions they might acquire. By the time they realized what was happening, the corps would be so deep in enemy territory that turning back would be suicidal. In fact, the corps would be surrounded all the way to Versailles. Schwarzenberg had issued orders for the French to be flanked discreetly by Allied cavalry and followed by other Allied troops to prevent a retreat. He had also given orders for the town of Versailles to be heavily guarded "due to the unreliability of its inhabitants." For fear that Marmont's men might turn on him or Napoleon might discover the plot and attempt a counter coup, the entire Army of Silesia and the Grand Allied Army's Third, Fourth, Fifth, and Sixth Corps were on notice to be ready for any event throughout the night.

Whether or not the plan to defect Marmont's corps was called off after Marmont's talk with Prince Schwarzenberg the night of April 4, the Allied alert was never canceled. The Allied escort was ready to swing into action when Marmont's generals signaled the enemy's advance headquarters that they had decided to march.

It was nearly 3 A.M. when Marmont's corps started to move. At first, the troops marched confidently in the silence imposed on them. They thought they were going to surprise the enemy. They assumed any noise they heard behind them came from other French troops following for the attack. The sound of arms and horses on their left and right was more puzzling. Though some thought it a French cavalry escort, two officers became suspicious enough to slip away and gallop to Fontainebleau. A squadron of Polish lancers left the ranks of the rear guard with cries of treason, and returned to Essonnes to join General Lucotte and his troops. The rest of Marmont's army marched on. There were murmurs, but the habit of obedience was strong, the night obscure, the road the right one to take to Paris. Besides, the truth was hard to believe until dawn revealed it unmistakably.

It was daybreak when Baron de Bourgoing jumped off his horse at the steps to the palace of Fontainebleau. Ignoring the men who crowded around for news of Paris, de Bourgoing demanded to be led to the Emperor at once. Everyone he met as he passed through the anti-chambers expressed eagerness for the coming battle for Paris.

De Bourgoing found the Emperor with Berthier in the gallery next to his suite. When Napoleon heard that one of Marshal Mortier's aides had arrived to see him, he hurried toward the gallery entrance. Mortier had just left. The news must be sudden, important.

At ten paces he asked, "What is it?"

"Sire, I bear a heavy message."

"No preamble! The facts!"

"The Sixth Corps has just left Your Majesty's cause. The entire corps is marching toward Paris," de Bourgoing said, unaware the troops had turned toward Versailles.

"That's terrible news you bring me there, young man," said the Emperor, seizing the baron's forearm forcefully. "Are you quite sure?"

"Sire, I was at Essonnes myself tonight. I saw the troops take up arms and march in the direction of the enemy lines with my own eyes."

"Did the men know where they were being led?"

"Undoubtedly not. As usual, they obeyed in silence."

"Ah!" said Napoleon. "My soldiers have to be tricked to be taken from me. . . . Did you see Marshal Marmont when the troops started to march?"

"No, Sire, he wasn't at his headquarters when they left. I only saw him yesterday evening when I arrived at Essonnes with Marshal Mortier. It was from Marshal Marmont's generals I found out the purpose of this march. I had to leave abruptly for fear they would try to keep me from getting back to my marshal."

"Did the cavalry march too?"

"Yes, Sire. Infantry, cavalry, artillery, all marched off in the same direction.

"What is Mortier doing?"

"Sire, he sent me to assure Your Majesty of his complete devotion. He awaits your orders to march. 'We are devoted to the Emperor, life and death,' he said."

"Ah! I recognize him well there! I know I can count on him! —And his troops? My Young Guard," he said, glancing at Bourgoing's uniform. "Are they thinking of abandoning me too?"

The baron felt a sharp pang. "Sire, the Young Guard and all the youth of France are ready to die for you."

The Emperor moved closer. Looking into de Bourgoing's face, he passed his hand under the fringes of the baron's epaulettes to touch his shoulder.

"Ah, yes," he said, "the young, they're not the ones who'll abandon me.... Go, my friend. Tell your brave marshal I count on him. I thank him for his loyalty and I have every confidence in his troops. Tell him to stay ready, take care.... And then," he added sadly and unexpectedly, "tell him we shall fight no more."

As de Bourgoing left Fontainebleau, he passed regiments breaking camp to march and others already moving through the imperial forest toward their positions, confident they were about to fight the Allies. But the fight had been lost without a battle.

At the same moment that Baron de Bourgoing reached Fontainebleau, Pozzo di Borgo, who had spent the night in a salon next to Emperor Alexander's study, got up to enjoy the sunrise over the Tuileries gardens. He was leaning against the window when he felt a hand on his shoulder. It was Tsar Alexander, who had just gotten the happy news that the Sixth Corps had been led over to the Allies' side.

"It's an act of Providence," he said excitedly. "Providence is with us, Providence has chosen. No more doubts, no more hesitation!"

Ney, Macdonald, and Caulaincourt no longer had any backing.

"Are you certain you represent the army's will?" Alexander challenged them. "Do you know Marmont's entire corps has gone over to the Allies? Napoleon must abdicate unconditionally."

There was one last emergency. When dawn revealed the truth to Marmont's troops, they mutinied. Soldiers threw down their arms and swore they would die rather than allow themselves to be forced into enemy service. Line officers smashed their swords and tore off their epaulettes. When the generals tried to restore order, a hundred shots were fired at them.

The mutiny threw the allies and the provisional government into a new crisis, quickly resolved by Talleyrand's persuading Marmont to take complete responsibility. Talleyrand had a card up his sleeve to force Marmont's hand. The *Journal des Débats* of April 5 announced that the marshal had "abandoned Bonaparte's flag to embrace the cause of France and humanity" and had come to Paris, where he would soon be joined by his entire corps.

Marmont was committed. He rushed from Paris to Versailles, where he found his troops in full insurrection. Disregarding warnings that he might be shot by his men, he appeared before them. Who had authorized them to disobey him? he challenged. Had they forgotten who he was? Hadn't he been wounded twenty times in their midst? Didn't they know he cherished their honor as his own? They had never had any reason to distrust him before, and they had none now. The war had become pointless, and their duty as soldiers of France was to follow the will of their country.

Bewildered, surrounded by the enemy, the men yielded to their habit of obedience and allowed themselves to be led off to separate cantonments. Had an officer of enough authority and boldness stepped forward, the troops would have followed him and tried to break through to Fontainebleau. No such leader appeared, and the crisis, the last to shake Alexander and the provisional government, was settled to Talleyrand's satisfaction.

After convincing Marmont to go to Versailles to take charge of his men under the new banner, Talleyrand made certain the marshal would not change his mind again. He publicized what Marmont had done everywhere, even printing the text of the marshal's agreement with Schwarzenberg in the papers. Marmont did not protest; he was the hero of the day.

When Marmont arrived at Talleyrand's house from Versailles late in the evening of the fifth, covered with dust, he was greeted like a conqueror and seated at a little gueridon in the middle of the room where he was served dinner while everyone came up to overwhelm him with compliments. Drunk with vanity for two days, Marmont, Duke of Ragusa, faced a lifetime of remorse and shame. The name *ragusade* was coined for treason. Marmont's company of guardsmen was dubbed the Judas Company and shunned.

Left without the support of arms or generals, Napoleon was persuaded to write his unconditional abdication late that night at Fontainebleau after the marshals and Caulaincourt returned from Paris. Orders of 11 P.M., April 5, detailing the army's withdrawal to the Loire, are crossed out in red ink in Marshal Berthier's register with no explanation. Napoleon issued his army no further orders. He could no longer count on anyone.

When he was alone in his bedroom, Napoleon was overheard by his valet to say, "Marmont dealt me the final blow. Wretched man, I loved him."

EPILOGUE

As soon as Napoleon abdicated, he rebelled. "They've dragged my eagles in the mud," he protested. Again he contemplated withdrawing to the Loire and assembling the 100,000 men remaining in all the armies of France. He toyed with the idea of repairing to Italy. The roads from Fontainebleau were open.

"Will you follow me once again?" he asked his officers.

There was no response. More than once he sent to Paris to get his abdication back. The marshals refused, and each day made a fight less possible.

Napoleon became a prisoner in fact, if not in name. His officers deserted him daily. Everyone found a pretext to leave for Paris—to get money, see a sick wife, take care of business. Few took formal leave, many made no pretense of regret.

"The little bastard wouldn't have been satisfied until he'd gotten every last one of us killed," said General Lefebvre.

Some left discreetly to avoid dealing Napoleon the final humiliation of pity. The palace of Fontainebleau emptied little by little. "You would have thought His Majesty was already buried," wrote Pelet, the faithful soldier who had recorded Napoleon's speech urging the attack on Paris. Soon only the few who would accompany him to exile in Elba were left.

Almost everyone, the Allies, the provisional government, the royalists, the Bourbons, Napoleon's ex-officers, and Napoleon himself, would have been happy had he disappeared, but he remained very much alive. He regretted that he had not been killed in the explosion at Arcis. He tried to commit suicide, but the poison he had worn in a little bag around his neck for two years to use in case of capture had lost its potency. He escaped more than one plot to kill him, to the relief of Louis XVIII, who remarked, "In our family we are the murdered, not the murderers."

Napoleon never saw Marie-Louise or his son again. Emperor Francis took them to Austria. From Blois, Napoleon's brothers and sisters wrote him only about money, worried only about how to avoid sharing his exile. Napoleon's abdication was published on the eleventh. His court rushed back from Blois to fill Talleyrand's house with so many courtesans and solicitors that it was more difficult than ever to get in. The Count d'Artois received the post of lieutenant general from the Senate on the fourteenth. After a long delay caused by an attack of gout, Louis XVIII reached Paris on May 3, the day Napoleon's ship reached the island of Elba.

The royalists were wild with joy. "Everyone has a special way of expressing joy," wrote Chateaubriand's sister, the Countess of Marigny. "Mme. de Gois talks to anyone in the street who will listen and is unable to remain seated or sleep. . . . Mme. de Chamillard has lost her tongue. Mme. Duquesne has put a white cockade on her hat like the soldiers. Others radiate a sweet and pious joy. Some have completely changed character. Mme. Louise, who was so short and round she could hardly move, is twirling about with stupendous agility. . . . My chambermaid is so exalted I only send her out on the most indispensable errands. She reads all the posters, listens to all the proclamations, and when she came across a white flag the other day, followed it shouting *Vive le Roi!* until she ran out of breath, which is the only reason she came back at all."

Because the old republicans clung to the tricolor that the Bourbons refused to accept, Talleyrand arranged to present the white cockade in a new light. The morning of April 5, he told his secretary to make up a pedantic little article for the newspapers to prove that the white cockade was not the Bourbon color, but the true national cockade.

"Put in a number of quotes and some big words. Say things such as that Turenne and Marshal Catinat fought under the white flag—you see the idea."

Talleyrand's secretary saw, took fire, and started writing. Next, Talleyrand fooled old Marshal Jourdan at Rouen into being the first to have his troops wear the white cockade. Jourdan had kept his reputation of being a staunch republican through all ten years of the empire, but he was tricked into adopting the cockade when Talleyrand wrote him Marshal Marmont's troops had already done so. When Talleyrand showed Marmont Jourdan's letter announcing he had followed Marmont's example, Marmont protested, "But I haven't adopted the white cockade."

"That's embarrassing, I admit," said Talleyrand, "but what do you want to do about it now? Deny it? That would be a hundred times more embarrassing for you. Just adopt the white flag as I did." And thus a thorny question was resolved.

It won't last, Napoleon predicted. The Bourbons will be turned out within a year.

"Ah, Caulaincourt," he said, "men are tired. All they want today is peace at any price, but before the year is out, they'll be ashamed of having given in instead of fighting, ashamed of having yielded to the Bourbons and the Russians. Everyone will run to my banner."

Napoleon was right. Disillusion was immediate. Soldiers and officers returning to Paris assaulted foreign officers. Fights broke out. There were bitter cartoons showing Louis XVIII mounted behind a Cossack, riding to Paris over French corpses. Alexander was furious after his first visit to Louis XVIII at the Tuileries.

"Louis XIV wouldn't have received me worse at Versailles at the height of his power. You would have thought it was Louis XVIII who had just put me back on my throne instead of the other way around."

The old aristocrats sniggered in satin sleeves at Napoleon's new nobility. The bemedaled marshals burned with indignation. Old soldiers were shunted aside, forgotten and in want. Resentment mounted.

In less than a year, Napoleon escaped from Elba and was received by a jubilant army. His triumph was brief, just 100 days. His next exile, after Waterloo, was not Elba but remote Ste.-Hélène, off the coast of West Africa, where he was quite forgotten by the world. If remembered at all, he was dismissed as the ruthless, warmongering adventurer who had almost ruined France.

It was Talleyrand's turn to triumph again. He won universal admiration as the man who remade Europe at the Congress of Vienna and established a more lasting peace than Europe had known for decades. It took him less than a year to dissolve the coalition against France and turn her into a great power again, but, as Napoleon had predicted, the ungrateful Bourbons kicked him out. In 1821, the year Napoleon died, Talleyrand was biding his time in the chamber of peers. The story has it that Talleyrand was playing cards when the Emperor's death was announced. The hush that fell was broken by the hostess's exclamation, "What an event!"

"It is no longer an event," said Talleyrand, playing his next card, "merely a bit of news."

Napoleon died at fifty-two, Talleyrand at eighty-four. Both outlived their useful lives. Talleyrand returned to favor under Louis-Philippe, whom he helped to the throne in 1830. After four years as ambassador to London, he retired reluctantly to Valençay in the Loire valley. Like Napoleon on Ste.-Hélène, he busied himself with the administration of his lands, but found that no substitute for running the affairs of the world.

"I arrange my life to be monotonous," Talleyrand wrote. "I am neither happy nor unhappy. My health is neither good nor bad. I have no pain, no illness. I am simply failing little by little. . . . I'm through. I've planted some trees, built a house, and done a lot of other stupid things. Isn't it time to have done with it?"

In 1838, Talleyrand died, reconciled on his own terms with the church. As the years passed, his role as the peacemaker of Europe was eclipsed by a growing Napoleonic cult. History's greatest heroes are warriors, not statesmen, as Napoleon observed as a schoolboy. It is the names of the world conquerors like Alexander the Great and Charlemagne that live in men's imaginations. Napoleon occupies center stage today as the man who brought France glory, while Talleyrand, who betrayed him to bring France peace, hovers in the wings. Their places in history may change again. It is becoming more popular to admire Talleyrand and criticize Napoleon. As Talleyrand said, *"Plus ça change, plus c'est la même chose."*

On Napoleon's Return from Elba

What news? *Ma foi!*
The Tiger has broken out of his den.
The Monster was 3 days at sea.
The Wretch has landed at Fréjus.
The Brigand has arrived at Antibes.
The Invader has reached Grenoble.
The General has entered Lyons.
Napoleon slept last night at Fontainebleau.
The Emperor proceeds to the Tuileries today.
His Imperial Majesty will address his loyal subjects tomorrow.

—ANONYMOUS, 1815

APPENDIX

Alexander I, Emperor of Russia (1777–1825).

Angoulême, Duke of, elder son of the Count d'Artois (q.v.)

Artois, Count d' (1757–1836), younger brother of Louis XVIII, whom he succeeded as Charles X.

Barclay de Tolly, Mikhail, Prince (1761–1818), Livonian of Scotch descent, in Russian service from 1786, Russian Minister of War (1810–12), promoted to field marshal for his part in the 1814 invasion of France.

Beauharnais, Eugène de (1781–1824), son of Napoleon's first wife, Josephine. Archchancellor of State. Viceroy of Italy from 1805.

Belliard, Auguste-Daniel, Count (1769–1832), fought in every campaign of the empire. Commanded cavalry under Marshal Mortier in 1814. Accompanied Napoleon to Elba.

Bernadotte, Jean-Baptiste (1763–1844), Marshal of France. After being elected Crown Prince of Sweden in 1810, fought against Napoleon in 1813 and 1814. Crowned Charles XIV of Sweden in 1818.

Berry, Duke of, second son of the Count d'Artois (q.v.).

Berthier, Louis-Alexandre, Prince of Wagram, Sovereign Prince of Neuchâtel (1753–1815), Marshal of France, and chief of staff to Napoleon, whom he served for eighteen years.

Beugnot, Jacques-Claude (1761–1835), Prefect of Lille during the campaign of 1814, Minister of the Interior in the provisional government.

Beurnonville, Pierre de (1752–1821), abbé, general, and senator, member of the provisional government in 1814.

Blücher, Gebhard von (1742–1819), Prussian marshal commanding the combined Russian and Prussian armies known as the Army of Silesia in the 1814 invasion of France.

263

Bonaparte, Jérôme (1784–1860), Napoleon's youngest brother, King of West-phalia (1807–13).

Bonaparte, Joseph (1768–1844), Napoleon's elder brother, King of Naples in 1806, King of Spain (1808–13), and Lieutenant General of France during the 1814 campaign.

Boulay de la Meurthe, Antoine (1761–1840), magistrate and politician, Councillor of State in Napoleon's government.

Bourgoing, Baron Paul Charles Amable de (1791–1815), aide-de-camp to Marshal Mortier.

Bourrienne, Louis-Antoine Fauvelet de (1769–1834), Napoleon's companion in military school at Brienne, once his private secretary and for years French envoy to Hamburg, he became Napoleon's enemy after being recalled from his post for graft. Headed postal services in provisional government of 1814.

Burhgersh, Lord John (later Earl of Westmoreland, 1784–1859), British military commissioner to the Allied armies in 1814.

Cambacérès, Jean-Jacques, Prince of Parma (1753–1824), member of the Convention, of the Council of 500, then Minister of Justice, Second Consul, and, under the empire, Archchancellor.

Carême, Marie-Antoine (1784–1833), most famous chef of the early nineteenth century.

Castlereagh, Robert Stewart, Viscount, 2nd Marquess of Londonderry (1769–1822), English Foreign Minister from 1812 to 1822, and one of the most influential Allied diplomats following the campaign in France in 1814.

Caulaincourt, Armand Augustin Louis de, Duke of Vicence (1772–1827), son of a general, himself a general and a diplomat, chief equerry to Napoleon, ambassador to Russia (1807–11), and Minister of Foreign Affairs during the 1814 campaign.

Chabrol, Gilbert-Joseph-Gaspard, Count of Chabrol de Volvic (1773–1843), Prefect of the Department of the Seine during and after the 1814 campaign.

Chateaubriand, Viscount François René de (1768–1848), author and statesman, appointed to diplomatic posts after his return to France from emigration in 1802, resigned after the execution of the Bourbon Duke d'Enghien. His pamphlet *De Buonaparte et des Bourbons,* published in 1814, was a vitriolic denouncement of empire and Emperor.

Clarke, Henri-Jacques-Guillaume, Duke of Feltre (1765–1818), Minister of War from 1807 through the 1814 campaign.

Compans, Jean-Dominique, Count (1769–1845), division general, veteran of the Italian campaign.

Constant, Louis, Napoleon's valet, wrote memoirs with the aid of others.

Courlande, Dorothée, Duchess of, (1761–1821), Russian national, came to

Paris for marriage of her daughter to Talleyrand's nephew, was Talleyrand's mistress for many years.

Dalberg, Emerich Joseph, Duke of (1773–1833), nephew of the Prince Primate of the Confederation of the Rhine, served the Austrians, then the Bavarians. Became Baden's envoy to France before becoming French national in 1809. Made councillor of state and granted a dukedom by Napoleon, he conspired against the Emperor and became a member of the provisional government of 1814.

Dejean, Pierre François, Count (1780–1845), general and aide-de-camp to Napoleon in 1813 and 1814.

Dessole, Jean (1767–1828), general and politician, became commander of the National Guard in the provisional government.

Drouot, Antoine, Count (1774–1847), baker's son, major general of the Guard and aide-de-camp to Napoleon during the 1814 campaign. Accompanied Napoleon to Elba.

Dupont, Pierre-Antoine (1765–1840), general who fell into disgrace with Napoleon over surrender to the Spanish at Bailén. Appointed minister of war in provisional government of 1814.

Dupont de Nemours, Pierre-Samuel (1739–1817), economist, secretary general in provisional government of 1814.

Fabvier, Jean-Charles (1782–1855), colonel and aide-de-camp to Marshal Marmont in 1814.

Fain, Agathon-Jean-François, Baron (1778–1837), secretary and archivist in Napoleon's cabinet from 1795 to 1815.

Flahaut, Auguste-Charles-Joseph, Count (1785–1870), son of Talleyrand, division general and aide-de-camp to Napoleon in 1814.

Francis I, Emperor of Austria from 1804 to 1835, known as Francis II during his briefer reign as Holy Roman Emperor (1792–1806). Father-in-law of Napoleon after the marriage of his daughter, Marie-Louise, in 1810.

Frederick William III, King of Prussia (1770–1848).

Girardin, Alexandre de, Count (1776–1855), division general and aide-de-camp to Napoleon in 1814.

Gneisenau, August, Count Neidhardt von (1760–1831), Marshal Blücher's chief of staff in 1814.

Gourgaud, Baron Gaspard (1783–1852), Napoleon's orderly from 1811, accompanied him to St. Helena and collaborated on his memoirs.

Hulin, Pierre Augustin, Count (1758–1841), general commanding the First Military Division in Paris during the campaign of 1814.

Jaucourt, Arnail François de, Marquess (1757–1852), old friend of Talleyrand's, shared his exile in England. After being first chamberlain to King Joseph in Naples, he became a senator, then member of the provisional government of 1814.

Langeron, Alexandre Louis Audrault, Count (1763–1831), French émigré to Russia, fought against French in 1792 and subsequent campaigns, including that of 1814, in which he served as general in the Allied army.

Larochefoucauld, Louis-François-Sosthène de, Viscount, later Duke of Doudeauville (1785–1844), royalist, member of the Chevaliers de la Foi.

La Valette, Count Antoine Marie de (1769–1830), married to a niece of Empress Josephine. Former aide-de-camp to Napoleon, Director General of the Post in 1814.

Lebrun, Charles-François, Duke of Plaisance (1739–1824), former deputy to the States General, Third Consul, then Archtreasurer of the empire from 1804 through the campaign of 1814.

Lefebvre, François Joseph, Duke of Danzig (1755–1820), a miller's son who enlisted as private at eighteen and served as marshal of France commanding the Old Guard in 1814.

Louis, Joseph-Dominique, Baron (1755–1837), one of Talleyrand's intimates who shared his exile in England, then became councillor of state, and, in the provisional government of 1814, minister of finance.

Louis XVIII (Louis-Stanislas-Xavier), 1755–1824, brother of Louis XVI and King of France from 1814 until his death.

Macdonald, Jacques Etienne, Duke of Tarente (or Tarentum), 1765–1840, descendant of Scotch émigrés, son of an army officer, volunteered in 1785. He was at Napoleon's side in the coup of 18 Brumaire, was in disgrace for five years after defending a rebel general (Moreau), but was made marshal in 1809. Commanded the Eleventh Corps in the campaign of France, 1814.

Maret, Hugues-Bernard, Duke of Bassano (1763–1839), Minister of Foreign Affairs in 1813, accompanied Napoleon in the campaign of 1814 as secretary of state.

Marie-Louise (1791–1847), daughter of Francis I of Austria, Empress of France, 1810–14.

Marmont, Auguste Frédéric Louis de, Duke of Raguse (or Ragusa), 1774–1852. Born into petty nobility, infantry officer at age fifteen, Napoleon's oldest comrade at arms among his marshals in the campaign of 1814, in which he commanded the Sixth Corps.

Méneval, Claude-François de, Baron (1778–1850), *maître des requêtes* in the Council of State, accompanied Marie-Louise to Vienna in 1814.

Metternich, Clemens Wenzel, Prince (1773–1859), ambassador to France in 1806, Austrian Minister of Foreign Affairs from 1809 to 1848.

Molé, Louis-Mathieu, Count (1781–1855), served under Napoleon as minister of the interior and as grand judge.

Moncey, Bon Adrien Jeannot de, Duke of Conegliano (1754–1842), enlisted at sixteen, served in 1814 campaign as marshal and commander of the Paris National Guard.

Montebello, Duchess of, widow of Marshal Lannes and chief lady-in-waiting to Marie-Louise.

Montesquiou-Fézensac, François-Xavier, Duke of (1756–1832), abbé, royalist, member of provisional government in 1814 and Minister of the Interior under Louis XVIII.

Mortier, Edouard-Adolphe, Duke of Trévise (1768–1835), son of wealthy landowner, marshal commanding the Young Guard in 1814.

Nesselrode, Count Karl Robert (1780–1862), Russian statesman and diplomat, counsellor of the Russian embassy in Paris (1808–11), returned with Allied troops in 1814 as secretary of state.

Ney, Michel, Duke of Elchingen, Prince de la Moskowa (1769–1815), a cooper's son, volunteered at age nineteen, became marshal of France in 1804.

Orlov, Mikhail Fedorovich, Count (1788–1842), aide-de-camp to Alexander in campaign of 1814.

Oudinot, Nicolas-Charles, Duke of Reggio (1767–1847), a brewer's son, enlisted at seventeen and became marshal of France. Veteran of fifty-eight campaigns, known for being wounded in almost every engagement. Commanded Seventh Corps in 1814.

Pacthod, Michel-Marie, Count (1764–1830), general commanding division of National Guard in the 1814 campaign.

Pasquier, Etienne-Denis, Baron, then Duke (1767–1862), prisoner under the Terror, Prefect of Police (1810–14).

Piré, Rosnyvinen (1778–1850), general commanding light cavalry brigade in campaign of 1814.

Plancy, Adrien de, Count, Prefect of Seine-et-Marne in 1814.

Pozzo di Borgo, Carlo Andrea, Count (1764–1842), Corsican patriot, opposed to Bonaparte. Entered Russian diplomatic service in 1803. Diplomatic adviser to the Tsar from 1807. Followed campaign in 1814 with rank of general and post of aide-de-camp to Alexander.

Pradt, Dominique-Georges Dufour de, Abbé, Archbishop of Malînes (1795–1837), Napoleon's first chaplain, fell into disfavor with Napoleon after failure as ambassador to Warsaw in 1812. Became an active royalist and was made Grand Chancellor of the Legion of Honor in the provisional government of 1814.

Rémusat, Charles de, Count (1797–1875), was chamberlain to Napoleon. His wife, Claire Elisabeth, was one of Empress Josephine's attendants and the author of memoirs. Son Charles de Rémusat also wrote memoirs.

Roux de Laborie, Antoine-Athanase (1769–1842), lawyer, journalist, Assistant Secretary in the provisional government of 1814.

Rovigo (see *Savary*).

Savary, Anne Jean Marie René, Duke of Rovigo (1774–1833). After serving in

Napoleon's army as general, became minister of police (1810–14).

Schwarzenberg, Karl Philipp, Prince (1771–1820), once Austrian ambassador to France, after serving under Napoleon in the invasion of Russia in 1812, in 1814, fought against him as commander-in-chief of the Allied forces.

Ségur, Count Philippe Paul de (1780–1873), general, aide-de-camp to Napoleon in several campaigns, he served in 1814, but not under Napoleon's direct command.

Souham, Count Joseph (1760–1837), French general commanding division in campaign of 1814.

Vincent, Henri, Baron (1775–1844), cavalry general.

Vitrolles, Eugène, Baron de (1774–1854), former émigré who undertook mission to the Allies in 1814.

Winzingerode, Ferdinand, Baron (1770–1818), fought in Hessian, Austrian, and Russian armies. General and cavalry commander in 1814.

Yorck von Wartenburg, Count (1759–1830), Prussian officer who had served under Macdonald in Napoleon's invasion of Russia and fought against Napoleon in 1814.

CHAPTER NOTES

The classical historical works of Houssaye, Koch, and Weil have been particularly useful throughout. Weil's *Campagne de 1814*, which contains hundreds of excerpts from Allied archives, was my basic source of information on Allied military moves.

Sources are referred to by authors' names only unless further information is necessary to identify the works in the bibliography. A list of abbreviations follows:

A.N.   Archives nationales
A.G.   Archives de la guerre
C   *Correspondance de Napoleon Ier*
J   *Mémoires et correspondance du Roi Joseph*
T   *Mémoires du prince de Talleyrand*
Caul *Mémoires* of Caulaincourt

PART ONE

I. THE GAMBLE   *March 23*

PAGE

18 The size of the respective armies: The size of the armies and the numbers of men engaged on either side in any individual combat cannot be determined exactly. Both French and Allied sources of the times falsified figures deliberately, and it was often impossible to gauge accurately how many men in a specific unit were fit for combat and actually present on the battlefield.

19 "The trade of emperor has its tools," Fain, *Mémoires*, 75.

19 "I enjoy reading them the way a young **girl** enjoys a novel," Vachée, 160.

20 "A general-in-chief should never sleep," Napoleon to Gourgaud, Vachée, 241.

20 "Keeps men guessing and on their toes," Fain, *Mémoires*, 244.

20 "I was made for work," Bertaut, 169.

21 "But what's the good of it all?" and "I want to get to know my children," Watson, 204.

21 "Send a gendarme in disguise to Metz," C 21531.

23 "I admit I tremble," Schwarzenberg's letter to his wife of March 12, Weil III, 346.

24 "We no longer know what we want," Wolkonsky to Toll, March 16, Weil III, 378.

24 "The confusion and dismay," *Tagebüch* of Prince de Taxis, March 18, Weil III, 397.

24 "The fact is, our operations are very singular," Lord Burghersh to Castlereagh from Troyes, March 12, Castlereagh IX, 336–37.

24 "Blücher would have to be mad," C 21522.

24 "Twenty-four hours can bring about many changes," C 21532.

24 "I am going to St.-Dizier to wait," A.N. AF IV 906, #124 and #124 *bis*.

26 "I am closer to Munich than the Allies are to Paris," memorandum of de Rumigny, *Archives de Caulaincourt, liasse* 12, in Caul III, note 1 to pp. 15–16.

27–29 Caulaincourt's journey and the description of the French countryside: Caul, Gain de Montagnac, Oudinot, de Vitrolles, and the *Archives départementales de la Marne* (574/21).

29 "I had the fever of despair," Caul III, 35.

29 "Everyone was saying the same thing," Caul III, 13.

29–30 "Tell Caulaincourt we don't have an army anymore," Belliard to de Rumigny on February 9, 1814, quoted in de Rumigny's memorandum, in Caul III, note 3 to pp. 24–25.

30 "France needs peace," Fain, *Manuscrit de 1814*, 37–39.

31 "I hasten to our headquarters in order to see you again the sooner," Caulaincourt to Metternich, Gourgaud and Montholon, *Mémoires pour servir à l'histoire de France*, VI, 407.

32 "Write General St.-Germain," C 21532.

32 "Give me a pretty little piece of paper," Fain, *Mémoires*, 273–74.

32 "*Mon amie*, I've been on horseback all these days," #292, *Lettres inédites de Napoleon Ier à Marie-Louise*.

33 "I'm really anxious to see the Emperor," Gachot I, 40.

33 "I think I may soon like him very much," Gachot I, 42.

33 "Our Solomon is learning all the games of childhood," remark attributed to the Duchess of Abrantès, Gachot I, 22.

34 "to yawn and stretch"—"*pour me dégoudir un peu et bâiller sous les arbres,*" Gachot I, 234–35.

34 "To the Empress . . . To the lady of my thoughts," Fain, *Mémoires,* 273–74.

35 "melancholy role of regent," Marie-Louise to the Duchess of Montebello, March 30, 1813, Gachot I, 249.

35 "The health of the Empress is excellent," Bourgoing, *Marie-Louise,* 209.

35 "I would very much like my letters to have a good effect," Bourgoing, *Marie-Louise,* 210.

36 "Posterity will never know," Molé I, 157.

36 "Joseph is a pygmy," "Has everyone gone mad in Paris?" *et seq.,* C 21374, 21375, 21376, 21340, 21341, and A.N. AF IV 906.

37 "How could they? Don't they need me?" Molé I, 183.

39 "What's the reason for withdrawing troops from here?" *et seq.,* Macdonald, 253–55.

41 "The pear is ripe"—one of the Emperor's favorite expressions, Constant VI, 57.

42 "If the enemy comes, let the land that bore you be his tomb." French propaganda poster in the Ardennes, A.N. AF IV, Cart 1670, Plaq 1^{iv} #187.

42 "The enemy is concentrating at Brienne" *et seq.,* A.N. AF IV 1688.

44 "I cut the Allies' communications" *et seq.,* Caul III, 40–43.

46 "At the age of thirty, one becomes less fit for making war," Molé I, 132.

47 "Why are our soldiers still defending Milan and Barcelona?" Ségur, 405–06.

47 "We are on the verge of total collapse," letter of March 11, J X, 194; "Paris is unwilling," letter of February 22, J X, 153.

47 "Peace—do you think I don't want peace too?" note of de Rumigny, *op. cit.* and various letters written by Napoleon.

48 "You're seeking publicity and popularity, not the public good," Napoleon's speech to the legislature, January 1, 1814, Molé I, 199.

48 "Fire, rape, and killing," Faré, 322.

49 "General Dejean is impatiently awaiting," letter of March 22, J X, 208.

49 "Stirring up the populace is the greatest danger," Pasquier to Montalivet, March 16, 1814, A.N. F 7 9753.

49 "*dans le plus grand calme,*" Rovigo III, 184.

50 "Cowards!" Napoleon's letter of February 24 to Marie-Louise, *Lettres inédites.*

51 In the words of an English general: Robert Wilson, in Fain, *Manuscrit de 1814,* 175.

II. INTRIGUE   *March 24*

52 "I liked Napoleon," T II, 133.

53 "Twenty battles won," T II, 134–35.

53 "What we should fear is not Napoleon's ambition," Lacourt-Gayet I, 263.

53 "If he lasts a year, he'll go far," Lacourt-Gayet II, 14.

53 "My devotion will end only with my life," Talleyrand's letter to Napoleon of June 28, 1802 in *Lettres inédites de Talleyrand à Napoleon, 1800–1809.*

54 "Everything can be explained by my childhood," Fabre-Luce, 31.

55 "I want some great names" *et seq.*, T I, 401–02.

56 Paris in 1814: Lanzac de Laborie, Marigny, Pasquier, Poumiès de la Siboutie, Rovigo, Underwood.

57 "What is the Emperor thinking of?" La Valette, 292.

57 "I was unable to get anything precise" *et seq.*, Rovigo III, 221–229.

59 "Nevertheless, while deploring the sad state of affairs," Rovigo III, 219.

59 "I am less than that, yet perhaps much more," Dard, 124.

59 "Well, what is one to do," Rovigo III, 227–28.

60 "Everything is coming to an end," Pasquier II, 193.

60 "The fear of seeing hopes for peace fade," *Bulletin de la police générale*, March 23, 1814, A.N. F 7 3835.

61 "He is the scion of a great family," Dard, 344.

62 "I'm attached to this empire of his," letter to Mme. de Rémusat, Dard, 147.

62 "But you act as if we had never quarreled," Dard, 294.

62 "I no longer know your affairs," de Coigny, 190.

63 "Women *are* politics," Talleyrand's remark to Adolphe Thiers, Cooper, 276.

64 "The minds I encounter now seem to me slow," de Bernardy, 130.

65 "Do you want to put an end to the dangers," de Vitrolles I, 125.

66 "The enemy is, in my view, a source of danger much less to be dreaded," Lord Aberdeen to Castlereagh from Châtillon, February 28, 1814, Castlereagh IX, 297–98.

66 "That miserable Viennese garbage"—"*cette malheureuse verdure, ou pluôt ordure viennoise,*" Col. Bocke, aide-de-camp to Tsar Alexander, writing General Toll, March 12, 1814, cited in Weil III, 378.

66 "Whatever happens, in God's name" Petre, 145.

68 "I understood Talleyrand listened," de Vitrolles I, 38.

68 "At times he even seemed afraid of it," *ibid.*, 50.

69 "You don't know that monkey," *ibid.*, 68.

70 "Receive the person I send you," Nesselrode note, T II, note 2 to p. 149.

70 "We brought war to France," de Vitrolles I, 117.

71 "Do you know the royal princes?" de Vitrolles I, 119.

71 "You say Paris will receive us with open arms" *et seq.*, abbreviated from de Vitrolles I, 146.

71 "You must return to Paris," de Vitrolles I, 151.

71 "That's just time lost," *ibid.*, 152.

72 "was against every rule of military strategy," letter of January 26, 1814, Madelin, 81.

73 "He has a personal feeling about Paris," Castlereagh to Lord Liverpool from Langres, January 30, 1814, Castlereagh IX, 212.

73 "If the Allies insist on marching on Paris," Francis I to Schwarzenberg, January 29, 1814, cited in Weil I, 354.

73 "You will rejoice, I am persuaded," letter of March 22 from Sir Charles Stewart to Edward Cooke from Bar-sur-Aube, Castlereagh IX, 372–73.

73 "Supposing while you are moving on Paris," memorandum by Sir Charles Stewart, Langres, January 27, 1814, Castlereagh IX, 536–41.

76 "The treasury, arsenals, and powder stores are empty," Weil III, 545.

77–79 "We must unite our forces" *et seq.*: the Allied councils and the events leading to the decision to march on Paris were recounted by two participants, Diebitsch (letter to Jomini of 1817 in Langeron, 491–93) and General Toll *(Relation de Toll,* in Russian archives). The latter is the main source of Houssaye's account (361–63). An observor, Lord Burghersh, wrote a summary in his memoirs, and Weil (vol. III, p. 555) used the sources listed above and a letter from Wrède of March 31, 1814 to the King of Bavaria.

79 "Let us all march to Paris!" Maycock, 173.

79 "it is to complete that juncture," Schwarzenberg to Francis I, March 24, 1814, Weil IV, 2.

80 "This is no longer the only place you hear the cry, *Forward!*" Weil III, 563.

80 "Bonaparte's court knew neither relaxation nor pleasure," de Coigny, 202.

81 "The Emperor's maneuvers might require," Joseph to General Hulin, March 23, in Weil IV, note 1 to pp. 130–31.

81 "Have you had any letters from the Emperor?" *et seq.*, Rovigo III, 235–36.

82 "What a horrid turn," Marie-Louise to the Duchess of Montebello, Gachot I, 283.

82, 84 Napoleon's orders to Marmont and Mortier: Marmont VI, 327–33; C 21525, 21526, 21528, 21529; A.N. AF IV 1670.

III. INDECISION   *March 25, 26*

86 "must set down nothing by hearsay"—general rules to be followed in reporting as outlined by Napoleon to Ségur, cited in Vachée, 167.

86 "We have entered Bar-sur-Aube," C 21541.

86 "Nothing new on the enemy," Macdonald to Major General, *Ferme de la Marthée*, 10 A.M., March 25, A.G. C² 185.

87 "Everything points to a good day," Berthier to Ney, Oudinot, Drouot, *et al.*, March 25, A.G. C* 7 185.

87 "The Emperor asks me to renew negotiations," Caulaincourt to Metternich, in T II, 270–71.

88 The retaking of St.-Dizier: Chevalier, Grabowski, Macdonald, Parquin.

88 "Never since the beginning of the war," Macdonald, 258.

90 "I was pleased to see he was a good, handsome animal," Parquin, 160.

92 "Since the rule is never to do what the enemy wants," Gneisenau to Boyen from Fismes, 7 P.M., March 22, in Weil III, note 2, p. 536.

94 "At nightfall, I saw an immense horizon," Marmont VI, 231.

95 "We had been at table" *et seq.*, Bourgoing, *Souvenirs*, 285–87.

96 "All right, my friends, just huddle together," *ibid.*, 289.

99 "I want to save them!" Krestoffsky, *Historique du régiment de uhlans de la garde*, in Weil IV, note 1, p. 29.

99 "Men who use swords so well," Rochechouart, 317.

99 "The army's advance was crowned with success," dispatch of 10 P.M., March 25, in Weil IV, 31.

IV. THE RACE FOR PARIS   *March 27, 28, 29*

101 "It was easy to guess" *et seq.*, Macdonald, 258–61.

102 Allied notice printed on von Schwichow's orders, A.N. AF IV 1568. The *6* is, in fact, printed upside down.

104 Barclay de Tolly's intercepted dispatch, A.N. AF IV 1568.

104 "Leave the capital to its fate," Fain, *Manuscrit de 1814*, 177.

106 "All I ask for is orders and bullets," Piré to Berthier, 3:30 P.M., March 27, A.G. C² 186.

107 "Paris isn't the capital of France," Jomini, 44.

107 "Paris will never be occupied" *et seq.*, C 21089, 21210.

107 "With the French, as with women," Caul II, 126.

107 "I lacked character," *Mémorial de Ste Hélène*, II, 558.

108 "It is incomprehensible not to profit," March 28, A.G. C² 186.

108 "which must worry him greatly," from St.-Dizier, 4:30 A.M., March 28, A.G. C*7 185.

110–111 "Your Kaiser does not seem to love his daughter" and "lying on the ground on a mattress," Wessenberg's account in Arneth, 189–93.

111 The situation in Paris: de Boigne, La Bédoyère, Marigny, Méneval, Pasquier, Rodriguez, Underwood, Véron, J.

112 "swift and clever" and "I begged him to come," La Valette, 262.

113 "I come to ask you" *et seq.*, from Lamothe-Langon, 144–49, a source to be approached with caution since much of the memoir is reputed to be the product of the author's fertile imagination.

114–115 "The empire is crumbling," *Talleyrand Intime.*

115 "There were straw-filled carts," Vêron I, 218–19.

117 "For heaven's sake, hold out," Joseph to Ledru des Essarts, March 27, A.G. C² 186.

117 "My troops fell into the greatest disorder," Ledru des Essarts to Clarke from Meaux, 9 P.M., March 27, *ibid.*

118 "I am sure these *messieurs* are planning something," Gachot I, 283–84.

118 The Regency Council: Bourrienne, La Valette, Miot de Melito, Méneval, Rovigo, T.

119 "Madame, you must make the Hôtel de Ville your headquarters," La Valette, 294.

119 "I do not understand how men," Rovigo III, 242–43.

119 "I've answered you on the fate of Paris," Napoleon from Nogent, C 21210.

120 "if the enemy should advance on Paris," Napoleon from Reims, C 21497.

120 "If the government leaves Paris, all is lost," Rovigo III, 244.

121 "I felt as if we were taking a last leave" and "if I were minister of police," *et seq.*, Rovigo III, 249.

122 "I would have been quite brave enough," letter of March 29, *Correspondance intime de Marie-Louise.*

122 The departure of Marie-Louise: Bausset, Oudinot, Rovigo, Underwood, Méneval's *Souvenirs* and Méneval's note from text given in Rapetti, 200. The latter differs from Méneval's account in his *Souvenirs* in that in his note, he pictures Joseph as trying to persuade Marie-Louise to stay while she remains unmovable.

123 "I went to the Louvre" *et seq.*, Underwood, 144–45. Underwood, an English prisoner, was an exceptionally valuable observer, having freedom of movement and many important connections. When other English prisoners were removed from Paris, Underwood obtained special permission to remain through Josephine's appeal to Rovigo in January 1814.

124 "My God! Let them make up their minds," Méneval, 992.

125 "Citizens of Paris, an enemy column," *Choix des rapports*, XX, 471–72.

125 "I found it a bit too emphatic," Miot de Melito, 350–51.

126 "You can't reach Charenton too soon," Marmont VI, 341–42.

126 "Gaining time, that's what we need," March 29, A.G. C² 186.

126 "in a pitiful state of fatigue," Plancy, 217–18.

127 "Why disturb his sleep? *et seq.*, La Valette, 293.

127 Three hundred of Marmont's men fought barefoot: Fabvier *Journal* in Debidour, 80.

128 "I have hardly slept," letter of March 29, *Talleyrand Intime.*

128 "to attack the heights of Montmartre at 5 A.M.," Wolkonsky to Blücher from Bondy, March 25, *Journal des pièces expédiées* #244, in Weil IV, 149.

129 "I was unable to sleep," Boris Galitzine, *Souvenirs et impressions d'un officier russe,* in Bertin, 342.

129 "No news for five or six days," #293, *Lettres inédites de Napoleon Ier à Marie-Louise.*

130 Description of Napoleon at Dolancourt: Constant, Grabowski, Fain.

130 "We have just received our dispatches from Paris," Napoleon from Dolancourt, 3:30 P.M., March 29, A.G. C* 7 185.

130 "Men in league with foreigners," Pasquier II, 221 and Fain, 183.

131 "Go to the head of the column," Gourgaud, *Bourrienne et ses erreurs,* in Bertin, 304.

V. FOUR HOURS TOO LATE *March 30*

The battle for Paris is particularly well covered by eyewitness accounts: Belliard, de Boigne, Bourgoing, Bourrienne, Burghersh, Chevalier, Combe, Fabvier, Giraud, Joseph, Langeron, La Rochefoucauld, La Valette, Marigny, Marmont, Méneval, Miot de Melito, Molé, Orlov, de Pradt, Rémusat, Rochechouart, Rodriguez, Rovigo, and Underwood. In addition there are various accounts in Bertin, the letter of General Dejean to Rovigo in Rovigo, Peyre's account of his adventures in Rapetti, General Hulin's letter re Peyre in Houssaye, and excerpts from Allied memos and dispatches in Weil.

133 Napoleon felt that if his army could not defeat the enemy: La Valette, 286–87.

133 Napoleon decided in favor of fortifying Paris in early March: C–21497.

134 "We don't have enough men to resist," de Bourgoing, *Souvenirs,* 292.

135 *"Prenez la goutte, cassez la croute!"* Underwood, 160.

135 "My dear, we've been shooting at each other for two hours," J X, 215.

136 "Ah, *mon ami,* we renew acquaintance in one hell of an hour" and "Where the devil does he expect me to get them?" Underwood, 177.

138 "You can see the size of our army," Peyre, *précis de la mission,* Paris, April 2, 1814, in Rapetti, 331–35.

138 "I authorize you to agree to a cease-fire," Orlov, 6–7.

139 "If Marshal Mortier and Marshal Marmont can no longer hold their positions," J X, 23–24. Though some sources claim Joseph called a council of defense before sending authorization to capitulate, he did not consult Marmont or Mortier, nor did he verify their situation at that time.

140   *Le grand roi Joseph, pâle et blême,*
      Pour nous sauver reste avec nous.
      Croyez s'il ne nous sauve tous
      Qu'il se sauvera bien lui-même.
      Popular epigram, note 1, p. 79, Giraud.

140 "The pride and nobility of Marmont," Ségur, 452.

142 "Negotiations have been reopened," Rovigo IV, 10.

143 "The close and indivisible union," Rovigo IV, note 1 to pp. 10–11.

143 "The army will bury itself," Ségur, 456.

143 "From the heights of Belleville," Marmont VI, 245.

144 "He yielded to cruel necessity," Fabvier's *Journal* in Debidour, 83.

144 "We're not afraid, we don't want to hide," Koch II, 499.

145 "The Parisians seemed as blind," Underwood, 165.

145 "Cane in hand, they leaned over the wall," Boucher de Perthes, *Sous dix rois* in Bertin, 328–29.

146 "In that case, we shall defend Paris foot by foot," Weil IV, 206–07.

146 "Fortune has smiled on you," Orlov, 12.

147 "I leave further negotiations to Marshal Marmont," Orlov, 12–13.

147 Allied commanders' fears: Carl von Plotho, Prussian colonel and historian, said in vol. III of his *Guerre de 1814* (p. 102) that Allied authorities believed a firm resolution to defend the city to the end would have enabled Paris to resist for one day, and possibly two, had the National Guard been used to advantage and the population armed. In that case, the Allies would have been stopped long enough for Napoleon to arrive to save it with his army. Writings of various Allied generals, such as Yorck and von Bismarck, support this thesis.

148 "That's treason," Rapetti, 94.

148 "We stood motionless at our windows," Oudinot, 255.

149 "Who are you, what do you want?" *et seq.*, Mayor Lorne's account in Perrin, 131–35.

150 "Who is that?" "General Belliard, Sire," *et seq.*, Belliard I, 171–79.

154 "What a great rush everyone was in" *et seq.*, Caul III, 55–59. The presence of Berthier at Juvisy is disputed. Houssaye claims, largely on the basis of Gourgaud's account, that Berthier was left behind at Troyes to lead the army to Fontainebleau. However, Chevalier (who was a

member of the Guard accompanying Napoleon part way), Mayor Lorne, Caulaincourt, and Belliard all mention Berthier's presence at various points of Napoleon's journey between Troyes and Paris. It is my belief that Berthier remained at Troyes to send orders (orders were sent in his name at 10 A.M.), then followed Napoleon rapidly and caught up with him at Sens.

154 "his presence alone, without any escort," de Chastenay, 301. Langeron wrote in his memoirs (p. 476) that if Napoleon had appeared in Paris, the resistance would have become twice as strong, possibly strong enough to force the Allies back and give Napoleon's army time to reach Fontainebleau. The invaders would then have been in a position Langeron termed *"fort incertaine."*

155 "All they thought of was saving their own skins" *et seq.,* Caul III, 59–63.

157 "to ratify all Caulaincourt would do" and subsequent excerpts from Napoleon's instructions, C 21546.

157 "You'll get there too late," Caul III, 64–65.

157 *"Mon amie,* I came here to defend Paris, but there wasn't time," #294, *Lettres inédites de Napoléon Ier à Marie-Louise.*

158 Constant found Napoleon paler and more tired: Constant VI, 70.

159 "disposed to act for us," Lamothe-Langon, 162.

160 *"Chère amie,* people say the attack this morning was just a reconnaissance," letter of March 30, *Talleyrand intime.*

160 "Not only do I refuse to authorize your staying," Rovigo IV, 15.

162 "My dear, I found the barriers closed," letter of March 31, *Talleyrand intime.*

162 "The conversation reflected the opinion of the times," Marmont VI, 249.

163 "Eh, *Monsieur le Maréchal,* if we have written guarantees" *et seq.,* Marmont VI, 249–50.

163 "That's futile!" *et seq.,* Bourrienne V, 19–23.

163 "They're planning to get Marmont involved," La Valette, 297–98.

164 "From then on, I wanted to perform my duties loyally and wait," Marmont VI, 250.

164 "My Lord, please bear your sovereign the assurance" *et seq.,* Orlov, 20.

165 "It's vital for the Emperor to know the exact strength," Fabvier's *Journal* in Debidour, 83.

165 "General Flahaut asked me," A.N. AF IV 1670, #236.

166 "I've come to rejoice with you" *et seq.,* Lamothe-Langon, 165.

PART TWO

VI. TWO EMPERORS AT THE GATES *March 31*

169 "I liked Napoleon" and "beaten he had to disappear," T II, 133 and 134.

170 "There are two parties," Gain de Montagnac, 122–23.

170 "Well, what news do you have for me?" *et seq.,* Orlov, 27.

171 "When Talleyrand left his bed" *et seq.,* Molé I, 287–89.

173 The affability that, Napoleon predicted, would soon tire Parisians: Caul III, 324.

174 "Don't feel inhibited," Pasquier II, 245.

174 "Gentlemen, you see me at the gates," Bourrienne X, 53–54.

174 "I have only one enemy" *et seq.,* Pasquier II, 246–47.

175 "gave the measure," Caul III, 69.

175 "Your mission is useless now," Caul III, 70.

176 "I am always greatly pleased," Caul III, 72.

176 "Remain calm," proclamation of Pasquier and Chabrol, March 31, in Rodriguez, 83.

177–179 The Allied entry into Paris was recorded by numerous witnesses whose versions vary according to the individual's bias and the spot from which he observed the Allied parade. The following sources were used for this section: Bourrienne, de Boigne, Burghersh, Caul, de Chastenay, Fabvier (in Debidour), Giraud, Langeron, La Valette, Marigny, Nesselrode, Pasquier, de Pradt, Rochechouart, Rodriguez, Sir Charles Stewart (description in letter to Castlereagh of April 1 in Castlereagh IX), Underwood, Véron.

179 "Oh, here come some more," Fabvier note from *Archives de Caulaincourt* in Caul III, note 1 to pp. 90–91.

179–180 "Many saw this painful and humiliating day," Caulaincourt, letter to Napoleon, evening of March 31, from *Archives de Caulaincourt,* in Caul III, note 1 to pp. 99–105.

180 "I admit that the attitude of Alexander throughout the procession," de Rémusat I, 139.

180 "The Emperor lost everything" *et seq.,* Caul III, 85–86.

181 "I left with death in my heart," Caulaincourt letter to Napoleon of March 31, *op. cit.*

181 "Everyone who might have known," Caul III, 87.

182 *"Eh bien,* here we are," *et seq.,* T II, 164–65 and de Boigne, 332–33 (from an account brought her by one of the participants the following day).

184 As the Archbishop of Malînes recalled the scene *et seq.*: de Pradt, 68–70.

184 "Very well, I hereby declare," de Pradt, 70.

185 "under France's legitimate kings" and "They may do more," Allied declaration of March 31, A.N. AF 7 4292, #83.

185 "If we could not keep them from coming," de Pradt, 72.

185 "Emperor Alexander received me," Caulaincourt letter to Napoleon, evening of March 31, *op. cit.*

186 "decidedly against the Emperor," Caul III, 102.

186 "The old senators are bewitched," Caul III, 105.

188 "By the unexpected and welcome restoration of Louis XVIII to the throne of his fathers," Langeron, 479.

188 "It's easy to see you did not fight the campaign," from A.D.B.M.***, lieutenant de grenadiers, *Une année de la vie de l'Empereur Napoléon*, Paris, 1815, cited in Rapetti, 401–02.

190 "Take courage," #295, March 31, *Lettres inédites de Napoléon Ier à Marie-Louise.*

VII. TALLEYRAND'S TRIUMPH   *April 1*

191 "the sort who appear the minute you tolerate them," Beugnot, 88.

192 "M. de Talleyrand listened privately," Beugnot, 88.

193 "The Prince of Bénévent has been invited by His Majesty," Masson, *Napoléon et sa famille*, IX, 432.

193 *La Table de Whist de M. de Talleyrand*, Véron I, 308.

193 "spun in salons," Lamothe-Langon, 155.

194 "Eh! no one wants to shunt you aside" *et seq.*, Beugnot, 105–07.

196 "A warrior who speaks our tongue alarms us less," Rodriguez, 82.

196 "Everything, even the rhythm of their drums, was novel," de Chastenay, 312.

197 "The Prussian King always had a rather timid air," Pasquier II, 279.

197 "It was touching to see the two great monarchs," Rodriguez, 119–20.

197 "Your Majesty's arrival," La Bédoyère II, 706–07.

197 "With manners like Alexander's, one could ruin France and still be adored," Caul III, 243.

198 "I guarantee you a reply to any question in half an hour," Pasquier II, 265.

198 "to assist in deciding the great question at hand," Pasquier II, 268.

199 "To the Emperor!" *et seq.*, Pasquier II, 273–74.

199 "Matters of state aren't accomplished with the heart," de Vitrolles I, 314.

199 "Poor devils," Chateaubriand, *Mémoires d'outre-tombe*, II, 539.

200 "We felt we were in an enchanted palace," Rodriguez, 113.

200 "It almost caused an explosion," Pasquier II, 273.

200 "the enemy army at Fontainebleau," Rapetti, 123–24.

201 "The feebleness, ambition," Caul III, 133.

202 "Though I officially represent Napoleon," Caul III, 113.

202 "I can explain," *et seq.*, Pasquier II, 269. Caulaincourt confesses his violent intentions towards de Mâlines in Caul III, 117.

203 "*Hélas!* I knocked on every door in vain," Caul III, 119.

203 "You don't know what can happen," abbreviation of quote from Caul III, 60.

205 "They moaned softly," Caul III, 137.

205 "Anyone who used it appeared divine," Caul III, 130.

205 "Intrigue knocked at the doors," Caul III, 138–39.

205 "The mass of Parisians were for him," Caul III, 120.

206 "Alexander seemed greatly shaken," Caul III, 142.

206 "He told me," Caul III, 144.

207 The commanding general at Allied advance headquarters, General Pahlen, wrote Schwarzenberg that he believed he was about to be attacked: Pahlen's dispatch of 3 P.M., April 1, from the chateau of Petit-Bourg, cited in Weil IV, 242.

207 "I won't hold anything back" *et seq.*, Fabvier's note from the *Archives de Caulaincourt* in Caul III, note 2 to pp. 162–63, and Fabvier's *Journal* in Debidour, 84–85.

208 "The occupation of the capital," *Choix des rapports* XX, 508.

VIII. THE TRUMPS ARE PLAYED *April 2, 3*

209 "How long the hours seemed!" Caul III, 146.

209 "Emperor Alexander's reception froze me," Caul III, 153–54.

209 "The Allies felt sure enough of the course of events" *et seq.* Caul III, 155–58.

211 Talleyrand ensured a large imposing audience for the Tsar by filling in the ranks of the absent with actors: de Villèle I, 228.

212 "Until you have the army on your side, gentlemen, you have nothing," Pasquier II, 289.

212 "You have never fought for the motherland," *Choix des rapports* XX, 491.

214 "The fall of the empire had become the object of every wish," Oudinot, 379–80.

214 "He listened impassively," Caul III, 167.

214 "Talleyrand is right," Caul III, 167–68.

215 "It's legitimate vengeance," Caul III, 172.

215 "If I'd freed Poland and the serfs" and "I could have deposed the King of Prussia," III, 173.

215 "No one abandons the fight on the eve of battle," Caul III, 171.

215 "Napoleon is still lulling himself with hopes," Caul III, 176.

April 3

216 "We may be fighting," Berthier to Macdonald from Fontainebleau, 3 A.M., April 3, in Weil IV, 264.

216 "Focus all your attention," Schwarzenberg to Major-General Kaisarov at Allied advance post, April 3, in Weil IV, note 1 to p. 259.

216 "Our affairs are highly promising," Castlereagh to Lord William Bentinck from Dijon, April 3, Castlereagh IX, 427–28.

217 "When generals in their position," et seq., Pasquier II, 285–86.

217 "I know how incapable you are of being involved," Pasquier II, 287.

217 "It was one of the most painful positions," Pasquier II, 287.

218 "Don't count on me for anything more," Pasquier II, 288.

218 "reason to be troubled" et seq., Plancy, 225–30.

220 "We formed a circle," agenda of General Pelet, A.G. (Of the various versions of this speech, I chose Pelet's because he is said to have written it down immediately after hearing it.)

221 Napoleon confronts his marshals: Thiers and various other historians reporting only one confrontation between Napoleon and his marshals and generals claim there was no violence and dismiss talk of it by some of the participants as boasting. A careful study of material available today makes it clear there were two confrontations, one on April 3, in which Napoleon turned his generals' anger against the Bourbons, and one on April 4, in which the generals forced his hand.

222 "My marshals and many of my generals have lost their heads," Caul III, 180–81.

222 "I'm going to fight," Caul III, 181.

223 "From this moment, the French are our friends," Barclay de Tolly's ordre du jour addressed to the combined Allied armies and posted on the walls of Paris on April 3, Rodriguez, 138.

223 "a holy crusade against the monster Napoleon," French royalist placard addressed to the Emperor of Russia and King of Prussia, Rodriguez, 139–40.

223 "Messieurs, as you will see, my task didn't cost me much effort" et seq., Pasquier II, 316–19.

225 "I'll always remember how extraordinary he looked in that disguise," Pasquier II, 292.

225 By hanging the man, Fabvier answered: Ségur, 507.

IX. BETRAYAL *April 4*

227 "It is hard to express," Marmont VI, 255–56.

227–28 "He alone dug the abyss," *ibid*, 257. "When he finally made me a marshal," *ibid*, 282. "I don't have to feel any great gratitude," *ibid*, 284–85. "Napoleon was probably the person I loved most," *ibid*, 285–86.

228 "Hadn't I more than fulfilled my duties," *ibid*, 258.

228 "Take you, for example," Marmont V, 276.

228 "I devote myself to France"—Marmont's letter was given to Ségur by one of Marmont's former aides-de-camp on June 29, 1837. It appears in Ségur, 510–11.

229 "The people and the army having been released," *Choix des rapports* XX, 494.

229 "Unfurl those colors," Napoleon, 'Notes sur l'art de la guerre,' *Commentaires*, VI, 176.

229 The march of Napoleon's Guard: description taken from Koch, who was present (Koch II, 570).

230 "It was difficult to get an idea," de Vitrolles I, 325–26.

231 "Ask *M. le Comte d'Artois,*" de Vitrolles I, 342.

231 "As for me" *et seq.*, T I, 137, from account of de Bacourt.

232 "The only way I could get a private word," de Vitrolles I, 344.

232 "Happy to see an end," Pasquier II, 283.

233 "just an adventurer seeking fame," address of the Provisional Government to the French people, A.N. F 7 4292, *Police générale* #83, Dossier 7.

233 "I confess I do not like," Sir Charles Stewart to Lord Liverpool from Paris on April 4, in Castelreagh IX, 440.

233 Napoleon's orders from Fontainebleau in preparation for the attack on Paris: C 21554, A.G. C ^{2} 187, A.N. AF IV 1670, Plaq 2.

233 "Only an abdication can get us out of this" *et seq.*, Ségur, 494–500.*

235 "The Allied powers having proclaimed," C 21555 and A.N. AF IV 906.

235 "I've no news from headquarters," Macdonald to General Friant, April 1, 6 P.M., A.G. C^2 187.

236 "Damn it, let us have peace!" Macdonald, 262.

236 "Times have changed" *et seq.*, Macdonald, 264–67 and Ségur, 500–05.*

238 "As soon as the principle articles," Caul III, note 1 to p. 190.

239 Napoleon's envoys tell Berthier to obey orders from them alone: Ségur, 505* and Macdonald, 268.

* Ségur's version is based on accounts made to him by the following participants: St.-Aignan, Fain, Moncey, and Macdonald. The latter dictated his account to Ségur and subsequently verified Ségur's write-up.

239 "No one inspires me with more confidence," Caul III, 188–89.

240 "All acted more embarrassed than astonished," Caul III, 193. The hedging, evasion, and lying in memoirs about this and subsequent incidents connected with the defection of Marmont make it difficult to sort out the truth, or probable truth. When participants are not covering up for themselves, they are usually covering up for someone else. As a result, almost any statement about the events can be documented or disputed. In the haze of memory, and under the influence of changing public opinion, some participants wrote accounts years later contradicting their own earlier ones. Thus, in his memoirs, Marmont wrote that he assembled all his generals and consulted them prior to making his decision to take the Sixth Corps over to the Allies (Marmont VI, 260–61), while in his *Réponse à la proclamation du golfe Jouan* in 1815, he said Napoleon's envoys had arrived "just as I was getting ready to inform my comrades of the situation."

Main sources used for this portion: Macdonald's memoirs, his account to Ségur (in Ségur's memoirs), and to Belliard (in Belliard's memoirs); Caulaincourt's memoirs; Fabvier's *Journal* (in Debidour), Fabvier's note found in the Archives of Caulaincourt (*op. cit.*) and Fabvier's replies to General Gourgaud's questionnaire of April 3, 1843 (in Rapetti, 350–53); Marmont's memoirs, Marmont's reply to Napoleon's proclamation of 1815, and General Bourdesoulle's letter of 1830 to Mortier (in Rapetti, 132–34).

240 "First get me out of this," Macdonald, 270.

241 "Then come to Paris with us," Belliard I, 187 (as told to him by Macdonald).

241 Some historians doubt that Marmont left orders for his troops to be assembled and informed of Napoleon's abdication. Lucotte's dispatch to Napoleon from Corbeil makes it certain that he, at least, received such an order: "On orders of Raguse, I assembled the division to inform it of your abdication . . . ," A.N. AF IV 1670, Plaq 2, #12, April 4, 1814.

241 "What's wrong?" Macdonald asked, *et seq.*, Macdonald, 271–74.

242 "That was merely under discussion," Belliard I, 189.

X. CRISIS AND ABDICATION *April 5*

243 "This is just an incident," de Vitrolles I, 347.

243 "*Messieurs*, what are you trying to do?" Bourrienne X, 97.

244 "a mere detachment, almost all recruits" *et seq.*, Macdonald, 274–76.

244 "Has Napoleon abdicated?" *et seq.*, Caul III, 209.

245 "Will Your Majesty let us speak plainly" *et seq.*, Macdonald, 276–78.

246 "Gentlemen, you're forgetting you're under the roof" *et seq.*, Macdonald, 278, and Bourrienne X, 100.

247 General Dessole's speech: Bourrienne X, 102–03.

247 "I find I have neither the time," Rochechouart, 337.

247 "When we reached Marshal Ney's," Macdonald, 279.

248 "Afterward I hope we'll get rid," Marigny, 66.

250 "The Emperor will do whatever is necessary" *et seq.*, Lucotte to Napoleon from Corbeil, April 4, A.N. AF IV 1670, Plaq 2.

250 Napoleon's dispatch summoning key generals to Fontainebleau: C 21553.

250 "Where's the marshal" *et seq.*, Gourgaud's questionnaire in Rapetti, 350–53; Fabvier's *Journal* in Debidour, 86–87; and Fabvier's note from the *Archives de Caulaincourt, op. cit.*

252 "Go tell the Emperor at once," Bourgoing, *Souvenirs*, 311–12.

253 "due to the unreliability," Schwarzenberg's orders of 4 April, in Weil IV, 267.

253 Whether or not the plan to defect Marmont's corps was called off: there is no conclusive evidence. General Bourdesoulle, who may have been motivated by self-interest, wrote Mortier in 1830 that when Marmont left for Paris, he still intended to carry through the defection of his troops. Lord Burghersh, who had no personal motive for making the claim, stated in his memoirs (p. 298) that what Marmont told Schwarzenberg at Allied advance headquarters was not that he had abandoned the project of defecting the Sixth Corps, but that there would be some delay in its execution. Possibly Marmont made execution conditional upon the outcome of Napoleon's envoys' negotiations.

254 "What is it?" "Sire, I bear a heavy message" *et seq.*, Bourgoing, *Souvenirs*, 313–15.

255 "It's an act of providence," Pasquier II, 311 (as recounted to him by Pozzo di Borgo).

255 "Are you certain you represent," Belliard I, 190 (as recounted to him by Macdonald).

257 "Marmont dealt me the final blow," Constant VI, 86.

EPILOGUE

258 "They've dragged my eagles in the mud," Constant VI, 86.

258 "The little bastard," Lefebvre to Bourrienne, Bourrienne X, 67.

258 "You would have thought His Majesty was already buried," agenda of General Pelet, A.G.

259 "In our family, we are the murdered," Lamothe-Langon, 187.

259 "Everyone has a special way of expressing joy," Marigny, 70–71.

259 "Put in a number of quotes," Gain de Montagnac, 169.

260 "But I haven't adopted the white cockade," Lacourt-Gayet II, 391, and numerous memoirs.

260 "Ah, Caulaincourt, men are tired," Caul III, 234.

260 "Louis XIV wouldn't have received me worse," Villèle I, 223–24.

261 "What an event!" *et seq.*, Dard, 348.

261 "I arrange my life to be monotonous," Fabre-Luce, 60.

BIBLIOGRAPHY

Numerous works consulted for background information are not listed either because they do not cover the specific period that is the subject of the book or because they give little information on it. Historians will therefore note the omission of the memoirs of Grouchy, General Baron de Marbot, Mme. de Rémusat, Count Roederer, and others.

ARCHIVES IN FRANCE

Archives Nationales
    AF IV   906, 990B, 1047, 1099, 1100, 1147, 1186, 1588, 1670, 1688
    AF V^3
    AF V^4
    AF V^5

3782, 3783, 3835, 3875, 4289, 4290–4292. 6586
Archives de la Guerre
    Grande Armée, Campagne de France:
    C^2 184, 185, 186, 187
    Suite à la correspondance de Napoléon, C * 7 185

Archives départementales de la Marne
    201- M–19, M–28, M–43, M–233
    574/21

CORRESPONDENCE

Correspondance de Napoléon Ier
Correspondance inédite de Napoléon Ier

287

Lettres inédites de Napoléon Ier à Marie-Louise, écrites de 1810–1814
Lettres inédites de Talleyrand à Napoleon, 1800–1809
Talleyrand intime, d'après sa correspondance avec la duchesse de Courlande en 1814
Correspondance intime de Marie-Louise
Marie-Louise et Napoléon, 1813-1814
Mémoires et correspondance du roi Joseph
Correspondence, Despatches, and other Papers of Viscount Castlereagh
Lettres et papiers (Nesselrode)

MEMOIRS, DIARIES, AND COLLECTIONS OF PAPERS

Abrantès, Duchess of
Barante, Baron Guillaume-Prosper
    de
Bausset, Baron Louis-François
Belliard, Count Augustin-Daniel
Beugnot, Count Jacques-Claude
Boigne, Countess de
Bourgoing, Baron Paul Charles
    Amable de
Bourrienne, Louis A. F. de
Burghersh, Lord
Castellane, Marshal Esprit-Victor de
Caulaincourt, Armand Augustin
    Louis de
Chaptal, Count Jean-Antoine-
    Claude
Chastenay, Countess Victorine de
Chateaubriand, François-Auguste de
Chevalier, Lieutenant Jean-Michel
Coigny, Aimée de
Combe, Colonel Michel
Constant, Louis
Desmarets, Pierre-Marie
Dupont, General Pierre-Antoine
Fabvier, Jean-Charles
Fain, Baron Agathon-Jean-François
    (*Manuscrit de 1814* and
    Mémoires)
Faré, Charles A.

Guizot, François Pierre
Gain de Montagnac, Count J. R. de
Grabowski, Josef
Hortense, Queen of Holland
Kielmansegge, Countess of
La Bédoyère, Charles Angélique de
Langeron, General
Larorhefoucauld, Louis-François
    Sosthène de
La Tour du Pin, Marquise de
La Valette, Count Antoine-Marie
    de
Macdonald, Marshal Jacques-
    Etienne
Marigny, Countess de
Marmont, Marshal Auguste Frédéric
Méneval, Baron Claude François de
Metternich, Prince Clemens Wenzel
Miot de Melito, Count
Molé, Count Louis-Mathieu
Nesselrode, Count Karl Robert de
Noël, Colonel Jean-Nicolas
Orlov, Count Mikhail
Oudinot, Eugénie
Parquin, Capt. Denis-Charles
Pasquier, Baron Etienne-Denis
Plancy, Count Adrien de
Pontecoulant, Count
Potocka, Countess Anne
Poumiès de la Siboutie, Dr.
    François-Louis
Pradt, Abbé de (Archbishop of
    Malînes
Reiset, Lieutenant General Marie-
    Antoine de
Rémusat, Charles de
Rochechouart, Count Louis-Victor
Rodriguez, Julian Antonio
Savary, Anne Jean Marie, duke of
    Rovigo
Ségur, Count Louis-Phillipe de
Semallé, Count Jean René Pierre de

Talleyrand, Prince Charles-Maurice
de
Thibaudeau, Count Antoine de
Trefcon, Colonel Toussaint-Jean
Underwood, Thomas Richard
Véron, Dr. Louis-Désiré
Villèle, Count Joseph de
Vitrolles, Baron Eugène de
Wilson, General Sir Robert

HISTORIES,   BIOGRAPHIES,   AND   COLLECTIONS   OF DOCUMENTS

Arneth, Alfred von, *Johann Freiherr von Wessenberg*
Beauchamp, Alphonse de, *Histoire de la campagne de 1814*
Bernardy, Françoise de, *Talleyrand's Last Duchess*
Bertault, Jules, *Napoléon Iᵉʳ aux Tuileries.*
Bertier de Sauvigny, *Le Comte Ferdinand de Bertier et l'énigme de la Congrégation*
Bertin, Georges, *La Campagne de 1814 d'après des témoins oculaires*
Bourgoing, Baron Jean de, *Marie-Louise, Impératrice des français*
Brinton, Crane, *The Lives of Talleyrand*
Bulletins officiels de la Grande Armée
Choix de rapports, opinions, et discours prononcés à la Tribune Nationale depuis 1789
    (Vol. XX)
Cooper, Duff, *Talleyrand*
Dard, Emile, *Napoléon et Talleyrand*
Esposito, Brigadier General Vincent, *A Military History and Atlas of the
    Napoleonic Wars*
Fabre-Luce, Alfred, *Talleyrand*
Finot, assistant mayor of Arcis, "Notice sur les évènements dont Arcis a été le
    théâtre en 1814" in *Guide du Camp de Mailly de la Ville d'Arcis-sur-Aube*
Gachot, Edouard, *Marie-Louise intime*
Giraud, P. F. F. J., *Campagne de Paris en 1814*
Gourgaud et Montholon, *Mémoires pour servir à l'histoire de France sous Napoléon
    écrits à Ste.-Helene*
Guillaume de Vaudoncourt, General, *Histoire des campagnes de 1814 et 1814 en
    France*
Houssaye, Henri, *1814*
Jomini, General Antoine-Henry de, *Vie politique et militaire de Napoléon*
Koch, Jean Baptiste Frédéric, *Mémoires pour servir à l'histoire de la campagne de
    1814*

Lacourt-Gayet, G., *Talleyrand*
Lamothe-Langon, Etienne, *Mémoires d'une femme de qualité*
Las Cases, Count de, *Mémorial de Ste.-Hélène*
Légende de la bataille de Paris [anon.]
Madelin, Louis, *Le Consulate et l'Empire*
Masson, Frédéric, *L'Affaire Maubreuil*
Masson, Frédéric, *Napoléon et sa famille*
Maycock, Captain F. W. O., *The Invasion of France, 1814*
Napoléon, *Commentaires*
Perceval, Emile de, *Un Adversaire de Napoleon, le Vicomte Laîné*
Perrin, Joseph, *Siège de Sens*, Vol. III of *Société Archéologique de Sens*
Petre, F. Loraine, *Napoleon at Bay, 1814*
Rapetti, Pierre-Nicolas, *La Défection de Marmont en 1814*
Rivollet, Georges et Albertini, Paul-Louis, *Les Maréchaux d'empire et la première abdication*
Robin-Harmel, Pierre, *Le Prince Jules de Polignac*
Thiers, Adolphe, *Histoire du Consulat et de l'Empire*
Vachée, Colonel Jean-Baptiste, *Napoléon en campagne*
Vialles, Pierre, *L'Archicancelier Cambacérès*
Viel-Castel, Baron Louis de, *Histoire de la Restauration*
Watson, S. J., *By Command of the Emperor, A Life of Marshal Berthier*
Well, Commandant Maurice Henri, *La Campagne de 1814*

MISCELLANEOUS

Jomini, General Antoine-Henry de, *Précis de l'art de la guerre*
Lanzac de Laborie, *Paris sous Napoléon*
Dictionnaire historique des rues de Paris (Hillairet)
Le Moniteur Universel, 1814
Le Journal des Débats, 1814

INDEX

293

DATE DUE

MAR 1 5			
DEC 1			
DEC 1			
GAYLORD			PRINTED IN U.S.A.

NAPOLEON